AIDS and the Ecology of Poverty

AIDS and the Ecology of Poverty

Eileen Stillwaggon

2006

OXFORD
UNIVERSITY PRESS

Oxford University Press, Inc., publishes works that further
Oxford University's objective of excellence
in research, scholarship, and education.

Oxford New York
Auckland Cape Town Dar es Salaam Hong Kong Karachi
Kuala Lumpur Madrid Melbourne Mexico City Nairobi
New Delhi Shanghai Taipei Toronto

With offices in
Argentina Austria Brazil Chile Czech Republic France Greece
Guatemala Hungary Italy Japan Poland Portugal Singapore
South Korea Switzerland Thailand Turkey Ukraine Vietnam

Published by Oxford University Press, Inc.
198 Madison Avenue, New York, New York 10016

www.oup.com

Library of Congress Cataloging-in-Publication Data
Stillwaggon, Eileen, 1949–
AIDS and the ecology of poverty / Eileen Stillwaggon.
p. cm.
Includes bibliographical references.
ISBN-13 978–0-19–516927–0
ISBN 0–19-516927–1
1. AIDS (Disease) 2. Poor—Diseases.
2. [DNLM: 1. Acquired Immunodeficiency Syndrome—prevention and
control. 2. Acquired Immunodeficiency Syndrome—epidemiology.
3. Poverty.] I. Title.
RA643.8.S75 2005
362.196'9792—dc22 2005002240

9 8 7 6 5 4 3 2 1

Printed in the United States of America
on acid-free paper

To Larry Sawers

Acknowledgments

My family, my employer, my colleagues at home and abroad, my students and research assistants, and very numerous nurses and doctors who have shared their work with me have all supported the creation of this book.

Larry Sawers has been my right arm throughout the writing of this book and for the many years of research that preceded it. He read many drafts and made copious suggestions. Brian Sawers read and commented helpfully on much of the book. He was especially insistent that I write the article on critical theory and race on which chapter 7 is based. Catherine Sawers was very helpful in my work on cell biology and other research tasks. Robert Sawers created tables and found countless articles in print and electronic collections. His enthusiasm for the project was particularly helpful.

Gettysburg College has been unfailingly supportive of my research since I joined the faculty in 1994. Through research grants every year, the college financed my work in Ecuador, in Lithuania and throughout the transition countries of Eastern Europe, and in Zimbabwe, South Africa, and the Dominican Republic. The college has been very indulgent, allowing me to take research leave when I wanted, and has generously supported my presentations at the international AIDS conferences in Bangkok and Durban and at American Economic Association meetings.

Gettysburg College has been supportive in other ways as well. True to the college's commitment to interdisciplinary and multidisciplinary inquiry in a liberal arts environment, my department and the administration have cheered me along every step of the way and awarded me tenure in the economics department when my work includes not only economics, but also epidemiology, biology, critical theory, and public policy. The two chairpersons during the period of this research, Jean Fletcher and the late Derrick Kanyerere Gondwe, were extraordinarily helpful. They made it possible for me to juggle all the demands of teaching and writing, and economics department administrator Sue Holz made everything work smoothly. The librarians were wonderfully helpful. Susan Roach and Cinda Gibbon were my electronic lifeline when I was living in Lithuania.

Two people, Mwangi wa Githinji and Barbara Stillwaggon, kept up a years-long pipeline of articles, sending me everything they found on HIV/AIDS. I could not have arranged the many interviews and visits without the help of colleagues and friends—in Dominican Republic, Rev. Vince Kobida; in Ecuador, Dr. Julio Gómez, Susana Cabeza de Vaca, and Susana Chiriboga; in Lithuania, Birute Jatautaite and Dr. Saulius Caplinskas; in Slovenia, Urška Velikonja; in South Africa, Dr. Philip Kotze, Leona Kleynhans, and Annemarie Bruwer; and in Zimbabwe, Clara Ndiweni and Rev. Dr. Libo Sifobela. Catherine Howard and Lisa Richey provided useful sources for the chapter on critical race theory. Jessica Brewster and Julia Baum were very able research assistants for the section on workplace prevention. Tony Barnett also helped direct me toward data for that section. Alan Whiteside read the manuscript and made many helpful suggestions. I have not followed all of his advice, so he should not be faulted for what remains. In a larger sense I am indebted to Tony and Alan for keeping the issue of AIDS as a development issue in the public conscience since the early days of the epidemic.

I recruited students from my first-year seminar, "Understanding AIDS," for various tasks. Ebru Ozsoy, Tim Dougherty, Nikolett Molnar, and Roberto Laratro found materials and created some tables. Emily Cunningham conducted a comprehensive search of sexuality studies for the appendix to chapter 1 and organized the materials in a convenient way. Nachiket Doshi organized data on food balance sheets and also did some interviewing when he was home in India. Michael Denholtz checked all the citations carefully.

Stephen McGroarty was the Associate Editor for Economics when Oxford acquired the book and was very helpful. Catherine Rae took over the project and has been very enthusiastic and efficient. Linda Donnelly managed the production very well, and Cynthia L. Garver did a great job as copy editor.

Three journals—*South African Journal of Economics, Journal of Development Studies*, and *Development and Change*—permitted the use of material from my articles in their publications. Some of the material on workplace prevention appeared in William Kosanovich (ed.), *Bureau of International*

Labor Affairs Research Symposium Papers, Vol. 2: *HIV/AIDS and the Workplace in Developing Countries.* That work was written under a grant from the Bureau of International Labor Affairs, US Department of Labor, administered by DTI Associates. I am also grateful to the Fulbright Senior Scholar Program, which supported me during a year in Ecuador.

Contents

AIDS and the Ecology of Poverty

1

Perspective

Global AIDS policy has failed to stem the epidemic spread of HIV.[1] This book explains why HIV/AIDS exacts such a devastating toll in sub-Saharan Africa and why the epidemic continues to spread in Latin America, the Caribbean, Eastern Europe, the former Soviet republics, and South, Southeast, and East Asia. This book also explains the failure of international AIDS policy that is built on flawed analysis and inadequate tools. Policy makers and researchers working on HIV/AIDS have asked the wrong questions about the causes—not of AIDS itself, but of its epidemic spread. Global AIDS policies attempt to stop HIV transmission at the last possible moment, instead of grappling with the underlying causes of the epidemic.

The grim facts are numbingly familiar. Almost 40 million people are infected worldwide with HIV, more than 90 percent of them in developing countries. That includes almost 30 million people in sub-Saharan Africa, more than 6 million people in South and Southeast Asia, 2 million in Latin America and the Caribbean, almost 2 million in Eastern Europe and Central

1. AIDS is the acquired immune deficiency syndrome, the umbrella term that indicates illness with one or more of the opportunistic infections associated with infection with HIV, the human immunodeficiency virus. The term HIV/AIDS conflates two distinct phenomena, a virus and the illnesses from which a person might suffer as a result of being infected with the HIV virus.

Asia, and 1 million reported in East Asia. At least 20 million people have already died from the opportunistic infections that constitute the syndrome. There are 15 million AIDS orphans, 12 million in sub-Saharan Africa alone. While the epidemic may be slowing in a few countries, prevalence still appears to be growing in most of Africa, Asia, Latin America, Eastern Europe, and the former Soviet Union (UNAIDS, 2004).

HIV/AIDS epidemics emerged in distinct forms in industrialized countries and in the developing world. In affluent countries, national rates of HIV prevalence remain below 1 percent of the adult population. In sub-Saharan Africa, prevalence of HIV exceeds 2 percent of the adult population in almost all countries; in 21 African countries, more than 5 percent of adults are infected. In South Africa and Namibia, more than 20 percent of adults are infected with HIV, in Zimbabwe, 25 percent, and in Botswana, 37 percent. In Asia, HIV has increased very rapidly in some areas since 1995, and 4 to 5 million people in India (1 percent of the adult population) are now infected. In Latin America, most national rates are below 1 percent, but in some cities in the region, HIV prevalence exceeds 20 percent among men who have sex with men and 60 percent among injecting drug users. Several Central American and Caribbean countries have the highest national rates in the Americas, from 2 to 6 percent of adults. The fastest rate of increase in the world is reported in the former Soviet republics, in particular Ukraine, Russia, Latvia, and Estonia (UNAIDS, 2004).

Transmission of HIV

To understand the causes of epidemic HIV, we must begin with an examination of the ways that the virus is transmitted. In affluent countries, HIV affects almost exclusively men who have sex with men, people who share needles for injecting drugs, female partners of bisexual men and needle sharers and their infants, and hemophiliacs. To the surprise of epidemiologists, HIV has made few inroads in the rest of the population in affluent countries, in spite of heterosexual epidemics of other sexually transmitted diseases. In Latin America and Southeast Asia, epidemics that began among drug users and men who have sex with men are spreading through heterosexual contact and from mother to child. In very poor countries, exposure through contaminated blood and medical equipment is also a much greater risk than in rich countries (UNAIDS, 2004). China and some parts of sub-Saharan Africa have been especially affected by iatrogenic infections. In the former Soviet republics, transmission is thought to be primarily through the sharing of contaminated drug equipment. In sub-Saharan Africa and in other very poor regions, the primary modes of transmission of HIV infection are heterosexual intercourse and vertical transmission from mother to child in pregnancy and lactation (UNAIDS, 2004), although unsterile medical procedures are an important cause of

HIV spread (Gisselquist et al., 2003), and sex between men certainly also plays some role.

The efficiency of transmission of HIV (the probability that an individual will be infected through direct contact with an infected person or through blood products or instruments) varies, depending on the mode of contact. Blood transfusions are the most efficient mode of transmission, with 90 to 100 percent of persons transfused with contaminated blood becoming infected. Needle-sharing is also highly efficient, with the result that local epidemics among drug users have spread very rapidly. Vertical transmission varies in efficiency among regions. Rates of transmission, before the introduction of prophylactic treatment of mothers, ranged from 14 to 40 percent of infants of HIV-infected mothers. Among men who have sex with men, unprotected receptive anal intercourse is conservatively estimated to result in 5 to 30 infections per 1,000 contacts; nonreceptive anal intercourse has a lower risk. Among medical personnel, the risk of infection from accidental needle pricks is estimated to be about 3 per 1,000 accidents, without adjusting for any other possible sources of infection, such as drug use or unprotected sex (World Bank, 1997).

Unprotected heterosexual intercourse between otherwise healthy adults is a relatively inefficient mode of HIV transmission. The transmission of HIV between healthy persons in industrialized countries is relatively rare and has been insufficient to maintain a heterosexual epidemic in the absence of other factors. In the United States and Western Europe, transmission from an otherwise healthy HIV-infected adult female to a healthy adult male will occur in about one out of 1,000 contacts. Transmission from an otherwise healthy HIV-infected adult male to a healthy adult female occurs about once in 500 contacts (World Bank, 1997). (For statistical purposes; not for individual use.) This book is primarily about the heterosexual and vertical epidemics of HIV/AIDS. It is in those epidemics that the greatest difference in rates of infection between rich and poor countries occurs.

Epidemiology of HIV

While the immediate cause of much HIV transmission in sub-Saharan Africa and other very poor regions is heterosexual intercourse, the individual transmission and epidemic spread of HIV are not simply mathematical functions of sexual behavior. HIV is an infectious disease. Epidemiological, clinical, and laboratory evidence show that HIV infection is influenced by the same factors that promote transmission of other infectious diseases. An established literature in public health and a century of clinical practice demonstrate that persons with nutritional deficiencies, with parasitic diseases, whose general health is poor, who have little access to health-care services, or who are otherwise economically disadvantaged have greater susceptibility to infectious diseases, whether they are transmitted sexually or by food, water, air, or other means. Regarding the conditions necessary for the transmission of infectious disease, Louis Pasteur is reported to have said: "The microbe is nothing, the terrain everything."

Living conditions in poor regions provide a very different terrain for the propagation of infectious disease from that of industrialized countries. The real annual income of the average person in the United States is more than 60 times that of the average Tanzanian or Malawian (UNDP, 2004). Calorie intake per capita in sub-Saharan Africa has not increased since 1970 and is still only 70 percent of the consumption level of industrialized countries. Public and private spending on health services in Canada is about US$2,800 per person per year; in Nigeria, it is US$31 per person per year; and in Ethiopia, it is US$14 per person per year (UNDP, 2004). In affluent countries, virtually everyone has access to biologically safe piped water and sanitation systems, such as sewer connection, cesspool, or outhouse. In developing countries, many people do not have access to clean water, and for sanitation many do not even have latrines. In Haiti, only 28 percent of the people have any form of improved sanitation, and only 46 percent have access to an improved water source (any form of piped water). In Cambodia, only 17 percent of the population have adequate disposal facilities for human wastes, and only 30 percent have access to clean water. In most developed countries, more than 95 percent of the population have sustainable access to affordable essential medicines, but that is true for less than 50 percent of the population in Brazil, Paraguay, Ecuador, Haiti, Georgia, Tajikistan, India, and many countries in sub-Saharan Africa, Central America, and Southeast Asia (UNDP, 2004). If we look at HIV as we do other infectious diseases, we should expect the HIV epidemic to develop differently in regions with widespread malnutrition and other sanitary and health-service deficiencies known to contribute to disease susceptibility.

The question of how, and to whom, HIV has spread in different parts of the world is not just an interesting puzzle for epidemiologists. The design of effective prevention strategies hinges on an understanding of the causes of the pandemic and its regional epidemics. Early explanations of the syndrome were chiefly virological, seeing HIV as a virus that barges in and clobbers the host's immune system until the person dies from one or more opportunist infections. Since HIV appeared to kill all those infected, the focus of the first decade of research was on the virus itself. Yet, the standard epidemiological model of disease causation recognizes the importance of host factors in disease transmission and progression. Drawing on that tradition, more recent work has focused on the immune response to HIV—that is, on the interaction of HIV with the host's own immune system (Whitaker, 1997).[2]

2. The host here is the person becoming infected—that is, serving as host to the infecting pathogen. In other contexts, the term *host* means the carrier, or the person already infected.

Host susceptibility is considered a key to the emergence of the new and resurgent infectious diseases, of which HIV/AIDS is only the most notorious (Morris and Potter, 1997).

The importance of a person's immune response to HIV was first noted in the industrialized countries in the more rapid transition from HIV to AIDS in malnourished persons (Baum and Shor-Posner, 1998; Baum et al., 1997; Semba et al., 1993; Fawzi and Hunter, 1998). Another indicator of the importance of host characteristics (in both mother and child) is the significant difference between rich and poor countries in the rate of transmission of HIV from mother to child (vertical transmission). Before medical intervention was available, 14 percent of infants born to HIV-infected mothers in Europe became infected, and in the United States, 17 to 25 percent were infected without intervention. In Africa, vertical transmission occurred in 25 to 40 percent of births to untreated mothers with HIV or AIDS (Fowler and Rogers, 1996). In rich countries, where antiretroviral prophylaxis and delivery by Caesarean section are available, mother-to-child transmission is now rare. But in most poor populations, the likelihood of transmission from mother to child is still at least 30 percent (UNAIDS, 2004).

Greater attention to host factors also helps to explain the extremely high rates of heterosexual HIV transmission in sub-Saharan Africa and increasingly in other poor regions. Two factors that we find across sub-Saharan Africa and among poor populations in Asia and Latin America that are known to undermine immune system response are malnutrition and parasite infection. Throughout the world, nutrition is the most important determinant of susceptibility to disease because of its impact on both the protective barriers (skin and mucous membranes) and on immune response at the cellular level (Morris and Potter, 1997). Parasite infection is also widespread in poor populations and produces chronic immune response to the foreign bodies (the parasites), leading to immune system exhaustion (Bentwich et al., 1995). (The roles of both nutrition and parasite infection are explained in chapters 2 and 3.)

Malnutrition and parasite infection contribute to greater susceptibility to any infectious disease, including those transmitted sexually. The conditions of poverty increase HIV susceptibility, not only to opportunist diseases after HIV infection but also to HIV transmission itself, just as they increase susceptibility to other infectious diseases. There are also certain diseases prevalent among poor populations in Africa, Asia, and Latin America, but rare in the rest of the world, that sharply increase the probability of transmission of HIV in particular (see chapter 3).

Ecology of disease transmission

The enormity and speed of the AIDS pandemic are menacing. It is understandable that observers initially tended to lose perspective, unable to explain how such a pandemic could come about, even though the conventional model of infectious disease is quite adequate for interpreting HIV spread. Some 20 years into the pandemic, it is harder to understand why the failure of global AIDS policy to halt the spread has led to so little reflection on its underlying causes. What is lacking in HIV/AIDS policy is both context and historical perspective.

The living and working conditions of some 2 to 3 billion people in the world promote epidemic and endemic diseases, both infectious and parasitic. People live on garbage dumps and survive by scavenging. Others take their drinking water from streams, rivers, and lakes contaminated by household and industrial waste. Residential crowding contributes to transmission of many diseases, including tuberculosis and meningitis. More than half of early childhood deaths around the world are attributable to malnutrition and its synergies with infectious disease. Malnutrition in young girls and malnutrition in pregnancy are important contributing causes of maternal mortality. In at least 20 African countries and in numerous countries in Southeast, South, and Southwest Asia, as well as in Latin America, a woman still has a much greater chance of dying in childbirth than from AIDS (derived from WHO, 2000b, and UNAIDS, 2004). And those deaths occur not just in the hinterland of the poorest countries but also in the urban slums and close-by suburbs of Buenos Aires, Rio de Janeiro, and other elegant cities of the middle-income countries. Mortality tells only part of the story of human suffering and wasted potential. Nutritional deficiencies, aggravated by parasite infection, also lead to physical and mental disability and thereby perpetuate a cycle of unproductive labor, poverty, and impairment (Stillwaggon, 1998).

We already know a great deal about why epidemics spread. Pathogens abound, but they do not always cause disease in a particular individual. Nor does the presence of disease in some members of a population always cause an epidemic. Random introductions of pathogens into human populations occur continually, but they rarely lead to epidemics or pandemics. Propitious conditions are necessary for a microbe to make a person sick or for the disease to spread throughout a population.

Throughout history it has been clear that the epidemic spread of a disease requires favorable conditions. Rats (or soldiers) aboard a ship from an eastern port carried plague-infected fleas into Italy in 1348 and sparked the epidemic spread of plague in Europe, wiping out one-third of the population in most of the continent. This introduction was a random event, but it was certainly not Western Europe's only exposure to rats or plague. In 1348, plague entered a continent weakened by 30 years of falling per capita food consumption and increasing immiseration of the peasantry due to increased feudal demands. The population of Europe had already been falling in the decades leading up to 1348, and a series of disastrous harvests exacerbated the effects of war (Pounds, 1994). Even though many nobles and townspeople perished in the Black Death, the ecologic context for the epidemic was the worsening economic situation of the peasantry: "The generation born in this age of crisis was so debilitated by hunger, disease, exploitation, war and disorder that a few years later it succumbed to a still greater catastrophe, the worst in world history" (Fischer, 1996, 41). That depiction of Europe in the early 1300s could describe parts of sub-Saharan Africa, Asia, and the Americas from the 1970s to today.

Plague is not merely a historical curiosity. It is endemic among rodents in the southwestern part of the United States, and there are about 10 to 15 human infections every year, with a case fatality rate of about 14 percent (CDC, 2003). Yet that low but steady transmission has not provoked a plague epidemic in the United States. When an epidemic of plague did break out in India in 1996, the presence of eight rats for every person in that country (that is, 8 billion rats) was perhaps a contributing factor, but it was the filthy conditions of the slums of the port city of Surat that allowed the disease to spread (Badhwar, 1994).

One way that pathogens are introduced into previously unexposed human populations is through zoonoses, animal viruses that become human diseases through mutation. Influenza is a zoonosis, and every year a new strain of influenza emerges from the pork and fowl ecology of southern China. The flu virus that raged through the world in 1918 might have been a particularly virulent strain, but it also found propitious terrain in populations ravaged by World War I, when more people died of hunger and disease, even before the influenza pandemic, than from combat. The increased mobility of populations—of troops and refugees—also facilitated its spread.

For 100 years there was no cholera outbreak in the Americas, although cholera vibrio were introduced into coastal waters throughout the region, from the United States to Argentina, on countless occasions over the twentieth century by trade with Asia. In 1991, however, the discharge of cholera vibrio in the bilge water of a ship in Lima harbor caused an outbreak that reestablished cholera as an endemic disease in the Americas. The years leading up to 1991 had seen rapid growth of the slums of Lima, without the necessary expansion of water lines and sanitation systems. The government did not invest in new infrastructure in the poor settlements, or *pueblos jôvenes*, and, even if it had been willing, it faced the continuing destruction of power plants, clinics, and other facilities by Sendero Luminoso (the Shining Path) guerrillas.

A relatively high dose of contaminated food or water is necessary to make a person sick with cholera compared to many other pathogens. The return of cholera to the hemisphere followed substantial deterioration in sanitary conditions throughout Latin America during the "lost decade" of the 1980s, a period of economic crisis, decreased government social expenditures, falling incomes, and increasing inequality. From one squalid slum to another, cholera spread north and south from Peru across Latin America, and it remains today an endemic disease throughout the region.

HIV is thought to be a zoonosis deriving from simian immunodeficiency viruses (SIVs) that infected humans, perhaps from hunting or butchering injuries that allowed blood contact. (Even if that origin is disputed by some, what remains true is that some virus was introduced into human populations, regardless of where and how that first occurred.) SIVs were introduced no fewer than seven times into human populations, although HIV only became epidemic after 1980. A similar virus might have been introduced on numerous other occasions but did not have epidemic results. The discoverers of the simian viruses observe that their findings "illustrate the classic maxim that the epidemiology of an infectious disease reflects complex interactions between the infectious agent, the host, and the environment" (Hahn et al., 2000, 612). The introduction of SIV was random, but the continuation and spread of HIV are not.

When HIV came on the scene in the early 1980s, it was barely noticed in some countries because of the routine enormity of suffering. Even today, HIV is far from the only threat to poor people. A study of the workplace impact of AIDS in 15 large firms in Tanzania in 1998 reported that 50 percent of employee deaths were AIDS-related (Baruch and Clancy, 2000). It is likely that workers in large firms would have steady employment and relatively higher wages than the average for Tanzanians. Since Tanzania has a relatively mature epidemic (at least 15 years since the first reported infections of AIDS) and high HIV prevalence, one would also expect that AIDS deaths would be a high proportion of all deaths of working-age people. Even allowing for underreporting due to the stigma of AIDS, it is remarkable that only half of employee deaths were from AIDS. Even in that relatively privileged population (for Tanzania), other maladies are killing employees at roughly the same rate as AIDS.

Another workplace study of a plantation in Malawi reported that there were, on average, three deaths per month from AIDS, certainly a terrible toll. But there were six non-AIDS deaths of adult workers per month, and 15 deaths per month of workers' dependents (Morris, 2003). Malawi has a very serious AIDS epidemic (adult prevalence 14 percent at the end of 2003), but only one-third of the workers' deaths were from AIDS. AIDS flourishes where people are dying of other diseases. Nowhere in the affluent countries is the death toll among working-age people and children so high, nor is the toll from AIDS comparable. That is not mere coincidence.

Limitations of global AIDS policy

International AIDS policy seems to exhibit amnesia regarding everything that epidemiologists know about disease transmission, in poor populations in particular, and everything economists and other social scientists know about the environment of poverty in the developing world. Most policy documents written since the Thirteenth International AIDS Conference in

Durban, South Africa, in 2000 begin with the acknowledgment that HIV disporportionately afflicts poor countries. Rarely is that statement accompanied by an adequate analysis of how poverty contributes to the spread of AIDS, and then only to suggest that poverty can provide the impetus to risky behaviors, which is certainly true, but it is only part of the story. Even when the economic and social context of AIDS is noted, that is not matched by policies that address the environment of poverty in which HIV is spreading.

Why did people formulating AIDS policy forget almost everything they knew about the requirements of disease transmission? Sex is part of it. People get distracted by sex, and because HIV is sexually transmitted many people ignore the fact that even sexually transmitted diseases require the combination of pathogen, host, and environmental factors. Syphilis provoked the same stigmatizing and unscientific reaction in earlier decades. Moreover, HIV has had its most devastating spread thus far in Africa, a part of the world about which most Europeans and North Americans have little correct information and plenty of erroneous notions, and this fact has had a crucial role in the misunderstanding of the AIDS epidemics. Economists, other social scientists, and policy makers from international organizations, all of whom should understand the complexity of African poverty, made little use of their knowledge of poor populations and relied on cultural explanations of the African epidemic. Deep-seated Western stereotypes of African sexuality hijacked the AIDS-in-Africa discourse, and, consequently, a behavioral bias continues to limit AIDS analysis and policy. HIV seemed to confirm Western notions of African hypersexuality and derailed investigation of other causes of the epidemic spread of HIV.

The narrow individual focus of what I call the behavioral paradigm was exacerbated by the methodologies employed in contemporary epidemiology and economics, as well as the current trend in public health to favor individual, curative interventions over "upstream" prevention. Consequently, prevention policy is restricted, almost exclusively, to interventions aimed at influencing individual sexual or needle-sharing behavior, rather than addressing the social and biological context in which those behaviors occur.

The limitations imposed on AIDS policy by the African stereotype and by the methodologies employed in the social and health sciences were only part of the reason the HIV/AIDS epidemics have been misunderstood. The grave impact of the epidemic has made policy makers reluctant to consider more remote causes, and the immediacy of the epidemic's human toll seems to have a paralyzing effect on devising creative solutions. The impact of the epidemic will continue to be devastating for decades to come. In several countries it is predicted that 25 percent or more of the adult population will die 30 to 40 years before normal life expectancy. Disease causes disruption of social and economic networks, loss of income for families, and loss of output for the economy. Children are taken out of school to care for sick parents and to earn incomes. Orphans generally do not continue in school after the death of a mother, and so investment in human capital for the country as a whole shrinks. Agricultural production is falling in severely affected countries, and in many cases surviving family members switch to production of less labor-intensive, but also less nutritious, crops. Widows and orphans lose rights to land and sometimes are compelled to enter commercial sex work to survive, compounding and accelerating the epidemic's effects. (For a thorough recent treatment of the impact of AIDS, see Barnett and Whiteside, 2002.) Policy makers must shift out of panic mode and create long-term policies for this now-permanent crisis.

A few economic analyses of the impact of AIDS have argued, correctly, that forecasts comparing a future "with AIDS" and "without AIDS" are no longer relevant (Loewenson and Whiteside, 2002). It is not possible to talk meaningfully about the future of sub-Saharan Africa, or any other region seriously affected by AIDS, without considering the impact of the epidemic. One paper suggested the useful concept of endogenizing AIDS: that is, recognizing AIDS as an endogenous variable in growth models for sub-Saharan Africa. Any predictions about the region would have to incorporate the AIDS variable (McPherson et al., 2000). That recognition is important, but it is only part of the answer.

Along with AIDS, numerous other afflictions, including malaria, tuberculosis, worms, and malnutrition, are, as they always have been, endogenous variables for growth projections for Africa and other very poor regions. Those endemic problems and myriad others provide an important, but neglected, part of the reason why people in Africa remain poor and why rates of HIV in the region are many times higher than in more prosperous regions.

Not only is AIDS an endogenous variable in future growth, but the AIDS epidemic was itself endogenously determined. The conditions of poverty, malnutrition, parasite infection, war, economic disruption, and rapid urbanization were essential elements of the epidemic spread of HIV. Consequently, stopping AIDS requires attacking the underlying causes. Models that fail to recognize the interactions among those endogenous variables that produced the AIDS epidemic cannot fully incorporate AIDS into future projections. Without discerning the complex causes of the AIDS epidemic, they conclude that "[u]nder present circumstances, African countries will remain in a downward spiral so long as behavior patterns do not change" (McPherson et al., 2000, 25). Behavior change is important, but the downward spiral can only be stopped if there is substantial change in the health profile of sub-Saharan Africa and other poor regions.

The answer cannot be to treat poverty eradication as an expensive diversion of funds from AIDS prevention, as some have suggested, but to strengthen poverty reduction as a necessary component of health promotion. The enormity and urgency of AIDS have led to pressure to concentrate all health spending on HIV prevention, instead of expanding comprehensive primary health care and health education. Mainstreaming AIDS is interpreted to mean that AIDS-specific programs take a bite out of every other budget, such as having the transport ministry paint AIDS ribbons on rail cars or having agricultural extension agents lecture farmers about sexual behavior. It is far more effective to find ways for each sector—whether it be trucking, commerce, agriculture, health care, government, or mining—to combat the conditions that produced the epidemic, whether they be biological, social, behavioral, economic, or environmental.

Recognizing underlying causes is especially important now that resources are finally becoming available for AIDS programs. The momentum that has been building since 2000 to allocate more funds to AIDS prevention and treatment has run up against a new obstacle, the supposed lack of absorptive capacity for the amount of money that is now offered. There is some truth in the statement: it would be a waste to send $3 billion worth of antiretroviral medicines if they spoil on African wharves for lack of transport, or to deliver them to Latin American governments only to find that corrupt administrators appropriate $5 billion of illegal profits, with very little improvement in the health of the population. Certainly, putting all the money into treatment or narrowly conceived condom and peer-education programs is a bad idea. But there is plenty of scope for using US$3 billion, or even US$15 billion, right now in ways that will help prevent HIV transmission immediately and for the long run.

AIDS policy currently ignores what we know about epidemics and why they spread. It lacks historical perspective. It disregards the social context of disease, except to the extent that the social context is used to explain individuals' sexual or drug-using behavior. Global AIDS policy is based on a model of HIV transmission that assumes "one risk fits all" in regions of vastly different economic and ecological conditions. It attempts to address those very varied risks with an extraordinarily limited set of solutions that hardly go beyond the provision of condoms, peer education, needle exchange, and voluntary counseling and testing. In 2003 WHO made an urgent call for a minimum of 24 billion condoms a year, particularly for Southeast Asia, to solve the AIDS crisis (Kaisernetwork, 2003b). But spending billions of dollars leaving Southeast Asia ankle deep in used (and unused) condoms would change little in the region's health profile or the economic, social, and ecological setting that promotes epidemic disease.

Global AIDS policy is missing the big picture. The pieces of the puzzle are all around, and numerous scientists, social scientists, and other observers in the past two decades have made some of the arguments in this book. In spite of the evidence, however, AIDS policy remains narrow, short-sighted, and even counterproductive. Documents of policy organizations report the failure of, and even resistance to, AIDS-prevention strategies, and yet policy makers respond by spending more money on the same failed strategies. They fail to see that the epidemic spread of HIV derives from the same context as the propagation of so many other afflictions. AIDS policy has asked very little about that context and so has generated strategies that cannot solve the problem of poor health, of which HIV is only a part.

Structure of the book

This book explains the rapid spread of HIV in the context of poverty, malnutrition, and parasitic and infectious disease. It describes the health conditions that derive from the social and economic context in three regions of developing and transition economies. It critiques some of the methodological limitations in the social and health sciences that encumber research on HIV and AIDS in developing countries, and it criticizes the policies that derive from those limited and limiting methodologies. Finally, it offers pragmatic solutions to social, economic, and biological factors that promote disease transmission, including the spread of HIV.

The appendix to this chapter presents survey data on sexual behavior in many countries. AIDS discourse is colored by the explicit or implicit premise that differences in national prevalence of HIV reflect differences in sexual behavior between populations. Assertions to that effect rely on anecdotal evidence, or no evidence at all (see chapter 7). The data presented in the appendix demonstrate that there is no correlation between higher rates of HIV and countries with higher rates of early initiation of sex, premarital sex, or multipartnered sex.

Chapter 2 brings together the results of numerous scientific studies on the biology of immune function and disease. It presents the biomedical evidence that malnutrition and parasite infection contribute to greater susceptibility to any infectious disease, including those which are transmitted sexually. The conditions of poverty increase HIV susceptibility, not only to opportunist diseases after HIV infection but also to HIV transmission, just as they increase susceptibility to other infectious diseases. Chapter 3 explains the biological synergies of malnutrition, parasitic and infectious diseases, and immune response that are specific to HIV transmission and that are widespread among poor populations in Africa, Asia, and Latin America, and increasingly in the former socialist countries.

Chapters 4, 5, and 6 describe the economic conditions in three world regions that provide the context in which HIV is spreading most rapidly. Chapter 4 examines the biomedical effects of economic conditions in Africa that contribute to high rates of HIV transmission. Economic and health variables distinguish sub-Saharan Africa from affluent countries with lower rates of HIV. This economic/biomedical conclusion implies a broad policy response for confronting HIV/AIDS in Africa, Asia, and Latin America.

Chapter 5 applies the lessons of HIV in sub-Saharan Africa to Latin America and the Caribbean. Economic and biological factors are important determinants of HIV transmission there, as they are in Africa. Statistical analysis shows high correlation between HIV prevalence and GDP per capita, international migration, urbanization, and calorie supply. The results reflect the dualism of the Latin American and Caribbean economies and their dual HIV epidemics and suggest the reasons why HIV is spreading fastest in lower-income groups.

Chapter 6 examines the health profile of the countries of Central and Eastern Europe and the former Soviet Union as the context for an emerging HIV epidemic. The HIV epidemics in the transition economies of Europe are apparently fueled by needle-sharing and prostitution, unlike the epidemics in most of the developing world. The emphasis on the behavioral conditions, however, masks the important role played by falling living standards and the collapse of public health services. This chapter broadens the analysis of declining health in the former socialist economies and situates the study of HIV epidemics there within a biomedical analysis of disease vulnerability, rather than the reigning behavioral model.

The conventional model of epidemiological inquiry should have spotlighted the conditions detailed in chapters 4 through 6, informed by the recognized synergies discussed in chapters 2 and 3. Since global AIDS policy does not reflect most of what is known about the regions of the world in which that policy is promoted, it is necessary to investigate what prevented social scientists and health scientists from using the information at hand. Chapter 7 examines Western preconceptions regarding African sexuality that distorted early research on the social context of AIDS in Africa and still limit the scope of preventive policies. Key works cited repeatedly in the social science and policy literature constructed a hypersexualized pan-African culture as the main reason for the high prevalence of HIV in sub-Saharan Africa. Africans were portrayed as the social "Other" in works marked by sweeping generalizations and innuendo, rather than useful comparative data on sexual behavior. Chapter 7 offers a critical analysis of the discourse on African "exceptionalism" and the historical and philosophical origins of treating Africa as a special case.

Chapter 8 discusses the methodologies employed by health scientists and social scientists that prevent them from seeing the interactions that produce epidemic spread of HIV, from measuring those interactions, and from using that information in prevention policy. It examines the methodological limitations in the fields of public health, epidemiology, and economics that are impediments to understanding health in the developing world and specifically obstruct prevention of HIV/AIDS.

Chapter 9 examines the impact of misguided development policy and inadequate epidemiology on the choice of interventions for HIV and other health problems in poor countries. Since 2000, there is increasing recognition that HIV/AIDS is a development issue, but policy prescriptions still do not reflect a development agenda. HIV/AIDS prevention plans are narrowly focused on provision of condoms, behavior modification, and treating cofactor STDs (sexually transmitted diseases). From a development perspective, those interventions come very late in the process. Chapter 10 examines workplace HIV/AIDS programs as an example of the limitations of global AIDS policy.

Chapter 11 uses the economic concept of externalities to evaluate the positive spillovers that exist in health interventions. It argues for mainstreaming AIDS prevention by addressing a broad array of development problems, rather than by employing a just-in-time approach to HIV intervention. The lesson from the biomedical literature on disease interactions is that the best investments in health require us to look beyond the immediate problem. There are serious conceptual and practical difficulties with the use of interventions that are narrowly focused on HIV and other STDs, including the divorce of sexuality from other aspects of a healthy lifestyle and the waste of health services infrastructure, squandering opportunities for economies of scale and scope. Fundamentally, HIV-only programs do nothing to change the environment that produces unhealthy people, unhealthy behaviors, and high transmission rates.

What this book is not

This book is not part of the debate about whether HIV causes AIDS. This work accepts that HIV is a necessary causal factor in AIDS. Of course, it is important to continue to evaluate anomalies in the HIV-AIDS link because that work may yield important information about HIV and AIDS and about other diseases and conditions. It is not useful, however—and, in fact, is irresponsible—to assert that there are sufficient anomalies in the data to deprioritize safe sex. I accept the mainstream explanation for HIV and AIDS because it is plausible and it has been substantiated adequately to pursue research and policy on the basis of causality.

Regrettably, this book does not address the epidemic in the United States or other affluent countries. That is the result of time constraints and my particular expertise. Many of the arguments of this work also apply to poor and marginalized populations in the developed countries. There is also not very much in this book about the Asian epidemics, although they are very important. I preferred to concentrate my analysis on the parts of the world in which I have lived and worked over the past 30 years—sub-Saharan Africa, Latin America and the Caribbean, and Eastern Europe and the former Soviet Union—which are also the parts of the world with the highest prevalence and the fastest reported spread of HIV. The lessons of this book, however, apply to the Asian epidemics as well, and at least to some extent to marginalized populations in rich countries.

This work also deliberately avoids ideology as much as possible. I know what the sides are in each of the methodological and policy disputes discussed here, and I do not think it furthers the cause of health to encamp with one side or the other in the pages of this book. Dogma only narrows the range of options for solving concrete problems. Even in the current political and economic context, there are pragmatic, affordable, and feasible solutions that will immediately improve the lives of poor people and stem the spread of HIV and other plagues of poverty.

This book also does not take a side in the debate over what has been labeled "public health nihilism" (Fairchild and Oppenheimer, 1998): the argument between changing only the socioeconomic context or only the curative inputs. Dichotomies such as prevention versus cure do not promote good health. Clearly, this book supports a comprehensive approach to public health. But I would not squander all the wonderful, life-saving innovations that we in this era are privileged to enjoy and wait for economic change to bring about good health for poor people.

This book does not dichotomize the debate on treatment versus prevention. I heartily support both treatment and prevention (including the preventive interventions that I repeatedly refer to as end-game, last-minute, and even paternalistic). We should use every means we have to save lives. But the means that have been tried thus far are not enough. The prevention of disease and other forms of oppression needs to be moved upstream *as well as* being continued in the behavioral forms that it now takes. Although I repeatedly emphasize that global AIDS policy depends too heavily on condom provision and behavior-change communication, I do not propose abandoning those tactics. They must be part of the wider strategy to bring the enjoyment of good health to more people.

In this book I cannot say all that must be said about gender roles. From birth to death, those roles impinge on every aspect of the lives of women and men. That is as true in the affluent countries as it is in Africa, Asia, and Latin America. Radical change in the status of women and girls worldwide is necessary.

Finally, this book is not pessimistic. There are myriad known solutions to the problems of poverty and poor health. Many of them are simple and low-cost. Some would even raise incomes and profits. And all of them provide positive spillovers in economic and human development. The means are at hand for preventing the spread of HIV/AIDS and for improving lives. The only problem is convincing people that those two objectives are one and the same.

◣ *Appendix: sex, everywhere*

Since HIV can be transmitted sexually, and most HIV is transmitted sexually in poor countries (and increasingly in transition countries), it is reasonable to include sexual behavior as one of the determinants of HIV prevalence. Nevertheless, differences in sexual behavior between different populations do not adequately explain differences in HIV prevalence.

In much of the popular and professional discourse, there is a presumption—generally unstated—that populations with high rates of HIV must have higher rates of early initiation of sex, multipartnered sex, and commercial sex than countries with low rates of HIV. Below are a few examples of assertions published by a multilateral organization and two academic publishers that sexual behavior is the key determinant of rates of HIV in different populations. These overt statements, together with less-explicit versions, are examples of the behavioral paradigm. It is a paradigm, in Kuhn's (1970) sense, because it determines what questions can be asked and what solutions can be sought regarding HIV/AIDS.

> HIV transmission has been much faster in societies where there are high levels of unprotected sexual interaction with prostitutes, who have very many sexual partners, than in societies where the majority of people have few or moderate numbers of partners in their lifetime. (Ford, 1994, 88) [Note: this statement was not followed by supporting evidence.]

> In contrast to Americans, who usually view sex morally and think that people who have multiple partners (even if unmarried) are immoral and unfaithful, most Africans do not judge sexual behavior in such terms at all. They experience little guilt about sex, and they enter into sex more casually and have more sexual partners than Westerners do. (Rushing, 1995, 62) [Note: there are no citations for these statements in the original.]

> "Promiscuity, and the Primacy of Cultural Factors: A Lethal Mixture in Africa" was the title of the largest of several text boxes in the *AIDS Update 1999* published by United Nations Population Fund (UNFPA, 1999, 6).

Chapter 7 addresses, at length, important and representative works in the AIDS discourse that unequivocally posit a behavioral explanation for differences in HIV prevalence or imply a behavioral explanation by presenting non-Western societies as exotic and different from the West, even in matters quite mundane. Chapters 9 and 10 discuss the policies that originate in an acceptance of the behavioral paradigm.

Since the "lots of sex" assumption plays consciously or unconsciously in discussion of HIV/AIDS and in AIDS policy, it interferes with seeing the epidemic in any other way. I present here comparative data on sexual behavior in various countries that demonstrate that there is no empirical basis for a presumption that high rates of sexual activity correlate with high HIV prevalence. Once we recognize that differences in sexual behavior cannot explain differences in HIV rates between countries, we can proceed with the subject of this book: what *is* causing the high and rising prevalence of HIV in developing and transition-economy countries, and what can be done to prevent further spread of HIV/AIDS and other crippling diseases.

The data on sexual initiation, premarital sex, multipartnering, and commercial sex tell us very little about the distribution of HIV around the world. What follows are the findings of a number of studies on sexual behavior from UNAIDS, WHO, UNDP, and scholarly journals. In some cases I have added comments to situate the findings within the HIV discourse.

Africa

UNAIDS. 1999a. *Fact Sheet on Differences in HIV Spread in African Cities.* Geneva: UNAIDS.

This study surveyed sexual behavior in four African cities in 1997 and 1998 and found significant variation in sexual behavior and in HIV prevalence, but it found no correlation between the two. Adult HIV prevalence in the four cities was: Cotonou (Benin), 3 percent in both men and women; Yaoundé (Cameroon), 4 percent in men and 3 percent in women; Kisumu (Kenya), 20 percent in men and 30 percent in women; Ndola (Zambia), 23 percent in men and 32 percent in women. Among the findings were: the highest rate of partner change was found in Yaoundé, where men reported more than twice as many lifetime partners as in the other sites, and women reported slightly more. Fewer married men reported extramarital relationships in the high-HIV sites. Very few married women (1–3 percent) reported extramarital relationships, except in Yaoundé (12 percent).

The researchers found that in the high-prevalence sites the age at which women became sexually active was slightly lower, there was a higher prevalence of herpes-2, and there was a much lower rate of male circumcision. Rates of partner change, concurrent sexual relationships, and contacts with sex workers were not correlated with rates of HIV. None of the factors taken into consideration could account for the high prevalence among teenage girls, soon after first sex and with few exposures. They state that, "In fact, behavioural differences seem to be outweighed by differences in HIV transmission probability," although it is unclear if they would consider factors beyond those they mentioned as contributing to that difference in probability.

> *Comment:* This study provided a clear empirical challenge to the behavioral assumption. Unfortunately, UNAIDS has not followed up on unanswered questions, in particular why young women in Kisumu have such high rates of HIV (see chapters 3 and 4 of this book for further discussion).

Africa, Asia, South America

John Cleland and Benoît Ferry (eds.). 1995. *Sexual Behaviour and AIDS in the Developing World.* London: Taylor and Francis for the World Health Organization.

This book reports on 16 surveys of heterosexual behavior in 15 countries (nine in Africa; four in Asia; Brazil and Mauritius) conducted from 1989 to 1991 under the auspices of the WHO Global Programme on AIDS (WHO/GPA). Almost all of the surveys were national, and an attempt was made to standardize the methodology because the stated intention of the surveys was to collect empirical data on behavior to understand the AIDS epidemic. The authors lamented: "The dearth of empirical studies that directly address sexual behaviours reflects a lack of interest from anthropologists. This is evident from reviews of the literature on human sexuality in sub-Saharan Africa (Standing and Kisseka, 1989; Larson, 1989; Caldwell, Caldwell, and Quiggin, 1989; Caldwell, Orubuloye, and Caldwell, 1992) and in Asia (Sittitrai and Barry, 1990) where most of the evidence about sexuality is anecdotal" (Caraël, 1995, 76).

The Cleland et al. summary of the WHO/GPA surveys contains useful data on premarital sex and multipartnering that the authors themselves found surprising: "Unexpectedly large proportions of men and women reported no sex during the last month, more so in Africa than elsewhere" (Caraël, 1995, 104). The surveys also contained questions intended to evaluate people's sense of subjective efficacy, or the belief that one's own actions can influence a situation. They found that in all the African surveys a very high proportion believed that they could change their behavior and their life situation, a finding which they felt contradicted the assertions that superstition and magical beliefs about transmission were more common in Africa than elsewhere.

Finally, as stated in the "Summary and Conclusions," written by Cleland, Ferry, and Caraël: "To return to the key point, the majority of men in all sites reported no sexual associates outside of regular partnerships in the year preceding the survey. . . . WHO/GPA surveys are thus immensely valuable in correcting wildly inaccurate perceptions of sexual behaviour, that were based on guesswork or small unrepresentative studies" (Cleland et al., 1995, 211).

▶ *Africa, Latin America and the Caribbean, Asia*

Ann K. Blanc and Ann A. Way. 1998. "Sexual Behavior and Contraceptive Knowledge and Use among Adolescents in Developing Countries," *Studies in Family Planning* 29(2):106–116.

This article reports data from the Demographic and Health Surveys, which are large-sample, nationally representative surveys of population, health, and nutrition in developing countries, sponsored by USAID and carried out by Macro International. Among the findings reported in this article: from the late 1960s to the early 1990s, the percentage of women who had sex by age 18 fell in 12 out of 17 African countries surveyed (in East, West, and Southern Africa) and increased by only 0.1 percentage point

Table 1.1
Percentage of 15- to 19-year-olds, never married, male and female, who have had intercourse (selected countries with year of survey and adult HIV prevalence)

Country	Male %	Female %	Adult HIV prevalence %
Great Britain (1991)	62	49	00.1
Brazil (1996)	61	16	00.7
United States (1995)	55	42	00.6
Dominican Republic (1996)	45	4	01.7
Haiti (1994–1995)	44	12	05.6
Tanzania (1996)	38	24	08.8
Mali (1995–1996)	32	16	01.9
Ghana (1993)	31	37	03.1
Zimbabwe (1994)	31	9	24.6

Source: Data for the first and second columns are provided by S. Singh. The third column data are from UNAIDS, 2004.

in another. It also decreased in the two Asian countries for which data were available, and in four of the eight Latin American and Caribbean countries surveyed.

Comment: The hypothesis that a sexual revolution (at least as regards earlier initiation of sexual activity) accompanied urbanization and modernization in the developing world is not supported by these data.

Africa, Caribbean, United States, Great Britain

Susheela Singh, Deirdre Wulf, Renee Samara, and Yvette P. Cuca. 2000. "Gender Differences in the Timing of First Intercourse: Data from 14 Countries," *International Family Planning Perspectives* 26(1):21–28, 43.

Tables 1.1 and 1.2 are derived from this article and from data provided to me by S. Singh. HIV prevalence data are from UNAIDS (2004). The point is not that sexual behavior is unimportant; it is that behavior does not explain differences in rates of HIV between different populations. Early initiation of sex is also frequently mentioned as one of the factors contributing to high rates of HIV in developing countries. But the United States has the highest rate of early initiation as seen in Table 1.2. In Mali, early marriage is common for women and is the reason for the high percentage of sexually experienced 17-year-old women there.

Table 1.2
Percentage of 20- to 24-year-olds sexually active before age 17, and median age at first intercourse (selected countries, sorted by male sexual activity percentage)

	Sexually active by age 17 (%)		Median age at first intercourse	
Country	Male	Female	Male	Female
United States (1995)	64	47	16	17
Brazil (1996)	63	29	16	19
Dominican Republic (1996)	49	32	17	19
Great Britain (1991)	47	42	17	17
Haiti (1994–1995)	44	30	18	19
Tanzania (1996)	42	45	18	17
Ghana (1993)	33	52	18	17
Zimbabwe (1994)	28	26	19	19
Mali (1995–1996)	26	72	19	16

Source: Derived from S. Singh et al., 2000.

Latin America

Chile

Nancy J. Murray, Lauri S. Zabin, Virginia Toledo-Dreves, and Ximena Luengo-Charath. 1998. "Gender Differences in Factors Influencing First Intercourse among Urban Students in Chile," *International Family Planning Perspectives* 24(3):139–144, 152.

This study surveyed 4,248 urban Chilean students, aged 11 to 19 years. "Results: Overall, 21% of the young women and 36% of the young men had ever had sex, with the median ages of first intercourse being 15 years and 14 years, respectively" (Murray et al., 1998, 139).

Peru

Mahler, K. 1997. "Increased Risk of STD Infection among Peruvian Women Linked to Their Partners' Sexual Practices," *International Family Planning Perspectives* 23(1):39–40.

In Peru, in a random sample of preemployment health screenings, 59 percent of men reported sex with a sex worker, and only 30 percent reported always using a condom with sex workers; 13 percent of the men reported having had urethritis, 19 percent reported genital ulcers, and 3 percent had had syphilis. The mean age of the men was 25, mean age for first sex for men was 16 years, and 21 percent had their first sexual experience with a sex worker. Those young men reported a lifetime mean of 11 partners, and 56 percent had multiple partners in the previous year. Some 60 percent of men with a regular partner also reported sex with a casual partner; 27

percent of men with a regular partner reported having sex with a prostitute in the year prior to the interview. None of the figures on women's behavior came anywhere close to the men's, and yet 33 percent of women and 12 percent of men had one or more STDs.

Dominican Republic

Abel, David. 1999. "Aids Linked to Infidelity in Dominican Republic," *Boston Globe*, December 28, pp. A2, A4.

The article states that Dominican Health Ministry studies report more than 50 percent of men have extramarital affairs, and 44 percent of boys and 36 percent of girls have had sexual intercourse by age 14.

United States

Susheela Singh and Jacqueline E. Darroch. 1999. "Trends in Sexual Activity among Adolescent American Women: 1982–1995," *Family Planning Perspectives* 31(5):212–219.

In surveys from 1982, 1988, and 1995 of U.S. women, aged 15 to 19: "In each of the surveys, about 40% of all 15–19-year-olds [female] had had sexual intercourse in the last [previous] three months" (Singh and Darroch, 1999, 212).

Olga A. Grinstead, Bonnie Faigeles, Diane Binson, and Rani Eversley. 1993. "Sexual Risk for Human Immunodeficiency Virus Infection among Women in High-Risk Cities," *Family Planning Perspectives* 25(6):252–256, 277.

This article contains data from 3,482 women in 23 cities in the United States who were 18 to 49 years old. The study showed that 15 percent of women engaged in sexual behavior that put them at risk of acquiring HIV, including "having multiple sexual partners, having a risky main sexual partner or having both multiple partners and a risky main partner. An additional 17% of women with no other risk factor report that they do not know their main partner's HIV risk status. . . . In general, women with a risky main partner are the least likely to use condoms consistently" (Grinstead et al., 1993, 252).

John O. G. Billy, Koray Tanfer, William R. Grady, and Daniel H. Klepinger. 1993. "The Sexual Behavior of Men in the United States," *Family Planning Perspectives* 25(2):52–60.

This article reports on a 1991 nationally representative survey of U.S. men aged 20–39, of whom 95 percent had had vaginal intercourse. Of those, 23 percent reported 20 or more female partners. "About one-fifth of never-married and formerly married men had had four or more partners over a recent 18-month period" (Billy et al., 1993, 52).

June M. Reinisch, Stephanie A. Sanders, Craig A. Hill, and Mary Ziemba-Davis. 1992. "High-Risk Sexual Behavior among Heterosexual Undergraduates at a Midwestern University," *Family Planning Perspectives* 24(3):116–121, 145.

This article reports on a 1998 survey of undergraduate students (generally the age group 18–22) at a large Midwestern state university in the United States. About 80 percent reported having ever had intercourse. Mean age at first intercourse was 17. Average number of sexual partners for women was six, and men reported an average of 11 partners.

Tom W. Smith. 1991. "Adult Sexual Behavior in 1989: Number of Partners, Frequency of Intercourse and Risk of AIDS," *Family Planning Perspectives* 23(3):102–107.

This article reports on a 1988/1989 survey of U.S. adults. The average reported number of partners since age 18 was seven, with men claiming many more partners than women.

Kathryn Kost and Jacqueline Darroch Forrest. 1992. "American Women's Sexual Behavior and Exposure to Risk of Sexually Transmitted Diseases," *Family Planning Perspectives* 24(6):244–254.

This article reports on surveys in 1988 and 1989 of U.S. women aged 15 to 44. The percentages of women and their reported number of partners are as follows:

67% of sexually experienced women had more than one partner
41% had four or more partners
23% had six or more partners
8% had more than 10 partners
71% had one or more nonmarital partners

They also reported that 27 to 39 percent of women aged 18–44 who were sexually active had had contact with more than one sexual partner, directly or indirectly, during the previous year.

► *Canada*

N. MacDonald, G. Wells, W. Fisher, et al. 1990. "High-Risk STD/HIV Behavior among College Students," *Journal of the American Medical Association* 263(23):3155–3159.

This article reports on a 1988 survey of 5,514 first-year students at Canadian community colleges and universities. Of the men, 74 percent were sexually active, and of the women, 69 percent. "Among the 21.3% of the men and 8.6% of the women with 10 or more partners, regular condom use was reported in only 21% and 7.5%, respectively" (3155). "40% of the men and 25.2% of the women reported at least 5 different partners" (3156). "Knowledge per se [of safe sex methods] was not typically translated into safer behavior" (3158).

Europe

Romania

M. Breslin. 1998. "Abortion Rate among Young Romanians Declines: Those Not in Union Report Rise in Contraceptive Use," *International Family Planning Perspectives* 24(3):150–152.

This article reports on a survey of Romanian 15- to 24-year-olds. Some 20 percent of women and 41 percent of men in the 15–19 age group had had sexual intercourse. Of sexually active men aged 15–24, 73 percent had initiated sexual activity by age 17. Of men who were sexually experienced, aged 15–24, 99 percent had had sex before marriage. Of sexually experienced men, 60 percent had had four or more partners, and 13 percent reported only a single partner.

France, Great Britain

R. Turner. 1993. "Landmark French and British Studies Examine Sexual Behavior, Including Multiple Partners, Homosexuality," *Family Planning Perspectives* 25(2):91–92.

This article reports on surveys in France (1991–1992) and Great Britain (1990–1991). In France, the average number of sexual partners reported by men was 11, and by women, three. In urban areas, 18 percent of men and 10 percent of women had two or more sexual partners in the previous year. Of those, the percentage whose multiple partnerships were concurrent increased with age group. In Britain, the proportion in each age group, by gender, reporting 10 or more lifetime partners was as shown in Table 1.3.

Table 1.3
Britons reporting 10 or more lifetime sexual partners (by age group and gender)

Age	Male (%)	Female (%)
24	16	5
25–34	31	10
35–44	29	9
>45	21	4

Source: Derived from Turner, 1993.

Poland

Zbigniew Izdebski. 2002. *Selected Aspects of Evaluation of the National HIV/AIDS Prevention Program.* Warsaw: National AIDS Center, UNDP.

This report presents the findings of national surveys in Poland in 1997 and 2001. Of all people interviewed, 15–49 years of age, 13 percent of women and 25 percent of men reported having had a sexual partner other than spouse or regular partner, while in the relationship. Of those interviewed who were sexually active, 15 percent of women and 29 percent of men had had another sexual partner while in a relationship.

From 1997 to 2001 the percentage of those who reported having had sex with a person other than their regular partner in the previous 12 months had dropped from 17 percent to 14 percent. Of those having partners other than their regular partner, half had one additional partner, 26 percent had two additional partners, and 28 percent had three or more additional partners. Most irregular contacts were persons known to the other, but 14 percent of irregular sexual contacts in 2001 and 12 percent in 1997 were met for the first time at the time of sexual contact. In 1997, 9 percent of all men reported paying for sexual services, and 12 percent reported using a commercial sex worker in 2001. From 1997 to 2001 the proportion of people going to a clinic or hospital in response to symptoms of STDs dropped from 39 percent to 26 percent, an increase of 3 percent went to a private doctor, and an increase of 10 percent asked advice of a friend.

Conclusions

The survey data presented here demonstrate that everywhere people have sex, everywhere some people have lots of sex, and everywhere most people do not. The numerous articles, books, and monographs asserting or assuming that differences in sexual behavior can explain variations in HIV prevalence rely on anecdotal evidence, not on survey data. Anecdotal evidence (such as in Caldwell and Caldwell, 1987, and Caldwell et al., 1989, discussed in chapter 7) cannot present an accurate assessment of broad patterns of sexual behavior. Only carefully randomized sampling techniques designed to ensure that respondents fairly represent the populations being studied can prevent sampling error. The use of anecdotal evidence in the attempt to understand the wide variation in the prevalence of HIV among different populations is fatally undermined by sampling bias in the study of sexual behavior.

Anecdotal evidence can be an important source of information and can illuminate and illustrate what would otherwise remain sterile and abstract observations. Nevertheless, anecdotal evidence cannot give us any information about the frequency of a behavior or of a condition in a population. The behavioral paradigm asserts or assumes widely different frequencies of certain types of sexual behaviors in different populations, and anecdotal evidence is useless in verifying that assertion or assumption. Even though survey data have well-known potential flaws (undersampling of certain subpopulations despite the best efforts of those who construct the sample design, inappropriately constructed interview schedules that generate misleading results, and poorly trained interviewers, for example), it is the only appropriate instrument for generating statements about frequencies in different populations.

The survey data that do exist show that differences in sexual behavior cannot explain differences in HIV rates between countries. We need to look at what are the important differences between populations that affect their vulnerability to disease. Chapters 2 through 6 explore those issues.

I

Ecology of Disease

2

Biological Synergies and Disease

Global AIDS policy is insufficiently grounded in scientific research. Although scientific studies of various aspects of HIV and AIDS abound, the specialized nature and conservative methodology of scientific research dictate that relatively few scientists cross the boundaries of their narrow subdisciplines. Those scientists who do make the connections between HIV and the ecology of disease are not well represented in AIDS policy circles.

Most social scientists and policy makers do not read much of the scientific literature. Consequently, their understanding of the AIDS pandemic is unduly influenced by unscientific notions that derive from unsupported but familiar preconceptions about behavior, a field in which social scientists feel more at home. HIV-prevention policies simply adopted the behavioral interventions of population-control programs because of the assumption that sexual behavior was of paramount importance. Devising successful HIV-prevention strategies, however, demands that social scientists and policy makers become more scientifically literate. The physiological complexity of HIV transmission in varied social and economic contexts should be the basis of policy.

Conventional epidemiology recognizes the importance of both pathogen and host characteristics in disease transmission and progression. The practice of much AIDS research, however, has failed to use the cross-disciplinary methods of epidemiology that situate the development of a disease in its social context. In the study of HIV/AIDS, most biomedical researchers investigate the molecular characteristics of the pathogen, while social scientists study human behavior. More AIDS research needs to cross disciplinary boundaries so that biomedical research might explore the "behavioral" characteristics of the pathogen—that is, the way that HIV behaves in different human ecological settings. Social science, for its part, needs to incorporate the physiological characteristics of the human population in its analysis of the dynamics of disease spread.

There is considerable recent research on the nutritional impact of HIV and on the effect of malnutrition in accelerating the transition from HIV to AIDS. There has been much less work incorporating what we already know about nutrition into an analysis of the determinants of individual transmission and of epidemic spread of HIV. This chapter presents the biomedical evidence that physiological characteristics of the host population contribute to greater susceptibility to any infectious disease, including those that are transmitted sexually.

Nutrition, disease, and the immune system

The human immune system protects the body from pathogens we encounter in our environment. It comprises nonadaptive immune responses and adaptive responses. Nonadaptive or natural immunity consists of nonspecific responses to any nonself intruder. The nonadaptive system includes barriers—the skin and mucous membranes—which are the first defense against infection, and phagocytic cells called natural killer (NK) cells, whose function is to recognize virus-infected cells and kill them. Adaptive immunity is the reaction (adaptation) to specific pathogens and has two main divisions: cell-mediated immunity (blood cells that are processed in the thymus, or T cells) and humoral immunity (bone marrow–derived, B cells) (Cunningham-Rundles, 1998). (For a very readable description of the immune system, see Powell, 1996, chap. 1.)

The epidemiological association between malnutrition and susceptibility to disease has been recognized for decades. Furthermore, research of the past 20 years demonstrates the specific mechanisms by which malnutrition compromises the immune system at the cellular level. With that information we can see more clearly that, regardless of the number of sexual contacts, the risk of contracting HIV associated with each contact is far greater for malnourished persons (Sanders and Sambo, 1991). Some of that research on immune response is summarized below.

Increased susceptibility to infection results from both protein and energy malnutrition (macronutrition) and deficiencies of specific micronutrients, such as iron, zinc, and vitamins. Infection and malnutrition are synergistic; minor illnesses can cause lack of appetite, which is very dangerous in a person who is already nutritionally deficient and parasite-laden. Fever increases the demands for energy at the same time that intake decreases.

Diarrheal diseases cause a rapid loss of nutrients. Children with diarrhea lose as much as 40 percent of protein ingested, 55 percent of energy content, and 30 to 70 percent of the vitamin A in food consumed (Scrimshaw and SanGiovanni, 1997). Nutritional deficiency combined with infection leads to 10 million child deaths a year (Beisel, 1996).

Both undernutrition and micronutrient deficiency, even in the absence of readily observable symptoms, weaken every component of the immune system, both its adaptive and nonadaptive responses. Numerous studies have demonstrated the effects of even moderate protein-energy malnutrition (PEM) on the physical barriers, epithelial (skin) and mucosal protection (Woodward, 1998). The humoral response is also affected through atrophy of the lymph system, and reduction in size and weight of the thymus results, affecting T-cell production (Beisel, 1996; Chandra, 1997). Children with PEM, regardless of degree or type (stunting or wasting), have reduced cell-mediated adaptive immunity (Chandra, 1997; Woodward, 1998). Protein is very important in resistance to infection because most elements of the immune system depend on cell replication, which requires protein (Scrimshaw and SanGiovanni, 1997). Protein deficiency has been shown to impair resistance to tuberculosis, for example, by preventing containment of the mycobacteria within the primary lesions (McMurray, 1998). Measles, relatively benign in well-nourished children, is often fatal in children with PEM because T-cell production is suppressed by the malnutrition and by the virus itself, thereby overwhelming the cellular immune response (Cunningham-Rundles, 1998).

The evidence demonstrates that macronutrient malnutrition affects mortality and morbidity in children and adults. Malnourished children have more episodes of illness and those illnesses are more serious and prolonged. Moreover, malnutrition acts synergistically with infection: fever uses up calories, and diarrhea robs the system of needed nutrients.

Micronutrient deficiencies

Micronutrient deficiencies also weaken every component of the immune system, even when the deficiencies are relatively mild (Chandra, 1997). Some diseases, such as scurvy (from vitamin-C deficiency) and pellagra (from a lack of niacin, a B vitamin), are the result of specific nutrient deficiencies. Besides their role in deficiency-specific diseases, many nutrients are needed both singly and in conjunction with others to maintain an immune system that can resist the entire array of infectious, parasitic, and even chronic degenerative diseases.

Iron

Iron deficiency, which results in anemia, is the most widespread nutritional deficiency in the world and is especially common in women and children.

Iron is essential in promoting resistance to infection, through humoral response (B cells), T cells, and NK cells (Scrimshaw and SanGiovanni, 1997).

Zinc

Even mild zinc deficiency can cause a large decrease in NK cell activity and reduced production of thymic hormone, affecting T-cell production (Beisel, 1996; Cunningham-Rundles, 1998). Zinc deficiency also impedes wound healing, undermines skin integrity as a barrier to infection, and weakens resistance to parasite infection, which aggravates malnutrition (Chandra, 1997). Growth retardation, common in malnourished children, is a clinical manifestation of zinc deficiency, but zinc supplementation by itself does not enable children to catch up in height and weight. Adequate protein intake is also necessary for zinc utilization (Wapnir, 2000). Zinc deficiency is a common result of prolonged diarrhea, and supplementation reduces diarrhea in children. This has been found to be a low-cost way to reduce malnutrition and boost immune response (Ruel et al., 1997). Zinc supplementation has also been found to result in "markedly lower incidence of anorexia [loss of appetite] and morbidity from cough, diarrhoea, fever, and vomiting in the stunted children" (Umeta et al., 2000, 2021).

Vitamin A

Research over the past 30 years has confirmed the role of vitamin A as a super-vitamin for the immune system and insufficiency of vitamin A as the deficiency that is most synergistic with infectious disease (Semba, 1998). Vitamin-A deficiency is very common in tropical areas because the diet of poor people often does not include vitamin-A rich foods (Fawzi et al., 1997) and because the stress produced by the tropical sun increases vitamin-A demand. Infection increases excretion of vitamin A, producing a deadly synergism of malnutrition, infection, and increased vitamin-A deficiency (Stephensen et al., 1994). Even children with subclinical (that is, not apparent upon examination) vitamin-A deficiency show a lower immune response and greater vulnerability to infection, particularly of the skin and mucous membranes (Solomons, 1998). Subclinical vitamin-A deficiency is more likely to occur in children who also show signs of PEM (Khandait et al., 1998). Vitamin-A deficiency reduces the number of NK cells, diminishing nonspecific, or natural, defense mechanisms against antigens. Vitamin A also is required for the production of T cells, or specific defenses (Semba, 1998).

The role of vitamin A in the promotion of physical barriers to infection is significant for the discussion in this book. The skin and the mucous membranes provide the most basic protection from infection by preventing or impeding the entry of pathogens, and "Vitamin A deficiency compromises mucosal immunity by altering the integrity of mucosal epithelia, including those of the eye as well as the respiratory, gastrointestinal, and genitourinary tracts" (Semba, 1998, S39). The alterations in the eye, for example, lead to xerophthalmia, the leading cause of blindness in children in the world. Respiratory infections are also promoted by disturbance of mucosal integrity because mucus captures and deactivates pathogens that enter the lungs. These same changes in epithelial tissue and mucosa seen in other diseases may make people more susceptible to sexually transmitted diseases, such as HIV (Semba, 1998), since the protective effect of those barriers in the genitourinary tract is decreased.

Not only is vitamin A essential for epithelial integrity to promote barriers to infection, but deficiency can also lead to toughening (keratinization) of the lining of the lungs, uterus, and other organs (Sommer et al., 1996). This suggests another possible explanation for the high rates of female sterility in Central Africa, which had been presumptively attributed to STDs. Vitamin-A deficiency is also associated with premature birth and low birth weight (Fawzi and Msamanga, 2000), both of which are associated with impaired immune function in infancy and later in life.

Numerous studies demonstrate the role of other micronutrients, including the B vitamins, vitamin E, and selenium, in maintaining the integrity of the immune system (Beisel, 1996; Scrimshaw and SanGiovanni, 1997; Meydani and Beharka, 1998). Furthermore, the interactive aspects of nutrients are extremely important. In some cases, supplementing with a single nutrient creates an imbalance rather than correcting one (Harbige, 1996). Repletion of a deficient micronutrient can increase function up to the level at which another nutrient becomes the limiting factor (Friis and Michaelsen, 1998). Problems with single-nutrient supplementation point to the fact that the long-term solution is nutrition through diet and food security, not pills, but supplementation can reduce mortality and increase disease resistance.

Vitamin-A deficiency impairs iron utilization and so interacts with anemia. Even vitamin A alone can improve iron utilization (Sommer et al., 1996, 152). Supplementation with vitamin A along with iron in pregnancy can virtually eliminate anemia. Considering the low cost of supplementation with vitamin A, its cost-effectiveness improves even more if we calculate its interaction with iron.

Nutritional deficiencies interact with parasite infection to make a combined assault on nutrition and immune support. Vitamin A strengthens immune response to malaria, including its most severe form, *Plasmodium falciparum*, which is most widespread in sub-Saharan Africa. Vitamin-A supplementation is an effective low-cost strategy to reduce malarial illness in young children (Shankar et al., 1999). Interventions that address nutritional deficiencies and parasitic infection are important for their own sake and for HIV prevention, especially since blood transfusions are a common therapy for malaria, which is endemic in areas where blood supplies may also be unsafe.

In sum, overall malnutrition combined with micronutrient deficiency is widespread in sub-Saharan Africa, South Asia, and elsewhere among very poor people and is responsible for suppression of immunity through all three routes: physical barriers, humoral immunity, and cell-mediated immunity. In particular, vitamin-A deficiency produces a greater susceptibility to STDs, particularly of the ulcerative type, in malnourished populations in tropical areas. It is important to reiterate that STDs (including HIV) are not a special case; they are infectious bacterial and viral diseases that can most easily be transmitted to a host whose immune system is weakened by malnutrition and by the synergistic effects of other infectious and parasitic diseases. STDs find their most fertile ground in the most nutritionally immunosuppressed population, such as we find in many countries in Africa and Asia. In particular, malnutrition that disturbs epithelial integrity promotes access for any disease, including genital ulcer infections that provide entry points for HIV.

In addition to increasing host susceptibility to infections, host malnutrition can play a role in increasing the virulence of the pathogen (Semba et al., 1994; Beck, 1997; Levander, 1997). A well-nourished immune system can mount defensive responses that clear the system of most types of invaders. Impaired humoral and cellular immune function delays or prevents viral clearance, leading to a larger pool of viral mutants in the body, including more virulent strains (Domingo, 1997). This effect was observed in a severe epidemic of Keshan disease from the normally mild Coxsackie virus in a selenium-deficient population in China (Beck, 1998). In Cuba in the 1990s patients with multiple nutritional deficiencies also developed severe variants of a normally avirulent Coxsackie virus with resultant eye disease (Beck, 2000). The possibility that HIV could mutate into a more virulent (and more transmissible) form in malnourished hosts should be investigated since the highest prevalence of HIV/AIDS occurs in areas with high rates of malnutrition.

Is there a threshold effect in malnutrition?

While it makes sense to lay and professional people alike that malnutrition contributes to susceptibility to disease, there has not been full agreement among researchers on the degree of malnutrition that is dangerous to health. The increased emphasis on targeted interventions and cost-effectiveness for health investments produced a spate of articles that disputed the mortality effects of moderate malnutrition.

In a series of important papers, Pelletier and colleagues responded to those who minimized the importance of moderate malnutrition. They showed that, in countries of varying levels of malnutrition prevalence and intensity, malnutrition is a factor in 56 percent of child deaths, and 83 percent of the children who died were in the mild to moderate malnutrition category, not severely malnourished (Pelletier et al., 1995). If interventions target only the severely malnourished, they will not prevent any deaths among the mildly to moderately malnourished children who constitute the vast majority of deaths. Where malnutrition is very prevalent, interventions to improve nutrition among children with all grades of deficiency would have broad effects on mortality and morbidity. Furthermore, to focus exclusively on the immediate cause of death, such as measles or diarrhea, and neglect the potentiating effect of malnutrition, is to intervene too late in the process.

Pelletier and colleagues also point out that statistical measures generally used to compare mortality risk from malnutrition (such as attributable risk, sensitivity, and specificity) have no intrinsic meaning in heterogeneous groups or across countries when studying synergistic conditions for which some populations have a high prevalence, of malnutrition for example, and others do not (Pelletier et al., 1993). Moreover, health-sector interventions, such as vaccinations and oral rehydration therapy (ORT), are less effective in reducing child mortality in an environment of widespread malnutrition (Pelletier, 1994b). Treating illness through ORT alone is not sufficient if the goal is to enhance child development. Recurrent malnutrition, even in the mild to moderate category, makes growth monitoring, the other strategy of child-survival campaigns, much less useful. Improving nutrition exploits the synergy of nutrition with numerous infectious and parasitic diseases simultaneously and can reduce mortality even if the environment of disease exposure does not change (Pelletier, 1994a).

The Pelletier evidence on nutrition is important for all infectious diseases. The method also has corollaries in HIV prevention. Since the late 1990s, several policy agencies have favored targeting prevention resources to risk groups, rather than to the population as a whole, arguing that it is more cost effective. But, just as Pelletier and colleagues found that most of the child deaths occur in the mild to moderately malnourished group, most AIDS deaths in poor populations with generalized epidemics do not occur in risk groups. The effectiveness of targeted interventions in countries with concentrated HIV epidemics cannot be generalized across heterogeneous populations.

Another methodological similarity is the observation that statistical measures of risk may have no intrinsic meaning when comparing heterogeneous groups; this also applies to comparisons of populations with and without endemic tropical diseases, which are discussed in chapter 3. Using a common risk variable for HIV transmission in heterogeneous populations leads to erroneous conclusions about the causes of epidemic spread and ignores the variables that are most important in differentiating populations, which is further discussed in chapter 8.

Parasitic disease

Endemic parasitic diseases aggravate the already bleak nutritional and epidemiological profile for poor people, especially in tropical areas. Malnourished persons are more susceptible to parasites, and parasites worsen the afflicted person's nutritional status (Storey, 1993). Malaria, caused by a protozoal parasite, is endemic in tropical Africa, Latin America, and Southeast Asia, and its endemic zone has increased in recent years due to climate change and inadequate resources for mosquito control (Nchinda, 1998). Of the 300 to 500 million malaria infections occurring annually worldwide, more than 90 percent are in tropical Africa. Africa accounts for the vast majority of malaria deaths, including about 1 million deaths annually of children under the age of 5. If one includes the deaths of low birth weight children born to malaria-infected mothers and the deaths of children from malaria-induced anemia, along with deaths from cerebral malaria and fever, the mortality toll may be as high as 1.7 million African children every year (Breman et al., 2001). Survivors are weakened by the disease, although they develop a degree of immunity through repeated reinfection (WHO, 1998c). Malarial fever significantly increases calorie needs. Malaria also causes anemia, and the treatment of anemic children with transfusions of HIV-tainted blood has spread HIV in Zaire (Hedberg et al., 1993) and elsewhere.

A recent study in Kenya found that malaria had a particularly serious effect on the nutritional status of early adolescents and might also affect nutritional status in older adolescents and adults (Friedman et al., 2003). Immune status entering adolescence and sexually active years is critical for susceptibility to any disease and is certainly important for young people in an area of high HIV prevalence and in a context of myriad other health threats.

Malaria is especially dangerous in pregnancy and contributes to anemia, premature birth, low birth weight, and maternal and infant mortality. In sub-Saharan Africa WHO estimates that more than 50 percent of pregnant women are anemic, due to malaria and iron deficiency, and prevalence is increasing. A study of malaria and anemia in Malawi found that more than 90 percent of pregnant women examined were anemic (Verhoeff et al., 1999). Some authors have suggested using a different threshold for calculating anemia prevalence in developing countries since, by the conventional standard, most women are anemic (Sarin, 1995), impeding identification of women in the highest risk group. But there are dangers to addressing nearly ubiquitous nutritional deficiencies and infections in poor populations by redefining the criteria. Such a tactic could be a pragmatic solution for the question at hand, such as targeting the most seriously anemic women. It would obscure highly prevalent conditions, however, and would hide the differences between such a population and one without those deficiencies in explaining differences in susceptibility to other infections, including HIV. The population in the Malawi study had multiple dietary deficiencies and multiple parasites. For this multideficient population, there are important synergistic effects of vitamin A and iron for treating anemia (Verhoeff et al., 1999).

Schistosomiasis (bilharzia), also caused by a parasite, is the second most prevalent tropical disease. Of the more than 200 million people with schistosomiasis, more than 80 percent are in sub-Saharan Africa. The eggs of the schistosome worms damage the intestines, the bladder, and other organs (WHO, 1998d), leading to anemia and protein-energy deficiency (Stephenson, 1993; Scrimshaw and SanGiovanni, 1997). (Genital schistosomiasis is discussed in chapter 3.)

Trypanosomiasis (sleeping sickness) is present in virtually all of tropical Africa. Prevalence has increased dramatically since the 1970s, with annual incidence estimated at 300,000 to 500,000 infections. Sleeping sickness invades all organs, multiplying and eventually overwhelming the immune system. The parasite also infects domestic animals, reducing availability of protein and worsening nutrition in endemic areas (WHO, 1998a).

Intestinal parasites of many kinds (including hookworms, roundworms, and amebas) are extremely widespread among poor populations in tropical areas, with an estimated 3.5 billion people infected worldwide. Numerous kinds of worm infections (including filariases, onchocerciasis, and elephantiasis) are endemic in sub-Saharan Africa, Asia, and Latin America, with serious consequences for nutrition and immune status. Worm infestation increases energy cost and depletion of vitamin A (Storey, 1993). People often carry several different parasites, with serious depletion of essential nutrients through intestinal blood loss and chronic diarrhea, resulting in aggravated malnutrition and retarded development (Hlaing, 1993; Oberhelman et al., 1998; WHO, 1998b). Table 2.1 lists just a selection of the studies that document the very high prevalence of parasites and polyparasitism in children and adults in poor communities.

Parasite interactions

Parasites interact in various ways; some parasites lessen the impact of other parasites, while some magnify the effects of others. The presence of *Ascaris* (a kind of worm) seems to enable the coexistence of two malaria strains. That could suggest that *Ascaris* offer immunomodulation, allowing people with this parasite to be vulnerable to more than one strain of malaria. At the very least, it suggests a complex web of interactions of tropical pathogens on human hosts (Nacher et al., 2001).

The bacillus Calmette-Guérin (BCG) vaccination for tuberculosis is less effective against TB in tropical areas, where immune response is complicated by the presence of parasites. Even though BCG does not protect against TB, it does protect against worms, leprosy, and Buruli ulcer. Among HIV-infected people in Uganda, it was found that individuals who had been vaccinated with BCG as children showed lower nematode infestation than

Table 2.1
Selected studies: prevalence of parasite infection

Authors	Date	Location	Findings/discussion
Kvalsig et al.	1991	Worldwide	1 billion people infected with *Ascaris* and 500 million with *Trichomonas trichiura*, 900 million with hookworm, 200 million with schistosomes. Discusses the difficulty of devising a measure of parasite load since most people carry more than one parasite. Measures of parasite burden need to reflect polyparasitism.
Nokes et al.	1992	Worldwide	Surveys numerous studies of infection in one-fourth of world's population, with resultant malnutrition, anemia, impaired cognitive ability and learning.
Needham et al.	1998	Vietnam, farming community	83 percent infected with *Ascaris lumbricoides*, 94 percent with *Trichomonas trichura*, and 59 percent with hookworm.
Brooker et al.	2000	Kenya, students aged 8 to 20	92 percent infected with hookworm, *Ascaris lumbricoides, Trichomonas trichiura,* or *Schistosoma mansoni*. Study also shows an association between concurrent infection and intensity of infection, with consequences for nutritional and educational status.
Thompson	2001	Australia, aboriginal population	Overall prevalence of hookworm infection, a major cause of iron-deficiency anemia, was 77 percent, and in 5- to 14-year-olds, 93 percent, but was reduced to 2.6 percent with regular treatment. Learning that it is possible to live without worms is an important educational tool for changing hygiene behavior.

those who did not. Even correcting for socioeconomic status, the difference remained significant, indicating an apparent protective effect of BCG vaccination (Elliott et al., 1999). Similar results were found in Brazil, where children with BCG vaccination had significantly lower hookworm infection, even after controlling for other factors (Barreto et al., 2000). It is essential to recognize immune-system interactions to adequately address disease susceptibility, including to HIV.

While several studies have suggested that helminth infection protects the host from severe bouts of malaria and cerebral consequences, helminth infections are correlated with increased incidence of *P. falciparum* (Nacher et al., 2002). This suggests that children who survive malaria in infancy are likely to be the ones who have higher loads of other parasites. They will face more frequent relapses of (albeit milder) malaria and reduced immune response to subsequent infections, including HIV.

As is the case for other nutrients, deficiency of zinc interacts with parasite infection. Parasites are better able to survive in zinc-deficient hosts. The gastrointestinal tract is an important part of the immune system, and because it contains the largest number of lymphocytes outside the thymus, it is the first line of defense against harmful elements ingested in food, water, or otherwise. Since the gastrointestinal tract is sensitive to changes in nutrition, zinc deficiency and undernutrition work together to undermine the mucosal immune function of the intestine, "leading to changes in systemically disseminated immune responses and prolonged parasite survival" (Scott and Koski, 2000, 1412S). Zinc also has been shown to have a large impact on the ability of the host to control cysticercosis (tapeworm) infection, which affects large numbers of people in poor regions (Fragoso et al., 2001).

Not all studies, however, show that micronutrient deficiency causes increased parasite load. A study in Korea showed that iron-deficient media reduced the growth of *Trichomonas vaginalis*, which generally flourishes immediately after menstruation, with increased vaginal acidity and presence of iron (Ryu et al., 2001). Of course, this demonstrates not the danger of micronutrient sufficiency but, rather, the complexity of nutrient balance and vulnerability. It also shows that vaginal hygiene and nutritional balance interact to protect against infection.

Besides undermining nutrition, parasites play another role in promoting infectious disease. The immune system protects the body by distinguishing between self and nonself. Protozoa, worms, flukes, and cysts are nonself, and so the immune system of a parasite-laden person is chronically activated by parasite infestation. An exhausted immune system cannot mount the response necessary to fight off new invaders. The continual immune activation produced by chronic parasitosis has been recognized as a possible cause of the more rapid transition from HIV to AIDS in Africa (Bentwich et al., 1995; Borkow and Bentwich, 2002).

Malnutrition and parasitosis are endemic in poor countries and have long been recognized as depressing immune function. Recent work in cell biology shows the particular mechanisms by which malnutrition and parasitosis depress both specific and nonspecific immune response by undermining epithelial integrity and the production of NK cells, B cells, and T cells. Protein-energy malnutrition, iron-deficiency anemia, vitamin-A deficiency, and parasite infection are widespread in Africa, Asia, and Latin America and have been shown in hundreds of studies to decrease disease resistance by weakening physical barriers, humoral immunity, and cell-mediated immunity. Malnutrition and parasitosis, therefore, make people more susceptible to infectious disease, including HIV. The next chapter examines the synergies of malnutrition, parasite infection, and disease that specifically increase vulnerability to STDs, and HIV in particular.

Medical transmission of HIV and other diseases

Although heterosexual contact and vertical transmission from mother to child may constitute the majority of new infections in sub-Saharan Africa and other developing regions, numerous infections have resulted from the use of nonsterile medical equipment and from contaminated blood transfusions. The importance of iatrogenic transmission has been noted frequently over the past two decades (see Drucker et al., 2001; Luby, 2001; Moore et al., 2001; Brewer et al., 2003; Gisselquist et al., 2003; and the citations in those articles).

Unfortunately, there has been a tendency in the scientific and social science literature and also in the policy realm to ignore such evidence. Part of the reason for that dangerous decision has been the constricting influence of the behavioral paradigm that dictates the limits of acceptable findings in HIV research. International organizations also seem to fear that people will avoid doctors altogether and that recognition of the dangers of medical transmission will lead to less emphasis on safe sex. Both of those fears underestimate people's ability to take in different but complementary information at the same time.

It is widespread knowledge in the developing world that health centers and hospitals, as well as untrained injectionists, did not and still do not practice universal precautions for infection control. Of the many hospitals and health centers that I have visited in developing countries, few have been in compliance with modern standards of infection control. In public hospitals and health centers in Buenos Aires, Argentina, when HIV was already well established, disposable syringes were rewashed so many times that the markings for dosage wore off. Rarely did hospital personnel wear gloves. Most doctors' bathrooms and wash areas did not have soap or towels, and most wards did not even have a sink. Health posts I visited in Mendoza, Argentina, had no autoclaves (to sterilize equipment) but performed numerous internal gynecological exams each day. A clinic I visited in a neighborhood with very high drug use and HIV prevalence within the city of Buenos Aires did not even have running water (Stillwaggon, 1998).

In Ecuador, only two of the country's hospitals, both in Quito, the capital, practiced universal precautions at the time that I worked there (source in Ecuadorian military medical corps, 2000). Thailand is lauded by UNAIDS and other AIDS policy organizations for its response to the epidemic. But even in its capital, Bangkok, in July 2004, an emergency room doctor told me that his hospital only used a complete set of disposable instruments and drapes if the patient tested positive for HIV. Anyone who has seen hospitals and health posts in the developing world knows that doctors and nurses have to do their job despite having little protection for themselves and their patients. In middle-income countries, where resources are available, a precautionary consciousness is too often absent. Even doctors, dentists, and orthodontists in private practice for affluent clients fail to follow universal precautions.

The consequences for HIV spread are important. Iatrogenic transmission has been frequently reported, and injections are a very common therapeutic treatment in poor countries. In government health posts and hospitals, injections and transfusions for anemia of malaria and pregnancy are routine. The widespread failure of hospitals and health posts to assure infection control was used as a defense in the Libyan case against foreign doctors accused of intentionally infecting children with HIV. The expert witness for the defense, Dr. Luc Montagnier, testified to the widespread accidental transmission of HIV in medical settings (Kaisernetwork, 2003a). Transfusions transmit a significant number of HIV infections in high-prevalence settings (Moore et al., 2001). Private injectionists administer vitamin therapies and folk remedies in storefront or informal settings. Government hospitals also widely promote injectable contraceptives as the "modern" method of family planning, even in high HIV-prevalence countries (hospital visits in Zimbabwe, June–August 1997).

There is plentiful evidence in scientific studies to support the observations of those who work in poor countries that medical and quasi-medical HIV transmission accounts for at least a significant minority of infections in Africa, Asia, and Latin America. In 2003, several important articles were published by David Gisselquist and colleagues that documented the probable transmission of HIV in medical settings. Those works were summarily dismissed by WHO in a meeting in March 2003, even though WHO's own reports document the inadequacy of sterilization in medical settings and the consequent transmissions of HIV, hepatitis B, and hepatitis C that result (Simonsen et al., 1999; WHO, 2003a; WHO, 2003c). WHO estimates that of the 16 billion medical injections annually worldwide, 30 percent are unsafe because of reuse of equipment (WHO, 2003a).

The organization, Physicians for Human Rights, estimates that at least half a million people are infected with HIV every year through unsafe medical injections and blood transfusions. They also provide a feasible plan for incorporating blood and injection safety into prevention programs and show that such programs have been successful in very low income countries, including Burkina Faso (Burkhalter, 2003). Even UNAIDS's low estimates that 5 percent of primary infections worldwide result from unsafe injections and blood products represents a very significant public health problem. And yet it devotes only one column of one page of its 2004 *Report on the Global HIV/AIDS Epidemic* (188 pages plus tables and references) to the prevention of transmission in medical settings (UNAIDS, 2004).

The decision by WHO and UNAIDS to downplay information about medical transmission of HIV is reckless. People need the same quality of information for demanding safe medical care as for demanding safe sex. In fact, it is an essential part of educating people about taking responsibility for their own health to alert them to their need to protect themselves from untrained injectionists and even from personnel at private or government health centers and hospitals. Furthermore, safe medical care is amenable to policy change, so those infections are the most easily prevented. Medical injection safety is carried out at a level that can be observed and regulated, whereas safe or unsafe sex occurs in private, far removed from the exercise of regulatory control.

It is essential to address medical transmission, and even when those problems are resolved, there will still be a need to prevent sexual transmission. As this chapter and the next demonstrate, sexual transmission will still be more likely in poor populations as long as other health needs are not addressed. The inadequacy of health systems is universally recognized as one of the contributory factors of morbidity and mortality in poor countries. That judgment is only more grave in the face of HIV epidemics.

3

HIV-Specific Synergies

There are numerous ways in which nutrition, parasite load, and other diseases promote not just infectious disease in general but transmission of HIV in particular.[1] The individual transmission of HIV depends on the characteristics of the virus, of the person transmitting the virus, and of the person to whom the virus is transmitted. This chapter is about the human ecology of HIV transmission, or the biological interactions that are specifically related to the transmission of HIV/AIDS, especially in poor populations. Most cofactors (diseases or conditions that promote transmission) of HIV are so intrinsically tied to widespread poverty and tropical location that they are not recognized as promoting HIV transmission. Epidemiology increasingly relies on controlled trials that abstract from all those variables that distinguish heterogeneous populations. Consequently, they cannot explain differences in prevalence between populations or suggest means of preventing diverse epidemics. (The limitations of individual-level models and controlled trials for the epidemiology of endemic conditions are discussed in chapter 8.)

The one HIV cofactor that is widely recognized and that has been

1. I have attempted to make the material accessible to readers who are not medically trained. Those interested in the specific biological effects are directed to the articles cited.

included in prevention policies is the presence of untreated STDs. Because both HIV and STDs are transmitted sexually, the connection was easier to recognize and incorporate into existing policy. But the biological reasons why STDs promote HIV transmission are the same as for other HIV cofactors that are not transmitted sexually. Some parasites, for example, have the same ulcerating and inflammatory effect on reproductive organs as STDs. Just because the HIV cofactors considered in this chapter do not have a sexual etiology should not make them ineligible for inclusion in HIV-prevention programs.

Viral load

Many of the HIV-specific synergies considered in this chapter affect transmission through their effect on viral load. Viral load is the concentration of HIV RNA in the blood and other body fluids. Higher viral load is correlated with higher rates of transmission. In a study in Uganda, viral load was found to be the chief predictor of transmission, and there was no transmission among people with a low serum viral load. The relationship was strong enough to identify a dose-response effect (Quinn et al., 2000). Interventions that reduce viral load have beneficial effects for the HIV-infected person and reduce the risk of transmission, horizontally or vertically. Reductions in viral load through antiretroviral therapy, better nutrition, antihelminthic treatment, antimalarial treatment, and treatment of STDs could potentially reduce rates of HIV spread. Lowering viral load is all the more important in generalized epidemics where a person's probability of sexual contact with an infected person is greater than in nascent or concentrated epidemics.

Nutrition

Poor nutrition has often been implicated in studies of progression from HIV to AIDS. There are also numerous studies that indicate the role of malnutrition in promoting transmission of HIV vertically and sexually. Much of the work on immune response and nutrition in general was presented in chapter 2. Additional studies that make a specific link between malnutrition and HIV transmission are presented here.

Maternal malnutrition in general and deficiencies of specific micronutrients, such as vitamin A, are associated with greater risk of vertical transmission. In Malawi, it was observed that mothers who were severely deficient in vitamin A had a much higher risk of transmitting HIV to their children, perhaps due to its effect on the vaginal mucosa or the integrity of the placenta (Semba et al., 1994; Nimmagadda et al., 1998). Increased viral load in the mother and decreased maternal antibody protection, both associated with impaired T- and B-cell production from vitamin-A deficiency, are also probable causes of greater transmission (Landers, 1996). Randomized trials in Tanzania found that multivitamin supplementation decreased fetal deaths and increased T-cell counts in HIV-infected mothers (Fawzi et al., 1998). Nutritional supplementation of mothers was expected to reduce vertical transmission by reducing viral load in secretions in the birth canal and in breast milk (Fawzi and Hunter, 1998). Although recent trials of vitamin-A supplementation have not yet been successful in reducing vertical transmission, they suggest useful avenues for research. The environment of poverty, malnutrition, and parasitosis in which HIV flourishes provides a complicated laboratory for trials of any single intervention. Complementary interventions in malaria treatment or other nutritional supplements might be necessary in order to detect the effectiveness of vitamin-A supplementation in this multiburdened population.

Systemic maternal virus burden is an important factor in HIV transmission to infants. Local virus burden (in the birth canal), however, may be even greater than systemic viral load, and therefore measures of systemic viral load might understate the risk of vertical transmission. Anemia is associated with greater viral shedding, with consequent locally higher viral burden in the birth canal, increasing the risk of transmission from mother to child. Anemia may be a marker for advanced disease, or it might be indicative of underlying nutritional deficiencies, which could be remedied with nutritional supplementation (John et al., 1997).

Malnutrition in its various forms promotes viral replication and consequently can contribute to greater risk of vertical or sexual transmission (Friis and Michaelsen, 1998). Various kinds of nutritional deficiencies are associated with progression to AIDS, both because malnutrition causes more rapid progression of HIV to AIDS and because disease progression causes malnutrition. In either case, supplementation improves health outcomes for HIV-infected persons, including children. Vitamin-A supplementation appears to rehabilitate mucosal integrity and boost immune response, reducing severity of diarrheal illness, rather than the number of episodes in HIV-infected children (Coutsoudis et al., 1995). Selenium deficiency has been found to be a good predictor of mortality in HIV-infected children, providing further support for the importance of nutrition in survival (Campa et al., 1999). In addition to helping people living with HIV, the reduction in viral load from improved nutrition reduces the risk of transmission in children and adults.

The next few sections report on research that links common diseases in poor populations with transmission of HIV. The vast majority of research on disease interactions focuses on the effect of HIV on other diseases. It is easier to find evidence of that because HIV is new, and it is brutally effective in magnifying the effect of other diseases. Those other diseases are often ubiquitous, subtle, familiar, and already interconnected. The funding for research on HIV interactions also favors studying the impact of HIV on other conditions rather than the role of other conditions in increasing the spread of HIV. Nevertheless, there is substantial evidence of the enhancing effects of other diseases on HIV transmission that is summarized below.

Malaria

Malaria is implicated in the spread of HIV in sub-Saharan Africa. As HIV spreads in Southeast Asia as well, the interaction between HIV and endemic malaria in the region increases the risk of transmission. Over 300 million people in Africa suffer from acute malaria each year. Given the large number of people in sub-Saharan Africa afflicted with malaria or HIV, or both, the potential impact of malaria on HIV viral load has serious implications for increasing HIV transmission.

Malaria stimulates HIV replication, and HIV viral loads are significantly higher in malarial patients than in HIV-infected persons without malaria. HIV viral load is higher in malarial patients, even after 4 weeks of treatment for malaria; this suggests that malaria could cause faster progression of HIV (Whitworth et al., 2000). Patients with malaria, and thus higher viral loads, are consequently more likely to transmit HIV to unprotected partners.

In the laboratory, malaria antigens have been shown to increase HIV replication in blood cells from 10 to 100 times that of non-malaria-exposed cells (Xiao et al., 1998). High viral load due to malaria coinfection correlates with risk of HIV transmission through blood, from mother to child, and through sexual contact. In Malawi, men with malaria were found to have seven times the median viral load of HIV-infected men without malaria. The reduction in viral load that results after treatment for malaria indicates that the causation is not from higher viral load to malaria but, rather, from malaria to higher viral load (Hoffman et al., 1999).

HIV-infected persons also have higher malaria-parasite densities in their blood, which increases the likelihood of malaria transmission in a population with high HIV-prevalence (Rowland-Jones and Lohman, 2002). In Uganda, adults with some immunity to malaria due to repeated exposure who were also HIV-infected had higher prevalence and severity of malaria than semi-immune adults who were HIV-negative (Whitworth et al., 2000). The greater prevalence of malaria and the higher parasite loads both mean that HIV also promotes malaria transmission.

There are other effects of HIV on malaria risk. First-time mothers are most vulnerable to the grave consequences of malaria in pregnancy. Additional pregnancies generally impart a degree of immunity that protects both mother and child, but HIV infection inhibits the development of that immunity to malaria that generally occurs in women after the first pregnancy (Verhoeff et al., 1999; Harms and Feldmeier, 2002). Maternal malaria also increases mortality among HIV-infected infants. A study in Malawi by the U.S. Centers for Disease Control compared mortality risks from maternal

HIV, maternal malaria, and low birth weight. Infants of HIV-infected mothers had 1.9 times the risk of dying in the first year, compared with infants born of HIV-negative mothers. (The fact that the difference was only 1.9 times, incidentally, illustrates that infant survival is precarious in Malawi and other poor populations, even without HIV exposure.) Normal birth-weight infants exposed to both placental malaria infection and maternal HIV had 2.7 times the mortality risk of infants born to HIV-infected mothers without malaria. Malaria is especially dangerous for pregnant women because it infects the placenta, and it is also an important cause of low birth weight and infant mortality, even without HIV. Low birth weight increased the odds of death for infants exposed to both placental malaria and HIV to 11 times that of normal weight children who were not exposed to either infection (Bloland et al., 1995). Maternal HIV presents a very great risk for infants, but so do maternal malaria, anemia, and other forms of malnutrition that cause prematurity and low birth weight.

In addition to 1 million infant deaths a year in Africa, there are countless cases of severe mental impairment in infants who survive cerebral malaria. Repeated exposure suppresses immune response to other diseases and results in recurrent bouts of debilitating fever throughout adulthood. Combined with high prevalence of HIV, endemic malaria causes additional problems. Malaria is also a common cause of anemia in children. The use of HIV-contaminated transfusions to treat malaria-induced anemia has already been mentioned as another source of HIV spread.

Malaria is a very serious health problem in the developing world, especially in sub-Saharan Africa. Malaria control is essential for reducing HIV transmission in children and adults through its effect on viral load for mothers and for sexual partners (Corbett et al., 2002). Controlling malaria would also alleviate one of the world's most devastating health problems. Table 3.1 shows all the countries with malaria prevalence greater than 100 per 100,000 people as of 2000. The Americas, Asia, and Oceania together have 24 countries with prevalence greater than 0.1 percent (100 per 100,000). More countries in sub-Saharan Africa (39) than in all the rest of the world have high malaria prevalence. Two countries outside of sub-Saharan Africa have prevalence exceeding 10 percent, whereas 14 African countries do. Particularly noteworthy are Burundi (48 percent), Guinea (76 percent), Malawi (26 percent), and Zambia (34 percent).[2]

2. In Table 3.1 I have replaced the prevalence given for Botswana in UN (2004) with data from WHO (http://www.afro.who.int/malaria/country-profile/botswana.pdf). The UN figure, which appears in the Millennium Development Goals data set, apparently overstates the actual prevalence tenfold. For all the other countries the two sources are reasonably compatible. For some countries (indicated by *), I used the country-profile data because it was more current.

Table 3.1
Malaria prevalence, 2000

Country	No. of cases per 100,000 people
Latin America and the Caribbean	
Belize	657
Bolivia	378
Brazil	344
Colombia	250
Ecuador	728
Guatemala	386
Guyana	3,074
Honduras	541
Nicaragua	402
Paraguay	124
Peru	258
Suriname	2,954
Asia and Oceania	
Bhutan	285
Cambodia	476
Indonesia	920
Lao People's Dem. Rep.	759
Myanmar	224
Papua New Guinea	1,688
Solomon Islands	15,172
Sri Lanka	1,110
Tajikistan	303
Thailand	130
Vanuatu	3,260
Yemen	15,160
Sub-Saharan Africa	
Angola	8,773
Benin (1995)*	11,279
Botswana*	4,634
Burkina Faso	619
Burundi	48,098
Cameroon (1998)*	4,678
Central African Republic (1999)*	3,518
Chad (1999)*	4,683
Comoros	1,930
Congo, Dem. Rep. of the (1999)	2,960
Congo	5,880
Côte d'Ivoire	12,152
Djibouti(1999)	715
Equatorial Guinea (1995)	2,744
Eritrea	3,479
Ethiopia (1995)	556
Gabon (1998)	2,148
Gambia (1998)	17,340
Ghana	15,344
Guinea	75,386
Guinea-Bissau (1999)*	20,543
Kenya	545
Malawi	25,948
Mali (1998)	4,008
Mauritania (1999)	11,150
Mozambique	18,115
Namibia	1,502
Niger	5,971
Rwanda	6,510
Senegal	11,925
Sierra Leone (1999)*	9,448
South Africa	143
Sudan	13,934
Swaziland	2,835
Tanzania (1999)	1,207
Togo	8,794
Uganda*	15,249
Zambia	34,204
Zimbabwe	5,410

Source: UN (United Nations), 2004. Millennium Indicators Database.

**Source:* WHO country profiles, available at http://www.afro.who.int/malaria/country-profile/index.html.

Leishmaniasis

Leishmaniasis is a protozoal parasitic disease transmitted by sand flies and is endemic in many parts of the developing world. Its three variants affect the internal organs (visceral), the skin (cutaneous), and the mucous membrane (mucosal). The cutaneous form is disfiguring, as is its variant mucosal form. Visceral Leishmaniasis, also called kala azar, is more often lethal. Large outbreaks of kala azar have occurred in recent decades in India, with about 200,000 cases per year, and in southern Sudan, with possibly as many as 100,000 deaths. Leishmaniasis has received more attention recently because it is increasingly common as an opportunist infection of HIV, particularly among needle-sharing drug users in southern Europe (Herwaldt, 1999). There are about 15 million people infected with various *Leishmania* species around the world, and *Leishmania*/HIV coinfection has been reported in 38 countries (Harms and Feldmeier, 2002).

Leishmania infection increases HIV viral load and viral shedding in coinfected individuals. The increasing occurrence of *Leishmania* and HIV coinfection is one of the numerous parasite-related causes of increased population viral load and viral shedding, which are important factors in the population dynamics of HIV transmission. Characteristics of the transmitter, such as high viral load due to parasite infection, are often overlooked in research trials that consider only behavioral variables or only the host factors of the receiving partner. In addition to increasing HIV viral load, another reason that Leishmaniasis could increase the transmission of HIV is that a major surface protein of *Leishmania donovani* enables HIV replication in $CD4^+$ cells (T cells that have receptors for HIV) (Bernier et al., 1998; Herwaldt, 1999; Harms and Feldmeier, 2002). HIV/*Leishmania* coinfection may also lead to increased transmission of Leishmaniasis among HIV-negative persons because coinfected persons are more parasitemic (have higher parasite load) and thus can increase transmission of Leishmaniasis through the sand fly vector (Harms and Feldmeier, 2002).

Helminthic and filarial infections

Helminthic and filarial infections (various kinds of worms) have also been shown to increase susceptibility to HIV acquisition and likelihood of transmitting HIV. Such infections are widespread in developing countries and virtually ubiquitous in shantytowns and many rural communities. Nearly 1.5 billion people are infected with ascariasis, 1.3 billion with hookworm, and over 1 billion with trichuriasis (PPC, 2002). (See Table 2.1 for additional data.) One of the reasons that ubiquitous health conditions, such as worm infection, are overlooked as cofactors is frequently the lack of a control group. In developing countries, virtually everyone harbors at least one parasite, so it is almost impossible to conduct research there on a population not affected by endemic parasitic disease. For a team of Israeli researchers, Ethiopian migration to Israel provided an excellent opportunity to study heterogenous populations. The researchers were able to compare recent immigrants from Ethiopia with earlier immigrants from Ethiopia and elsewhere. They showed that immune activation of the host caused by endemic infections, particularly helminthic (worm) infections, makes the host more susceptible to HIV infection and more vulnerable to HIV replication once infected (Bentwich et al., 1999).

There are several components of the parasite—HIV interaction that have important implications for HIV transmission in poor populations. The team of researchers found important differences in immune response of both HIV-negative and HIV-infected Ethiopian immigrants to Israel from other Israelis already resident. First they observed that more than 80 percent of Ethiopian immigrants had at least one helminthic parasite, 40 percent had two parasites, and 3 percent were infected with four different intestinal parasites. The Ethiopians who were HIV-negative and TB-negative still evidenced broad immune dysregulation[3] (Borkow et al., 2000). Blood cells taken from HIV-negative Ethiopians exhibited marked immune activation and when exposed to HIV were highly susceptible to the virus. In addition, treatment for helminths reduced HIV plasma viral load in HIV-infected Ethiopians (Bentwich et al., 1999). Furthermore, the team observed that BCG vaccination has relatively poor efficacy in Africa and Asia, and they suggested this could be due to immune activation from helminths, which are virtually ubiquitous in the population (Borkow et al., 2000). HIV viral load was also observed to be greater in people from developing countries and is positively correlated with helminth load. Helminths impair immune response, but treating people for worms enables immune response to recover (Borkow et al., 2001).

In another investigation by the same hospital, it was found that chronic immune activation by other coinfecting pathogens increased replication of HIV and thereby increased HIV plasma viral load. They found that the effects of schistosome infection on immune functions may be more prolonged and slower to change after eradication, in comparison with other more superficial helminthic infections (Wolday et al., 2002). Other researchers found that schistosome infection apparently inhibited viral clearance by reducing cell-mediated immunity (Actor et al., 1993). That has important implications in Africa and other areas with schistosomiasis (including Brazil and parts of Asia) for preventing HIV transmission. The

3. "The results of this study clearly show that chronic immune activation results in hyporesponsiveness, manifested by impaired T-cell signal transduction, significantly lower expression of CD28 with concomitant increased expression of CTLA-4, decreased ß-chemokine secretion, low proliferation to recall antigens, and decreased DTH responses" (Borkow et al., 2000, 1054).

immune dysregulation that results from all of these parasitic infections calls into question the possibility of developing an HIV vaccine for populations in parasite-endemic areas or, at least, the ability to conduct a meaningful test of vaccine efficacy under such circumstances (Borkow and Bentwich, 2002). And yet, as of December 2004, a search of documents available from the International AIDS Vaccine Initiative (www.iavi.org) yielded only one document from 1994 that mentioned, in one line, the need to test a vaccine in animals with parasites (IAVI, 1994).

Filaria worm infection is endemic in countries throughout Asia, Africa, and the Americas, and filariasis is also implicated in greater transmission of HIV. A study by the U.S. National Institutes of Health found that blood cells of people infected with filaria worms and exposed to HIV showed higher levels of HIV proliferation, compared with blood cells of healthy persons similarly exposed in vitro. Furthermore, blood cells taken after patients were treated for filarial infection were less susceptible to HIV infection. The authors conclude that people infected with worms can have increased susceptibility to HIV infection and that "aggressive treatment and control programs for filarial diseases and possibly other helminth infections in areas of Africa, India, and Southeast Asia where the HIV epidemic is rampant" are necessary (Gopinath et al., 2000, 1808). It is interesting that one of the coauthors of the Gopinath et al. article is Anthony Fauci, director of the U.S. National Institute of Allergy and Infectious Diseases. Even with such a prominent coauthor, interventions to control host factors such as parasites are still not part of global AIDS policy. Deworming is cheap and uncomplicated, and it has positive spillovers even for untreated people. Chapter 11 discusses the numerous solutions to cofactor conditions that are already available but are neglected in programs for HIV prevention.

There is an intergenerational effect of helminth exposure as well. Infants exposed in utero to helminths have an immune response to the worms that continues into childhood. Children who are exposed in utero to helminths and who grow up in a parasite-endemic environment suffer chronic immune activation that disadvantages them in the face of exposure to HIV (Harms and Feldmeier, 2002). That immune response interferes with the efficacy of childhood vaccines and speeds the development of HIV and also tuberculosis. Community-wide treatment for helminths would thus be an important and cost-effective component in a TB- and HIV-prevention program (Malhotra et al., 1999; Markus and Fincham, 2000).

Coinfections of two or more parasites have varying immune consequences. As noted in chapter 2, infection with helminths can suppress the manifestations of malaria, thereby enabling the person to survive the greater threat, the malaria (Nacher et al., 2000). But the risk of malaria (*P. falciparum*) increases with number of helminth species harbored (Nacher et al., 2001; Nacher et al., 2002). Helminths worsen nutritional status and increase the incidence, if not the severity, of certain malarial strains. In the context of the TB and AIDS epidemics, the benefit of a malaria-suppressing effect of some helminths is offset by the greater susceptibility to TB and HIV caused by helminth infections and the lesser efficacy of vaccines that may result (Nacher, 2002).

Genital schistosomiasis

With the possible exception of malaria, schistosomiasis, also known as bilharzia, is probably the most significant parasitic cofactor of HIV transmission because some schistosomiasis species colonize the genitourinary tracts. Urinary and intestinal schistosomiasis are generally the more recognized variants, but the importance of genital infection with schistosome worms and eggs has been known for decades. The interaction of female genital schistosomiasis with and contribution to HIV transmission was clearly described as early as 1995 (Feldmeier et al., 1995) and has been demonstrated in numerous studies reported in scientific journals since then, and yet schistosomiasis treatment and eradication are not addressed in HIV-prevention programs. Schistosome infection promotes HIV transmission by producing genital lesions and by its inflammatory effect of attracting cells, including $CD4^+$ cells, to the genital area. The coincidence of schistosome endemic areas with zones of high HIV prevalence provides epidemiological support for a biological mechanism by which the parasite increases vulnerability to HIV transmission (Harms and Feldmeier, 2002).

Schistosomiasis is a parasitic disease second only to malaria in its prevalence. It affects more than 200 million people in 74 countries (WHO, 1996/2003[4]). Of the five species of water-borne schistosome flatworms, *Schistosoma hematobium* is more common in sub-Saharan Africa than in other regions. Dam construction has caused an increase in schistosomiasis prevalence in a number of African regions, including a threefold increase in some countries (Sharp, 2003).

People become infected with schistosomiasis when they are in contact with fresh water in lakes and slow-moving streams infested with snails that harbor the schistosome worms. The worms enter through the skin and locate in the intestines (*S. mansoni* generally) or the urinary tract (*S. hematobium*). The worms leave eggs that further infect those regions. Since people use such streams for bathing, washing clothes, recreation, and collecting aquatic plants for food or thatching houses, schistosome infection is widespread.

Schistosomiasis is so highly endemic that it can be overlooked as a cofactor for other locally endemic conditions. As with helminth infection and immune suppression in Ethiopian immigrants, the opportunity to study

4. I use both dates because the fact sheet was last updated in 1996 but was still disseminated through the WHO Web site in 2003.

a comparison group exposed the high prevalence of schistosomiasis in an area thought to be schistosomiasis-free. Lake Malawi was considered schistosomiasis-free until two Peace Corps volunteers became infected and suffered the more conspicuous neurological variants of the disease. Subsequent investigation among 1,000 expatriates in Malawi found schistosomiasis prevalence of 32 percent among those who occasionally used Lake Malawi for recreation. Length of stay in the area was positively correlated with infection, with prevalence of 48 percent among people who had been resident for more than 4 years. Local Malawians, who also use the water for household purposes, would therefore be likely to have even higher prevalence. The lake study brought attention to increasing prevalence in the Malawian population. Whereas 46 percent of schoolchildren exhibited hematuria (blood in the urine, a symptom of urinary schistosomiasis) according to data for 1981, and 73 percent in 1991, prevalence had increased to 83 percent in 1994 (Cetron et al., 1996).

Schistosomiasis infection of the female reproductive tract was first reported in 1899 (Madden, 1899) and was described throughout the twentieth century in scientific journals in English, French, and German. Schistosomiasis infection was more often referred to as genitourinary schistosomiasis until the 1960s (Feldmeier et al., 1999). In spite of repeated findings of the genital manifestations, there has been greater emphasis in recent decades on the urinary consequences. The World Health Organization fact sheet on schistosomiasis, last updated in 1996 (WHO, 1996/2003) does not even mention female or male genital schistosomiasis, and yet 60 percent of women with *S. hematobium* have genital manifestations (Harms and Feldmeier, 2002). In other studies, 75 percent of women in endemic areas were estimated to have reproductive tract infections of schistosomiasis, with infestation of worms and ova in the vagina, uterus, vulva, or cervix (Feldmeier et al., 2001; Mosunjac et al., 2003).

It is now clear that female genital schistosomiasis (FGS) causes considerable morbidity in women in endemic areas. The species of schistosomiasis that is most associated with genital infection (*S. hematobium*) is most common in sub-Saharan Africa and not found in most other world regions. Prevalence in endemic zones is extremely high. In one area of Tanzania, 63 percent of residents were infected with *S. hematobium* and 34 percent with *S. mansoni*. Further study found that 37 percent of women and girls over the age of 15 had schistosomiasis in the lower reproductive tract. Women with FGS had higher frequencies of cervical lesions and other symptoms that could be confused with STDs than women in a control village in a nonendemic area. Both groups had low but similar prevalence of STDs (Poggensee et al., 2000).

In spite of numerous references in the medical literature, FGS has been overlooked and has often been mistaken for a sexually transmitted disease (Attili et al., 1983). The presumption by medical professionals and the local population that the symptoms of FGS were in fact symptoms of sexually transmitted diseases has inhibited women from seeking medical care and contributed to stigmatization of women with FGS symptoms (Feldmeier et al., 1995). Even in regions with prevalence exceeding 40 percent of the population, such as on the shores of Lake Victoria, people feel that schistosomiasis is a shameful condition. Because of its location in the genital organs, it is considered an STD, in spite of its transmission in water and the increasing prevalence with proximity to the lake (Mwanga et al., 2004).

Female genital schistosomiasis is difficult to diagnose because the symptoms are varied and nonspecific, and they resemble other reproductive tract problems and therefore do not afford an easy identification method (Mosunjac et al., 2003). FGS is easily overlooked because of inadequate access to health care and because the simplest diagnostic tool for reproductive tract health, the Pap smear, has very low sensitivity for the presence of genital schistosomiasis. Even in women who had sufficiently high schistosome egg load in the reproductive tract to produce infertility, only 30 percent of smears were positive for FGS (El-Mahgoub, 1998). Pap smears are still recommended, however, because they can show the immune reaction of the cervix to the presence of eggs in the form of inflammatory cells (Feldmeier et al., 2001). Genital infection very often is not accompanied by the presence of schistosome ova in the urine (Attili et al., 1983), which would be the easiest way to diagnose infection where health services are limited.

The effects of FGS are numerous. *S. hematobium* (urinary schistosomiasis) produces lesions in the lower genital tract in 30 to 75 percent of women infected (Leutscher et al., 1998). FGS lesions bleed spontaneously and from contact. In young girls, lesions are generally located in the vulva and vagina. At sexual maturity, the lesions become more numerous and cluster in the cervix, which is the area most vulnerable to HIV infection in young women (Marble and Key, 1995). Vascular changes in the pelvic areas of girls during puberty and of women in pregnancy make the genital area even more vulnerable to schistosome infestation. These changes also facilitate the movement of schistosome eggs further into the upper reproductive tract. It is likely that FGS explains some of the high prevalence of female sterility in the Central African region that generally has been presumed to result from STDs (Bullough, 1976). As mentioned in chapter 2, scarring (keratinization) due to vitamin-A deficiency can also be one of the generally overlooked causes of the Central African sterility belt.

Genital schistosomiasis promotes the transmission of HIV not only through the general effect of parasite load on nutritional balance and immune activation (as discussed in chapter 2) but also through its direct effect on the immune system barriers (skin and mucosa) and on the cell-mediated response. The numerous lesions produced by the eggs of the schistosome worm on the cervix, the vulva, and the vagina provide direct access to the blood stream for the HIV virus (Feldmeier et al., 1995). Both viable and dead ova also produce an inflammatory reaction in the tissue and attract to those sites $CD4^+$ T cells, which are HIV-susceptible (Poggensee et al., 2000;

Mosunjac et al., 2003). FGS lesions and inflammation can promote transmission of HIV, both male to female and female to male.

Additional evidence of the role that genital schistosomiasis plays in HIV transmission is epidemiological. HIV is more prevalent in areas with high schistosome prevalence than in low prevalence areas (Feldmeier et al., 1995; Marble and Key, 1995). Much has been made of the role of commerce in facilitating HIV transmission in Kenya, Uganda, and Tanzania in the regions around Lake Victoria. The emphasis has been on sexual partner change that might accompany the trade in goods across the lake. But the extremely high prevalence of schistosomiasis in the area around the lake has been virtually ignored, except by tropical disease specialists.

Genital schistosomiasis in males has been less studied, but there are also indications that it can promote HIV transmission through inflammation of the genital area. In one study in Madagascar, 43 percent of semen samples of a cross-sectional community-based study showed the presence of schistosome eggs. Bleeding associated with male genital schistosome infection is less often noticed than with urinary schistosomiasis, and so the genital form has been overlooked. In HIV-infected males, such bleeding also promotes viral shedding (Feldmeier et al., 1999; Leutscher et al., 2000). In Africa alone, 200 million people, men and women, are afflicted with genitourinary schistosomiasis (Feldmeier et al., 1999), constituting a very large population with increased susceptibility to HIV.

In the HIV literature and in global AIDS policy, there is a great deal of attention paid to the notion of risk behaviors. It is clear from the data we have about schistosomiasis and other parasites that one of the riskiest activities in Africa is to be a little girl or boy who gathers water for the family in a slow-moving stream, or helps with the family laundry at creekside, or bathes or plays in fresh water. When he or she grows up, that child will have a much higher risk of sexual transmission or acquisition of HIV because of schistosome infection than a healthy person with similar sexual behavior. AIDS policy needs to address the mundane risks of growing up in sub-Saharan Africa, Asia, and Latin America that burden people with sickness and make them more vulnerable to HIV.

Parasite load also has important implications for the development of an effective vaccine for HIV. Broad immune dysregulation is common in developing countries, as a consequence of widespread helminthic and other bacterial, viral, and parasitic infections, such as malaria, Leishmaniasis, hepatitis, herpes, and tuberculosis (Borkow and Bentwich, 2002). Helminth infection is almost universal in vast regions of the developing world, and some worms produce chronic debilitating diseases, as well as facilitating immune dysregulation. Most people in poor communities have worms most of their lives. That is an ecologic factor that must be taken into account in testing a vaccine that is effective for a developing-country population. The efficacy of vaccines has to be tested on populations that are immunologically the same as those for whom it is intended. Vaccines might fail, however, in trials in African or Asian populations because of helminth infection in the population, not because the vaccine is ineffective in an otherwise uncompromised person. So even a magic bullet for HIV, such as a vaccine, requires a broader health-promotion approach. "It is clear that eradication of helminths will enhance the capacity of the host to mount more efficient cellular immune responses following immunological challenges" (Borkow and Bentwich, 2002, 506).

The connection between parasite infection and HIV transmission makes treatment of schistosomiasis and other parasites a very high priority in an HIV-prevention program. "Deworming is a low-cost way of decreasing viral levels, which makes it an attractive addition to the list of therapy of coinfections associated with HIV/AIDS" (Wolday et al., 2002, 61). Effective treatment for schistosomiasis can be delivered for less than 25 U.S. cents per adult and even less for children (WHO, 1996/2003). Deworming, however, provides only temporary relief unless there are also parallel improvements in better water, sanitation, and health education. WHO chose deworming through drugs, not parasite eradication, because they concluded that resources would not be available to eliminate transmission with known methods, whether they were single, multiple, or integrated interventions (Chandiwana and Taylor, 1990).

An expert committee of the WHO came to the conclusion that eradication of schistosomiasis was not cost-effective. That position was revisited most recently in 1993 (WHO, 1996/2003). The time frame for such an evaluation must have been relatively short since the cumulative costs of perennial deworming would ultimately make eradication more cost-effective. In addition, the investment in clean water and sanitation would provide benefits far beyond schistosomiasis control alone. Evaluating programs for schistosome eradication without calculating any of the numerous collateral benefits of clean water understates the benefits. Attributing all of the costs of clean water to a schistosomiasis program (or to an antidiarrheal program) overstates the costs for any individual program. The demonstration that parasite infection interacts with HIV viral load and HIV transmission now makes a recalculation of the cost-effectiveness of eradication of *Schistosoma* and other parasites even more urgent. Eradication through water and sanitation investments is also attractive because once high-cost environmental measures are in place, they generate relatively low recurrent cost (Chandiwana and Taylor, 1990).

The biggest constraint on schistosomiasis eradication has been the lack of an adequate institutional framework for implementing control programs. But that is the same constraint that discourages investment in myriad complementary programs. A broad program of investment in a public health infrastructure—such as clean water, health care centers, and health and hygiene education—is the necessary base. Then the additional cost of a program for schistosomiasis control or other intervention would be minimal. Clearly, the method of calculating cost-effectiveness only for single-input investments shackles health policy. (The limitations of cost-effectiveness methodology are discussed in chapter 8.) It is a relatively simple matter to aggregate the costs and benefits of complementary interventions to see the logic of eradicating numerous water-borne problems with investments in water and sanitation that have positive spillovers. Numerous analyses of HIV-prevention and treatment programs argue that poor countries cannot absorb the billions of dollars of anticipated expenditures. That is only true in a very narrow and short-sighted view of developing-country needs. When the agenda is good health, not only HIV-prevention but including that, there is no problem of absorptive capacity in developing countries. There are ample opportunities for investments—in water, sanitation, nutrition, and health-care facilities—with known benefits for a broad array of problems.

Tuberculosis

Tuberculosis is the most lethal and most prevalent infectious disease in history. One-third of people worldwide now are infected with tuberculosis, of whom some 5 to 10 percent will develop active cases of the disease. Sub-Saharan Africa has the highest prevalence of TB, but there are other regions, including parts of Latin America and the former Soviet republics, where prevalence is extremely high. Table 3.2 lists the countries outside of sub-Saharan Africa with TB prevalence greater than 100 per 100,000 population, as of 2002. There are almost as many countries in sub-Saharan Africa alone with prevalence in excess of 100 per 100,000, as is shown in Table 3.3. Whereas only seven countries in the rest of the world have prevalence greater than 400 per 100,000, or 0.4 percent, 28 countries in sub-Saharan Africa do.

Although there had been some success against tuberculosis by the middle of the twentieth century, TB surged anew coincident with the spread of HIV. Tuberculosis is increasing rapidly in some parts of the world. The largest number of new cases is in Southeast Asia, with 3 percent of new infections in the world. But sub-Saharan Africa has the highest incidence: 350 new infections per 100,000 people (WHO, 2004). TB is the most common opportunist infection of HIV in sub-Saharan Africa and the leading cause of death among HIV-infected persons in the region (Corbett et al., 2002). HIV and TB are mutually exacerbating. HIV promotes the activation of latent TB, and TB infection accelerates the progression of HIV to AIDS and death. Treatment for TB has been shown to be effective in reducing viral load and improving survival in HIV-infected persons.

TB is an enormous public health problem that is not reflected in adequate research on the synergies between TB and HIV. There have been numerous studies on the effect of HIV on TB activation, on the interaction of HIV and TB, and on the accelerating effect of coinfection. What has

Table 3.2
Countries with tuberculosis prevalence over 100 per 100,000 population, 2002: world except sub-Saharan Africa

Region/country	No. of cases per 100,000
North Africa	
Morocco	100
Latin America and the Caribbean	
Bolivia	312
Dominican Republic	125
Ecuador	210
Guatemala	108
Guyana	157
Haiti	392
Paraguay	109
Peru	246
Suriname	103
West Asia	
Iraq	251
Yemen	145
East Asia	
China	272
Korea, Democratic People's Republic of	194
Korea, Republic of	138
Mongolia	270
South Asia	
Afghanistan	667
Bangladesh	447
Bhutan	205
India	344
Nepal	271
Pakistan	379
Southeast Asia	
Cambodia	734
Indonesia	609
Lao People's Democratic Republic	359
Malaysia	120
Myanmar	176
Philippines	540
Thailand	179
Timor-Leste	734
Viet Nam	263
Oceania	
Guam	147
Micronesia, Federated States of	111
New Caledonia	151
Northern Mariana Islands	112
Palau	130
Papua New Guinea	543
Solomon Islands	126
Vanuatu	147
Developed regions	
Romania	189
Commonwealth of Independent States	
Armenia	106
Azerbaijan	109
Belarus	125
Kazakhstan	149
Kyrgyzstan	164
Republic of Moldova	233
Russian Federation	181
Tajikistan	169
Turkmenistan	125
Ukraine	143
Uzbekistan	134

Source: UNDP, *Human Development Report 2004.*

Table 3.3
Countries with tuberculosis prevalence over 100 per 100,000 population, 2002: sub-Saharan Africa

Country	No. of cases per 100,000	Country	No. of cases per 100,000
Angola	398	Lesotho	449
Benin	131	Liberia	501
Botswana	338	Madagascar	407
Burkina Faso	272	Malawi	462
Burundi	531	Mali	695
Cameroon	238	Mauritania	437
Cape Verde	352	Mauritius	137
Central African Republic	438	Mozambique	547
Chad	388	Namibia	478
Comoros	121	Niger	386
Congo	435	Nigeria	565
Congo, Democratic Republic of the	594	Rwanda	598
		São Tomé and Principé	308
Côte d'Ivoire	634	Senegal	438
Djibouti[a]	892	Sierra Leone	628
Equatorial Guinea	362	Somalia	757
Eritrea	480	South Africa	366
Ethiopia	508	Sudan	346
Gabon	307	Swaziland	769
Gambia	325	Tanzania	472
Ghana	371	Togo	688
Guinea	375	Uganda	550
Guinea-Bissau	316	Zambia	588
Kenya	579	Zimbabwe	452

[a]Data for 2001.
Source: UNDP, *Human Development Report 2004.*

not appeared in the literature is any assessment of whether tuberculosis, latent or active, increases the transmission of HIV. That would be especially useful in understanding HIV dynamics in areas with very high prevalence of tuberculosis, including sub-Saharan Africa and the former Soviet republics. If TB increases HIV transmission, as do malaria and other parasites, the implications of high prevalence of TB for the future spread of HIV are ominous. Much attention is focused on the HIV/TB coinfection rates. What has received less emphasis is that the majority of tuberculosis cases are not HIV-related. In sub-Saharan Africa, for example, only 25 to 31 percent of TB is due to HIV (Pallangyo, 2001; Corbett et al., 2003). If the other 70 to 75 percent of people with active TB are more vulnerable to HIV acquisition because of depressed immune response, that has serious implications for the spread of HIV. In Russia, the Baltics, and other former Soviet republics with very high TB prevalence, the vast majority of people with active TB do not have HIV but are probably especially susceptible to it.

Sexually transmitted diseases

Sexually transmitted diseases are an important cofactor for HIV transmission, for reasons relating both to the person to whom the HIV is transmitted and the person transmitting the virus. STDs, especially treatable, bacterial, ulcerative STDs, are more common in poor populations because of lack of water and facilities for personal hygiene, lack of information, lack of access to health care, and lack of privacy in those facilities where care is available only in specialized STD clinics. Even symptomatic STD patients do not seek medical care (Grosskurth et al., 2000), probably because of the stigma and the difficulty of obtaining care. STDs are also more common in poor populations because of nutritional deficiencies that impair epithelial integrity and the protective capacity of mucosal membranes (see chapter 2).

While STDs are common in the industrialized countries[5] and can act as cofactors in the transmission of HIV, they play a more significant role in Africa and in South and Southeast Asia because of the kinds of STDs that are prevalent and because of the failure to treat them. In affluent countries, chancroid is virtually unknown. Cumulative cases in the United States for 1989 to 1996 were just over 17,000, compared to 4.1 million cases of gonorrhea, 2.6 million cases of chlamydia, and 1.2 million cases of syphilis in the United States in the same period (CDC, 1999). In Africa and South and Southeast Asia, in contrast, genital ulcer diseases such as chancroid constitute a much larger proportion of sexually transmitted dis-

5. One in six American adults reports having had a sexually transmitted disease. Incidence (new cases) was 1.5 percent of those polled (Michael et al., 1994). In the United States, STDs are the most common diseases reported to the Centers for Disease Control and Prevention (not all diseases are reported), with 12 million new cases annually, of which 3 million are in teenagers (CDC, 1998). Chlamydia is the most common sexually transmitted bacterial pathogen reported to CDC, even though reporting seriously understates the extent of the epidemic because 70 percent of women and 25 percent of men are asymptomatic (Webster et al., 1993). Almost half a million cases were reported nationally in 1995, but much higher rates, from 8 to 40 percent of women, were found in studies around the country (Webster et al., 1993; CDC, 1997). STDs are increasing rapidly in the United States and other industrialized countries. Herpes-2 has increased 30 percent since the late 1970s and now infects about one in five persons in the United States 12 years of age and older. Prevalence has quintupled among white teenagers and has doubled among whites in their 20s (Fleming et al., 1997).

cases. Chancroid is one of the most prevalent STDs in Zimbabwe; in Harare and Bulawayo, the two largest cities, chancroid is one of the top two complaints of men visiting STD clinics, along with urethritis (generally gonorrheal). Genital ulcer diseases are most common in areas where water is difficult to acquire and personal hygiene suffers. While there is convincing evidence that all STDs can increase the transmission of HIV, genital ulcers increase the risk five- to ten-fold (World Bank, 1993b).

Not only are the kinds of STDs in poor populations more likely to be cofactors for HIV transmission, but the STDs go undetected and untreated, increasing the likelihood of transmission of an ulcerative STD and HIV. In women, some symptoms of STDs may be mistaken for symptoms of pregnancy, or just one more discomfort of an infectious or parasitic disease. Health services are inadequate, drugs are not available, and women do not want the social opprobrium that would attend a visit to an STD clinic. Women reporting to a prenatal clinic in South Africa did not complain of STDs, but 52 percent were found to have at least one bacterial STD, and 18 percent had more than one. In that study, HIV was found to be more prevalent among women with at least one other STD (Sturm et al., 1998).

Access to health care is critical in diagnosing and treating STDs. Viral STDs can be treated symptomatically but are not curable. Bacterial STDs, including chancroid, syphilis, gonorrhea, and chlamydia, can be treated with a relatively short course of antibiotic. But the decline in health services in Africa and Latin America and parts of Asia, never adequate, has left people especially vulnerable to HIV. Even where health care is available, medications often are not.

For an HIV-negative person, the presence of other STDs, especially genital ulcer diseases, acts as a cofactor in the acquisition of HIV. STDs provide an easy entry for HIV by compromising nonspecific epithelial defense (Hitchcock and Fransen, 1998). STDs also compromise cell-mediated immunity and enhance HIV transmission (Fleming and Wasserheit, 1999). As is the case with genital schistosomiasis, STDs have an inflammatory effect on genital tissue, attracting T cells to the site where they can be most easily infected. In addition, gonorrhea seems to prevent or mute an immune response by inhibiting the development of immunological memory response (for adaptive immunity), which might be why gonorrhea increases the risk of infection with other STDs, including HIV (Boulton and Gray-Owen, 2002).

Coinfection with other STDs in an HIV-infected person also increases the likelihood of transmitting HIV. STDs promote more viral shedding in the genital tract of HIV-infected persons (Fleming and Wasserheit, 1999; Corbett et al., 2002). Treatment for STDs reduces viral shedding, decreasing the risk of HIV transmission. Consequently, calculations of the increased risk of acquisition of HIV attributable to STDs are likely to be underestimates since they account for cofactor effects of STDs on susceptibility of HIV-negative people but do not capture effects of enhanced infectiousness of HIV-infected people who also have other STDs. The protective effect for HIV-negative persons of treating HIV-infected persons with STDs has not been calculated in studies of the effectiveness of STD treatment (Grosskurth et al., 2000). This illustrates the limitations of individual-level studies that do not measure ecologic factors, such as viral load in the transmitting population, which will be discussed further in chapter 8.

Nonulcerative STDs, including gonorrhea and chlamydia, also increase HIV shedding (Fleming and Wasserheit, 1999). Additional evidence of the interaction between STDs and HIV transmission was found in Malawi where HIV-infected men with urethritis had much higher levels of HIV in their semen. HIV shedding was eight times greater in men with urethritis than in HIV-infected men with similar viral burdens but without STD coinfection. Treatment for urethritis, particularly gonorrheal urethritis, was associated with a 42 percent decrease of HIV in semen, bringing it to the levels of men without urethritis (Cohen et al., 1997). Nonulcerative STDs pose a large public health problem because, in some populations, they constitute a much larger part of the infection burden and they are often asymptomatic. Even the nonulcerative STDs increase risk of HIV transmission. Consequently, they might be a cofactor in a larger proportion of HIV transmission than ulcerative STDs.

STDs also increase the likelihood of vertical transmission. In Tanzania, early STD diagnosis and treatment reduced the infectiousness of people with HIV. In pregnant women, treatment of STDs has the additional benefit of reducing congenital syphilis and other serious medical complications for newborns (Urassa et al., 2001).

In areas with low HIV prevalence but high STD prevalence, it might be especially effective to treat STDs as an early intervention to prevent the spread of HIV. Standard cost-effectiveness studies may find that expenditure unjustified based on the number of HIV cases in a low-prevalence population at the time. For example, in Bangladesh a cost-effectiveness study was conducted on a syphilis-screening program at a maternal-child health and family planning clinic. The authors point out that standard measures of cost-effectiveness do not include prevention of secondary infections of HIV through treatment of syphilis, and in a low-HIV prevalence population, the benefit would appear small. But HIV prevention could be an important spillover of syphilis screening (Khan et al., 2002). Of course, we want to avoid HIV prevalence sufficiently high that it provides additional cost-effectiveness justification for STD treatment. In areas with high HIV prevalence, it is already clear that treatment of STDs is important for reducing the absolute number of cases of HIV transmission (Grosskurth et al., 1995; Grosskurth et al., 2000). In areas with low HIV prevalence, it should be possible to include an imputed value for future cases of HIV prevented in a cost-effectiveness model.

Parasites, STDs, and HIV

An important pair of research trials was carried out in Mwanza, Tanzania, and Rakai, Uganda, to test the effectiveness of treating STDs for reducing HIV transmission. In Mwanza, there was a significant difference in HIV transmission between the intervention group, treated for STDs, and the control, untreated group (Grosskurth et al., 1995). In Rakai, Uganda, in contrast, there was no significant difference in HIV incidence between the intervention and control groups (Wawer et al., 1999). Several good reasons have been proposed for the difference in results between the two trials, including stage of the epidemic, duration of the trials, and others (Hitchcock and Fransen, 1998; Grosskurth et al., 2000). One possible reason that has not been mentioned in any of the comparisons is that in the Rakai trial people in the control group were treated with antihelminthic medication and vitamins, whereas in Mwanza the control group was not treated. It is possible that in Rakai the STD intervention and the antihelminthic/vitamin intervention were roughly equal in their effectiveness in reducing, or preventing greater increase in, HIV transmission, resulting in the lack of significant difference between the two groups.

The Rakai study (Wawer et al., 1999) makes brief mention of historical estimates of incidence (1990–1991) as the presumed benchmark. But the study emphasizes prevalence in the two groups measured at the start of the trial as the basis for comparison of trial results. They did not estimate incidence at the beginning of the trial and consequently cannot (and do not) make a statement about any change in incidence as a result of the trial, although there is an inferred conclusion of no change in the STD-treated group. The comparison they make is actually not about change in incidence but about the difference (or lack thereof) between the group treated for STDs and the group treated for helminths.[6] What they found, then, was that treating for STDs and treating for helminths results in the same HIV incidence. There was in fact no control group of untreated persons. Other factors, such as stage of epidemic, may explain the difference between the Rakai and Mwanza results. What needs to be explored further is the effect of antihelminthic treatments.

The antihelminthic/vitamin intervention is noted in the methods section of the Rakai study but is not mentioned again by the authors or by the many people who have attempted to reconcile the Mwanza-Rakai results. It is a very Kuhnian problem, in that the paradigm cannot recognize data that are outside the questions it asks. The Rakai trials were considered, in a sense, a failure (for policy, not as research) because no difference in HIV incidence was found between the intervention group and the control

6. The problem of change versus difference will be recognized by economists familiar with Joan Robinson's critique of neoclassical economics.

group. Because of the blind pursuit of data that are behavioral or STD-related, potentially useful information about the role of antihelminthic treatment and vitamin supplementation was neglected.

Antiretroviral treatment and viral load

Widespread access to antiretroviral treatment has numerous reasons to commend it. Simple compassion and ethical considerations support the use of available treatments. In an instrumental sense as well, treatment is a pragmatic strategy. Antiretroviral treatment for parents postpones the time at which children become orphans. It keeps farmer-parents alive long enough to pass on farming skills, it supports social cohesion in the community, and it maintains the productivity of workers. Antiretroviral treatment also reduces viral load and thereby should reduce sexual transmission. Vaginal shedding of HIV can be reduced through antiretroviral treatment, thereby reducing the risk of vertical transmission as well (Fiore et al., 2002). Treatment is complementary to other forms of prevention and improves the cost-effectiveness of other prevention programs.

If we look at all the factors that affect transmission of HIV and map where those cofactors are most prevalent, the global distribution of HIV and AIDS becomes considerably more logical. The necessary interventions, or rather the myriad opportunities to intervene, are also more apparent. This chapter has brought together numerous studies from scientists in different fields and at different locations. Individually they present evidence of the connection between malaria and HIV transmission, helminths and HIV transmission, schistosomiasis and HIV transmission, and so on. Together they demonstrate that poor people in developing countries, especially in tropical regions, are at much greater risk of HIV infection because of endemic cofactor diseases.

It is the greatest failure of global AIDS policy makers that they looked at Africa, and only belatedly at the Americas and Asia, and saw sexual behavior, rather than hunger and disease, as the key differentiating characteristics of the pandemic. The next three chapters review the conditions that constitute the health profile in three world regions and provide the context for HIV transmission amidst poverty.

II

Health Profiles of Developing and Transition Regions

4

Sub-Saharan Africa

Fertile Terrain

The HIV/AIDS epidemic in sub-Saharan Africa is not an isolated phenomenon. It is a predictable outcome of an environment of poverty, worsening nutrition, chronic parasite infection, and limited access to medical care. In such circumstances, people are more susceptible to all infectious diseases, no matter how they are transmitted. Just as tuberculosis, diarrheal diseases, and respiratory infections are more prevalent and more quickly fatal among poor people, so, too, HIV is a disease of poverty in the African context. Prevalence of HIV in Africa is not a special case but a brutal indicator of the nutritional, infectious, and parasitic diseases that have afflicted African people all along, and it is a precursor of higher rates of HIV infection among similarly marginalized populations in the rest of the world.

As explained in the two previous chapters, based on experience with other infectious diseases, we should expect the HIV epidemic to develop differently in a region with widespread malnutrition and other host factors known to contribute to disease susceptibility. To assess the conditions under which HIV has spread in Africa, this chapter first reviews important economic and nutritional indicators relevant to Africa's health profile. Second, it examines how the biomedical effects of those economic conditions contribute to higher rates of HIV transmission in sub-Saharan Africa. Finally, there is a brief discussion of social and economic factors that affect the options people have and the choices they make. An appendix to the chapter presents the results of statistical analysis showing the correlation of economic and epidemiological variables, such as nutrition, distribution of income, and urbanization, with rates of HIV.

Economic and nutritional background of African health

Most of the poorest countries in the world are in sub-Saharan Africa; 31 African countries had per capita GDP in 2001 below US$500. All 25 of the countries that rank lowest on the Human Development Index are in sub-Saharan Africa, as are half of the next 25. In 15 African countries, more than half the population lives on less than US$1 a day, and in 25 countries more than two-thirds of the people live on less than US$2 a day (UNDP, 2003a).

In those African countries with relatively higher GDP per capita, the distribution of income is very unequal. In South Africa, the top 10 percent of the population receives more than 47 percent of income. Botswana and Zimbabwe have the highest rates of HIV/AIDS and the highest Gini coefficients (the most unequal income distribution) in Africa (World Bank, 1997; World Bank, 1999). Income distribution is important because it tells us more about the living conditions of the poor than does average income because a few very high incomes will skew the average. One-fourth of Botswana's population and more than one-third of Zimbabwe's and Namibia's populations live on less than $1 a day (UNDP, 2003a). In Botswana, GNP per capita increased at 8.5 percent per year from 1975 to 1990, but per capita daily supply of both protein and cereals fell 9 percent from 1970 to 1995 (UNDP, 1998; UNDP, 2000). Inequality is growing in Botswana, and the number of people categorized as "permanent destitutes" has increased five times as fast as the total population since 1980 (Good, 1999).

In the 1970s and 1980s, when the AIDS pandemic had its origins, sub-Saharan Africa suffered worsening poverty, drought, and malnutrition.[1] According to World Bank data, between a quarter and a half of the population of the region suffered serious malnutrition. Some 90 million people consumed less than 80 percent of the FAO/WHO caloric requirement, below which people face serious health risks and stunted growth. There were 150 million people in sub-Saharan Africa in 1980 who consumed less than 90 percent of the FAO/WHO requirement, which is considered to be sufficient calories to maintain an active working life (Kamarck, 1988).

Sub-Saharan Africa was the only world region to experience falling food production per capita in the 1980s. There were a number of reasons, including faulty government producer-price policies, rapid urbanization com-

1. The data for this chapter are both historical (1970 to 1995) and current because its focus is the nutritional and health environment that produced the epidemic.

bined with gender-biased land tenancy, and a drought of millennial proportions.[2] Average daily caloric intake fell in sub-Saharan Africa as a whole from 1980 to 1989 and fell in 25 of 44 countries of the region (Pio, 1994). Although food production increased in 33 out of 44 countries in the 1990s, daily per capita supply of calories was still 1.5 percent lower in 1997 than in 1970. Sub-Saharan Africa was the only region to experience a decline in calorie supply and also the only region in which daily protein supply per capita fell over the same period, more than 4 percent in the region as a whole (UNDP, 2000).

The economies of sub-Saharan Africa continued to decline in the late 1980s and early 1990s. Gross domestic product per capita fell in real terms between 1988 and 1992 by about 1 percent per year, and real per capita consumption declined in 23 of the 41 countries in that period. Even in countries with moderately successful economic reforms, in which the reported incidence of poverty fell nationally (Tanzania, Kenya, and Nigeria), the poorest of the poor were considerably worse off in 1991 than they were in 1983 (Demery and Squire, 1996). In 24 countries in the region, per capita income in 2001 was lower than in the 1970s or 1980s (UNDP, 2003a).

From 1988 to 1998, when nascent or concentrated AIDS epidemics developed into generalized epidemics in sub-Saharan Africa, 30 percent of the total population of the region was malnourished. In some countries, conditions worsened considerably for the poor. In Côte d'Ivoire, for example, the proportion of the population in poverty increased from 11 percent to 18 percent between 1985 and 1988, and reached 32 percent in 1993. Among children born between 1988 and 1993, the prevalence of stunted growth is 80 percent higher than among children born before 1988 (World Bank, 1998). Côte d'Ivoire has the highest reported rate of HIV prevalence in West Africa: 7 percent of adults by the end of 2003 (UNAIDS, 2004). For Côte d'Ivoire, as for other countries, it is not GDP per capita that is most relevant but the rapidly worsening situation of the poor.

Serious drought again affected numerous countries in eastern and southern Africa in the late 1990s and into the new century. The drought exacerbated a developing food crisis caused by the deaths of adult farmers from AIDS. As late as 2002, some regions lost the entire crop of maize, the dietary staple. Ongoing civil strife also threatened food security in several countries (FAO, 2003a).

Zimbabwe has one of the highest rates of HIV in the world. In the years in which adult HIV prevalence there increased steadily to 25 percent, Zimbabwe had higher income per capita than many of its neighbors, but

2. Unlike earlier Sahelian droughts caused by ENSO-El Niño that would last 1 or 2 years, the drought that began in the late 1960s lasted 17 years. (For more about the Sahel droughts, see Giannini et al., 2003).

its economic difficulties were similar to those in the rest of sub-Saharan Africa. At independence in 1980, the income of whites was 39 times the income of rural blacks while urban blacks had incomes five times those of rural blacks (Barry et al., 1990). A disastrous drought in the 1980s diverted much needed resources from other sectors. Economic restructuring pushed up the price of maize meal (the staple food) 100 percent over 1982/1983; bread prices increased 25 to 30 percent, and the price of edible oils increased by 25 percent (Davies and Sanders, 1988). The newly independent Zimbabwe expanded health services to the poor, but with only one physician per 10,000 population and 60 percent of the doctors in urban areas, access to health care was still very limited (Barry et al., 1990). The introduction of user charges in 1991 caused a significant drop in outpatient visits, inpatient demand, and prenatal visits (Logie, 1993). In 1980, 22 percent of Zimbabwean children were severely malnourished, and 13 years later the proportion was still 12 percent (World Bank, 1993b). In recent years, the combined effects of drought, HIV/AIDS, and the deteriorating political situation in Zimbabwe have gravely affected incomes, investment, and food security in what had been, in Africa, a relatively affluent country.

In 25 of 33 African countries surveyed, the nutritional situation from the 1970s to the 1990s was even worse than in Zimbabwe (Tagwiyeri and Greiner, 1994). Of 19 famines worldwide from 1975 to 1998, 18 occurred in Africa. Internal and external conflicts contributed to most of those famines, producing massive flows of refugees with consequent food shortages and crowding in unsanitary camps (von Braun et al., 1999). The immediate cause of death in refugee crises is generally a communicable disease, but the underlying cause is malnutrition, which increases case-fatality rates for all the common childhood and adult diseases, including measles, diarrhea, malaria, and respiratory infections (CDC, 1992).

In addition to protein-energy malnutrition caused by an absolute shortage of food, refugees suffer from micronutrient deficiencies. Low levels of dietary vitamin A prior to displacement are aggravated by relief rations deficient in vitamin A and by diseases that deplete vitamin-A stores, such as measles and diarrhea. Rates of scurvy (vitamin-C deficiency), pellagra (niacin deficiency), and iron-deficiency anemia soared in refugee camps in Ethiopia, Malawi, and Somalia. It is difficult to maintain statistics on refugee malnutrition because mortality is so high that the survey population keeps changing. In a Sudanese camp, for example, the proportion of malnourished children appeared to remain stable over a 2-month period although, in that time, 13 percent of the children died and were replaced in the data set by other malnourished children (CDC, 1992).

A 1998 report by the U.S. Centers for Disease Control and Prevention (CDC) on cholera and other disease outbreaks among refugees stated modestly: "Public health workers increasingly appreciate the fragile interaction between individual host, environment, and infectious and noninfectious agents capable of producing disease" (Cookson et al., 1998, n.p.). Cholera swept through the estimated 800,000 Rwandan refugees living in camps in Goma, Democratic Republic of Congo. In one month in 1994, 60,000 people fell ill and 10,000 died (Cookson et al., 1998). There were 20 outbreaks of cholera among Mozambican refugees in Malawi between 1988 and 1992, but the conditions in Mozambique from which they fled were so bad that crude mortality rates in Malawian camps were still one-third lower than in Mozambique. Internally displaced persons in Mozambique, Ethiopia, and Sudan had crude mortality rates from 4 to 70 times the mortality rates in those countries for persons not displaced (CDC, 1992).

Our subject, of course, is not those who died in refugee camps or elsewhere in Africa in the 1980s; it is those who survived. The old adage "if it doesn't kill you, it makes you stronger" is unfortunately not true. Recurrent malnutrition, infectious disease, and parasite infection, if they don't kill you, make you weaker. Child survivors of the 1980s famines are now in their 20s and face continued nutritional and parasitic stress in their reproductive years. Many of them are now dying of AIDS.

The decades in which Africa experienced falling food production, wars, and massive flows of refugees were also decades of fiscal and monetary mismanagement. The economic chaos, and for some countries, the attempts to correct it, weighed heavily on the poor, although reductions in social spending were less drastic in Africa than in Latin America. In half the countries for which data are available in sub-Saharan Africa, real per capita expenditure on health fell from 1980 to 1985. Most of the decline occurred in nonwage recurrent expenditure—for drugs, for example—so the quality of treatment suffered even more than spending figures alone suggest (Jespersen, 1992). In Zambia in 1986, government spending on drugs was only 10 percent of what it had been in 1983 (Sanders and Sambo, 1991). Adjustment continued into the 1990s. In Zimbabwe, for example, the Ministry of Health budget fell 35 percent in real terms from 1991 to 1993 (World Bank, 1993b).

Even the meager amounts allocated to health do not benefit poor people primarily. Public social spending on health and education generally benefits middle- and upper-income people far more than the poor. Urban, hospital-based health-care systems divert funds from services for the poor that are best delivered at the primary care level. In six out of seven African countries studied, the benefit accruing to the top income quintile was from 171 to 290 percent of that enjoyed by the lowest quintile. Physical inaccessibility and the effects of cost-recovery schemes, such as user fees, are also among the causes (Castro-Leal et al., 1999).

Tuberculosis

All of the countries of sub-Saharan Africa have very high prevalence of active tuberculosis. As Table 3.3 shows, 42 African countries had rates in excess

Table 4.1
Distribution of new tuberculosis infections in Africa, by age and by sex, 2002

Age group	Females (%)	Males (%)
0–14	6.8	4.0
15–24	23.9	17.2
25–34	34.3	31.5
35–44	19.3	23.2
45–54	9.0	14.9
55–64	4.1	5.7
65 +	2.5	3.5

Source: WHO, 2003b. *Tuberculosis Epidemiological Surveillance Report.*

of 300 per 100,000, as of 2002. Tuberculosis has increased rapidly along with the AIDS epidemic; it is also the leading cause of death among people with HIV in Africa and other poor regions. TB transmission is increasing at 6 percent per year in sub-Saharan Africa, an increase attributed chiefly to HIV (Corbett et al., 2003).

In a striking reflection of the HIV epidemic, new TB infections are concentrated in the adolescent and young adult population. Table 4.1 shows the distribution of new TB infections by age and by sex in 2002. Among women, nearly 60 percent of new active infections were in those between 15 and 34 years of age, and 78 percent were in women aged 15 to 44. Men are more likely to become infected with both HIV and TB at a slightly later age than women are. Nearly half of new infections were in men aged 15 to 34, and 72 percent were in men aged 15 to 44 (WHO, 2003c).

Parasitic disease

Africa is the continent with the greatest area in the tropics and therefore suffers more than other continents from parasitic diseases. More than 90 percent of acute malaria infections each year worldwide occur in tropical Africa. Africa accounts for the majority of malaria deaths, including about 3,000 deaths per day of children under the age of 5. Survivors suffer chronic immune activation through repeated reinfection (WHO, 1998c).

Schistosomiasis

Schistosomiasis (bilharzia) is the second most prevalent tropical disease, both in Africa and worldwide. As noted in chapter 3, more than 80 percent of the 200 million people infected worldwide with schistosomiasis are in sub-

Saharan Africa. Schistosomiasis has been eliminated in some non-African countries, but African health budgets cannot cover the necessary diagnostic and therapeutic measures to eradicate the disease. While Latin America and Asia also have schistosome species (including *S. mansoni*), genital schistosomiasis is more common with *S. hematobium*, the species more common in sub-Saharan Africa than in other tropical regions.

The construction of dams and lakes for water collection, irrigation, and hydroelectric power has accelerated in the past 50 years. By 1985, the surface area of artificial lakes in tropical regions equaled the surface area of all natural lakes in the entire world. Moreover, artificial lakes are more hospitable than natural lakes to the aquatic plants in which the snail hosts of schistosome worms proliferate (WHO, 1987).

Although schistosomiasis is considered primarily a rural concern, the rapid urbanization in sub-Saharan Africa in the 1970s and 1980s increasingly made it an urban problem. The cycle of transmission is repeated by human contamination of surface water. Consequently, urbanization spreads the parasite since dense populations lack sanitary facilities, bathing areas, and laundry and recreational sites. The construction of roads and railways spreads the foci of schistosomiasis because of lack of sanitary facilities in workers' camps and because the construction itself produces breeding areas for snails in new surface water sites (WHO, 1987).

Although the large lakes, including Lake Malawi, Lake Victoria, Lake Kariba, Lake Tanganyika, and Lake Tana, are obvious sources of infection, the parasite flourishes as well in small ponds and streams, especially when small dams are constructed to supply household water. Even arid areas are not exempt. Artificial lakes in arid areas can be even more propitious environments for the snail hosts of the parasite (WHO, 1987).

Schistosomiasis is endemic throughout tropical Africa and parts of subtropical Africa. There is considerable overlap of schistosome-endemic areas and high HIV-prevalence countries. Of course, the coincidence of areas of high prevalence of schistosomiasis and HIV does not prove causation. It does, however, corroborate known mechanisms that link the two, as discussed in chapter 3, including genital lesions and the inflammatory effect in genital areas caused by worms and ova. The most detailed prevalence data available on the WHO Web site date from a country-by-country mapping compiled in 1987. Although transmission of schistosomiasis may have decreased in some locations because of changing water use patterns, it has increased in most areas due to dam construction (www.who.int/wormcontrol; Sharp, 2003). Extremely high prevalence among children in endemic areas in the 1970s and 1980s has created a large population of young adults in the 1990s and 2000s with chronic lesions and genital inflammation, as well as anemia and overall debilitation. Country analysis shows that much of the region of high schistosome prevalence in the 1970s and 1980s corresponds with areas of high HIV prevalence today.

In a national survey in Botswana between 1976 and 1978, the prevalence of *S. hematobium* infection in the area around Gaborone ranged from 15 to 35 percent, depending on locality. In earlier years, Botswana's chief regional economic significance was that the railroad from Zambia to South Africa passed through its eastern region, near Francistown and Gaborone, which are today its two largest cities and centers of HIV prevalence. A large number of small dams in eastern Botswana, and even the railroad embankments, provided an ecological niche for the snails (WHO, 1987).

South Africa provides a very interesting example of the impact of climate on human health. In much of the country, streams are seasonal. In contrast, rainfall patterns and geography in KwaZulu Natal, Mpumalanga, Gauteng, Limpopo (Northern Province), and North West Province permit permanent rivers that support a snail population and, hence, schistosomiasis. According to the WHO country report, schistosomiasis prevalence in numerous districts of KwaZulu Natal at the time of the survey exceeded 60 and 80 percent. Even in Durban, one-fourth of schoolchildren were infected, and just a few miles inland, more than 80 percent of children were burdened with the parasite. KwaZulu Natal is the province with the highest estimated prevalence of HIV. All of the other provinces with high schistosome prevalence are also the provinces with the highest HIV, except Free State. There are certainly other factors in some provinces, including large urban areas and mines with single-sex barracks, that influence HIV prevalence. Urban areas in the drier half of the country, however, do not report as high HIV prevalence as in the wetter, northern and eastern half.

Numerous reports on HIV emphasize the border area near Messina and Venda as a center of HIV transmission between Zimbabwe and South Africa and the border with Botswana in North West Province, in particular among truckers and sex workers. The 1987 WHO report, however, spotlights those locations for their extremely high schistosomiasis infection rates. As in the rest of Africa, the species that is most prevalent in South Africa is *S. hematobium*, which causes genital lesions and inflammation of genital areas in the majority of those infected, especially in women and girls. Average prevalence of schistosomiasis in surveys of schoolchildren in the border area was 42 percent, although in more than half the locations surveyed, more than two-thirds of the children were infected (WHO, 1987). In the 1980s, prevalence of schistosomiasis in parts of Swaziland ranged from 33 to 60 percent (WHO, 1987). Adult HIV prevalence in Swaziland is 39 percent (UNAIDS, 2004).

In Tanzania, there is, as one would expect, high schistosomiasis endemicity in all of Mwanza (near Lake Victoria) and Kigoma (along Lake Tanganyika), along the Ruvuma River, and also in all the population centers, such as Dodoma, Dar es Salaam, and Tanga. In Uganda, fishing communities have high schistosome-infection prevalence. Migrant workers have spread the parasite into higher-elevation areas, and new sources of transmission have developed in the area of Owens Falls dam, in addition to the expected high prevalence around Lake Victoria from Busoga to Masaka (WHO, 1987).

In Kenya, there are increasingly numerous areas of transmission, and prevalence of schistosomiasis has also increased over the past few decades. In 1978, an estimated 3 million people were infected out of a national population of 13 million, three times as many as in 1960. As with other African countries, *S. hematobium* is more widespread in Kenya than is *S. mansoni* (intestinal). In the coastal plain and the Tana River area, 50 to 70 percent of schoolchildren were infected. In western Kenya, towns closer to Lake Victoria had higher infection rates, with greater than 50 percent prevalence in Kisumu, which is on the lake. In other areas, the introduction of irrigated rice farming increased prevalence of schistosomiasis from zero to 60 percent. By the 1980s, snails were present in all water projects and irrigation canals inspected in Kenya. As late as 1987, 85 percent of Kenyans used surface water for their household needs. The WHO report attributed increasing prevalence in Kenya to labor migration from endemic areas in Uganda and Tanzania, as well as to irrigation (WHO, 1987).

Ethiopia is characterized by great variation in schistosome prevalence. Even in areas a short distance apart, prevalence can range from 7 to 80 percent. Ethiopian prevalence data show the difference in risk by gender and age. Among children and adolescents, prevalence is often higher among boys because they have greater freedom to leave the house and play in ponds and streams. Among 20- to 40-year-olds, however, prevalence is higher among women because they gather household water, do laundry, and collect aquatic plants for food and for thatch. Those women often spend half the day immersed in water (WHO, 1987).

Filariasis

Lymphatic filariasis, or elephantiasis, afflicts over 40 million people in sub-Saharan Africa. It is caused by a worm transmitted by mosquitoes and lodges in the lymph system, a component of the immune defenses. The worms produce millions of larvae that circulate in the blood. Prevalence is increasing in Africa because breeding areas for mosquitoes proliferate with unplanned urban growth. People can be asymptomatic, even with millions of larvae in the blood or adult worms in the lymph system. Where the disease is highly endemic, however, 10 to 50 percent of men and 10 percent of women can have serious genital damage and enlargement of the legs or arms. Bacterial infections of the skin also result from the failure of immune response due to damage to the lymph system (WHO, 2000a).

African trypanosomiasis

Trypanosomiasis (sleeping sickness) is endemic with high prevalence across a broad belt of tropical Africa, with increasing transmission in 12 countries, and epidemic conditions in Uganda, Sudan, Angola, and Democratic Republic of the Congo (WHO, 2001b). Prevalence has increased dramatically since the 1970s, with annual incidence estimated at 300,000 to 500,000 infections. An epidemic that broke out in 1920 had almost been eradicated by 1965, but surveillance efforts slackened; a new epidemic began in 1970 and is still increasing. Distribution is scattered, but in highly endemic villages, prevalence is between 20 and 50 percent (WHO, 2001a).

Helminths and other parasites

Intestinal parasites of many kinds (including hookworms, roundworms, and amebas) are extremely widespread among poor populations in tropical areas, as discussed in chapter 2. The hundreds of millions of people in tropical Africa whose food supply has decreased since 1960 are sharing their meager supply of nutrients with billions of parasites.

The importance of helminth infection for promoting HIV transmission was discussed in chapter 3. Most HIV research, however, is still generally blind to the human environment in which transmission occurs. The HIV literature accepts that access to health care is critical in diagnosing and treating STDs and consequently in preventing HIV. Those same facilities, however, are essential for diagnosing and treating schistosomiasis, filariases, trypanosomiasis, and numerous other parasites. The inadequacy of health services puts virtually the entire population at risk for numerous serious diseases, as does the lack of safe water and waste-disposal facilities. To ignore the elevated risk for poor people in a tropical environment disregards most of the accumulated knowledge in epidemiology.

HIV had an additional advantage in Africa. From 1970 to 1990, sub-Saharan Africa had the highest rate of urbanization in the world. Seasonal and permanent labor migration increased viral traffic. New and distant populations, still burdened by other diseases, were exposed to viruses that would have remained in smaller populations without rapid urbanization. Some viruses, such as Ebola, are quickly fatal, with dramatic symptoms, and their epidemics tend to be relatively short-lived. As a lentivirus, however, HIV kills the host slowly, allowing more time for a person to transmit the virus (Morse, 1997). The combination of long latency, asymptomatic carriers, and rapid urbanization made HIV particularly lethal in sub-Saharan Africa.

This section explored just a few of the important findings of clinical and laboratory research on HIV/AIDS of the past decade. For all its complexity, HIV conforms to what we know about infectious disease and immunocompromised hosts. HIV is not a special case just because it is sexually transmissible. The way it attacks the immune system is different from other viruses, but it exploits host susceptibility as other pathogens do. Like other bacterial and viral pathogens, it is opportunist, patient, collaborative, and complex.

Behavior or biology?

The previous sections described some of the economic and sanitary factors prevalent in the era in which HIV spread across sub-Saharan Africa. That is the relevant context in which to examine the AIDS epidemic. Was it too much sex (as some have assumed), or too little food, too little medicine, and too many parasites that triggered the wave of susceptibility to HIV engulfing sub-Saharan Africa? Sexual transmission of HIV has distracted attention from the complexity of disease transmission and immune response. Not all of the AIDS literature explicitly attributes higher rates of HIV transmission in Africa to sexual behavior different from that of other world regions. Many social science works and policy documents merely imply that diagnosis by failing to acknowledge other epidemiologically relevant data or by prescribing solutions that only address sexual behavior (see chapter 7).

The argument that the prevalence of HIV in Africa can be explained by rates of sexual activity, however, is not something that was left behind in the 1980s or that appears only in the popular press. In the *AIDS Update 1999* published by the United Nations Population Fund, the statement is made quite explicitly: "The problem is promiscuity, and underscores the primacy of cultural factors," the report proclaims in a special box on the subject (UNFPA, 1999, 6). An implicit assumption or explicit assertion of higher rates of sexual partner change in Africa appears in numerous works.

The UNAIDS *Report on the Global HIV/AIDS Epidemic 2002* continues the propagation of an extremely narrow construction of HIV transmission. A text box entitled "What drives HIV/AIDS in Africa?" refers to a complex interplay of factors, but the factors it mentions only include cofactor STDs and male circumcision. It asserts that "sexual behavior is the most important factor influencing the spread of HIV in Africa" (UNAIDS, 2002, 25). The entire discussion of what drives HIV/AIDS in Africa is about sexual behavior and mentions nothing about nutrition, tuberculosis, malaria, schistosomiasis, or other assaults on immune status. The UNAIDS report refers to an important study that compared four cities in Africa and their rates of HIV, although it does not mention that the findings of the four-city study were an important break from the sexual behavior paradigm. The authors of the four-city article repeatedly emphasize that differences in sexual behavior were insufficient to explain the variation in rates of HIV, particularly the early infection of young women soon after initiating sexual activity (UNAIDS, 1999a). The UNAIDS report spotlights Kisumu, Kenya, which has a very high prevalence of HIV and early infection of young women. Neither the original four-city study nor the summary of it by UNAIDS mentions the proximity of Kisumu to Lake Victoria and the high prevalence (over 50 percent) of schistosomiasis there. Prevalence surveys in the area around Kisumu show that increasing schistosomiasis infection correlates with proximity to the lake and also to the town of Kisumu, which is on the lake (WHO, 1987).

The early infection of young women shortly after initiating sexual activity is very consistent with prevalence of schistosomiasis in excess of 50 percent. The four-city study was specifically focused on behavior, so the authors would not necessarily have information about the schistosomiasis prevalence that could resolve the unexplained high HIV rates among young women. The 2002 UNAIDS *Report*, however, found the HIV prevalence in Kisumu noteworthy and, therefore, should have employed better epidemiological methods before claiming to have the answer to their question, "What drives HIV/AIDS in Africa?"

The anomalies that researchers find in the Kisumu data and in the difference between Mwanza and Rakai in the STD-treatment trials (see chapter 3) cannot be explained by an analysis confined within a paradigm that considers only sexual behavior. Consideration of the ecology of disease in those areas helps to explain the seemingly odd results. Within the behavioral paradigm, an adequate answer cannot be found. The biological context of poverty makes the transmission of HIV more understandable and thus more preventable.

Economic/biomedical hypothesis

As we saw in chapters 2 and 3, biomedical research provides sufficient evidence for examining the HIV/AIDS epidemic by conventional epidemiological and economic means. In this section, I describe the results of a multivariate regression analysis that demonstrates a high correlation between HIV prevalence and several economic and nutritional variables. The complete discussion of the regression analysis appears in the appendix to this chapter. This exercise does not presume to use statistical analysis to prove a causal relationship between malnutrition and HIV transmission, nor does it ignore the fact that sexual contact is the most common source of transmission. Instead, it is meant to suggest new avenues for interdisciplinary research in the epidemiology of HIV/AIDS and new strategies for prevention and treatment.

In countries of medium and low human development the strongest correlations are found to be between HIV prevalence and change in calorie consumption and Gini coefficients (a measure of income inequality). The more severe the decrease in nutrition and the more unequal the distribution of income in a country, the higher is the rate of HIV. In the regression analysis, the prevalence of HIV is strongly correlated with income inequality, falling protein consumption, falling calorie consumption, and, to a lesser extent, rapid urbanization. There is much work to be done in this field using subnational data and time series. For a start, however, these correlations correspond to what we know about sub-Saharan Africa in the last 20 years, the era in which the AIDS epidemic was developing. These findings also correspond to what we know about malnutrition and parasitosis, and their effects on the immune system.

Other economic and social factors

Numerous other economic and social factors have an important role in the spread of HIV. Poverty and underdevelopment impose constraints on people's choices and their ability to avoid risky behaviors. Prevention policies limited to information, education, and provision of condoms can succeed only if people have the power to make decisions about their lives, including about their sexual behavior. In spite of their importance, this book devotes little space to socioeconomic issues because the social science literature addresses them. But to leave them unmentioned here would give the incorrect impression that they are unimportant.

Legal systems in many countries in Africa, as in Asia, perpetuate the inferior economic and social status of women. While gender inequality is a worldwide problem, it is rigidified and aggravated in those countries in which women have no rights to property. In many parts of the world, women are the primary agriculturalists and the main source of support for their children (especially in much of sub-Saharan Africa), but they do not have rights to land apart from their fathers or husbands. Although women may know the risk of having unprotected sex with their husbands, refusing sex risks personal injury and abandonment, leaving women without land to farm or other means of support and perhaps without their children.

After 20 years of AIDS prevention programs based on information and education, there have been few signs of success in halting the epidemic. Even in countries where condoms are widely available, such as Botswana, HIV infection continues to spread (Lush et al., 2005). Although in most countries people are now aware of the causes of HIV infection, their behavior has not changed because the chief determinants of that behavior are economic and social, not informational.

Key institutions that could protect people from HIV are lacking or inadequately accessible. Education protects young people from risks in numerous ways. Children are generally safer in school than out, especially if they live in shantytowns where there are gangs or widespread drug use. Young people in school are more likely to postpone initiation of sex, and schooling provides the opportunity for instruction about sexuality and safe sex. Literacy and learning empower people, girls in particular, to have control over their health and that of their children. Yet, poor countries have instituted school fees that have the perverse effect of motivating some girls who want to stay in school to accept the sexual advances of school administrators or of affluent men who pay their fees in return for sex.

Certain other legal or regulatory impediments common to less-developed and transition countries might seem unrelated to health conditions but, in fact, have serious repercussions for health. In many countries, trade regulations, corrupt officials, or outdated methods of clearing goods across national or provincial borders also promote the spread of HIV. Trucking routes have been an important path of HIV spread, in part because delays that can last for days keep truckers away from home. The men can often save money by staying with sex workers at border crossings instead of in hotels.

Another factor contributing to the spread of HIV and other diseases has been population movement due to economic and political causes. Government spending has tended to favor urban areas and populations. Many governments have kept producer prices low for agricultural products through commodity marketing boards, overvalued exchange rates and other means, making farming unprofitable and encouraging people to leave the land for the cities. Concentrated land ownership and the failure of governments to reform land tenure leave little opportunity for young people, who then migrate to cities in search of work. Some of the causes of rural poverty are international. Volatile world markets, external pressure to open markets too quickly, and trade barriers erected by the United States, Japan, and the European Union to the agricultural exports of poor countries have all contributed to the collapse of sustainable rural systems. Individual poverty and national underdevelopment are exacerbated by those external forces.

Migration creates conditions that encourage the spread of many different diseases, including HIV. Poor people crowd into refugee camps, urban slums, and suburban shantytowns. Water supply, sanitation, and other infrastructure have not kept up with population increase. Infectious and parasitic diseases spread under such conditions, worsening malnutrition.

In some regions, migration is circular. Laborers from all over southern Africa were recruited to work in the mines and factories of South Africa. The apartheid regime made no provision for the workers' families, so men lived in single-sex barracks and returned to their wives perhaps one month a year. After apartheid ended, the labor system of southern Africa did not change rapidly enough to prevent the spread of HIV in the region. Throughout Africa, mines, factories, and plantations rely on circular migrant streams, and similar labor systems fuel Asia's economic boom and the spread of infectious diseases there.

In the cities, there is not enough work, there are few opportunities for women, and there are few remunerative positions for the many migrants with little education. Consequently, many people—men, women and children—see no option for survival other than to engage in commercial sex with local clients and tourists. Poverty compels people to prioritize risk. Survival today for themselves or their children through selling sex may win out over the risk of illness and death in the future from AIDS. For women and children, and for racial and ethnic minorities, low social status reinforces the powerlessness of poverty. The economic and legal vulnerability of the sex worker makes negotiating safe sex extremely difficult.

Conclusion

A combination of environmental and economic factors made Africa almost a laboratory for retrovirus spread. Africa is the poorest continent, with the most countries at the bottom end of the income scale. The few exceptions (South Africa, Botswana, Namibia, and Zimbabwe) have highly skewed income distributions. Africa has the greatest area in the tropics and therefore suffers more than other continents from parasitic diseases and poor tropical soil. Low and falling food production and consumption, low food quality caused by the infertility of tropical soil, and endemic parasitic diseases that drain the population of essential nutrients are all conditions more descriptive of sub-Saharan Africa than of any other part of the world.

Nutrition and parasites are certainly not the only factors influencing the course of the HIV pandemic, nor is HIV a nutritional disease like pellagra or scurvy. But the same health and hygiene considerations that contribute to morbidity and mortality from other infectious diseases around the world are at play here. Those nutritional deficiencies weaken the immune system—including the body's first line of defense, skin and mucosal integrity—exposing malnourished people to infectious disease, especially to STDs whose transmission is promoted by skin and mucosal weakness. STDs are a very important cofactor for HIV transmission, especially those STDs that result in genitourinary ulceration, which are also more common among malnourished people in Africa and similarly poor populations in Asia.

Differences in sexual behavior cannot explain the vast difference in rates of HIV transmission between sub-Saharan Africa and most of the rest of the world. Models of HIV transmission for poor populations must include other variables, including the host factors that are conventionally recognized as influencing susceptibility to infectious disease.

The conclusion of this analysis is that an AIDS policy for Africa that relies only on behavior modification is misguided and dangerous. That approach has been effective in the United States and Europe and has also had some success in Uganda, demonstrating that behavior modification is one important element of prevention. But transmission depends on much more than sexual contact, as the low heterosexual transmission probabilities in rich countries indicate. Prevention has to involve a much broader health-promotion and poverty-eradication program that includes improved nutrition, treatment for parasitic and infectious diseases (including bacterial STDs), and health education (including education for safer sex).

The next chapter examines the economic and social context of HIV in

Latin America and the Caribbean and considers what lessons can be learned from the African epidemic for other poor regions.

Appendix: regression analysis

I began with all countries ranked by the United Nations Development Programme as having medium or low human development, according to the Human Development Index (excluding formerly socialist countries in Europe and Central Asia because the social and health changes in those countries involve a somewhat different dynamic from that of the developing world). A number of countries had to be excluded because no data were available for the dependent variable, HIV prevalence. One measure of HIV prevalence was based on numerous separate studies of urban low-risk populations, such as women attending prenatal clinics, collected in the HIV/AIDS Surveillance Data Base of the U.S. Bureau of the Census. A second measure of HIV prevalence was based on national estimates of adult HIV prevalence generated by UNAIDS, the joint organization of all United Nations affiliates working on HIV/AIDS.[3] Since measurement of HIV is problematic, we should have greater confidence in the results if they are confirmed using both measures of HIV prevalence.

Several variables normally associated with prevalence of infectious disease were used as independent variables. These included change in caloric intake between 1970 and 1995, change in protein consumption between 1970 and 1995, change in the urban population between 1970 and 1995, inequality in the distribution of income as measured by the Gini coefficient, real per capita GDP (on a purchasing power parity [PPP] basis), and change in real per capita GDP (on a PPP basis) between 1960 and 1995.

I used change in calories (rather than level of calories) because worsening nutrition in a population at the margin of good health is a better indicator of increasing vulnerability to disease as the epidemic unfolded. I used the Gini coefficient to correct GDP per capita. A more direct measure would have been the proportion of the population living on less than US$1 a day, but those data are not available for many countries. I also tried other variables normally associated with infectious disease prevalence, such as access to clean water and sanitation and attended births, but as I had anticipated, they were not significantly correlated, and I dropped them from the

3. Data for HIV prevalence came from the U.S. Census Bureau, 1999, and UNAIDS, 1998. Economic, health, and social variables came from UNDP, 1998; World Bank, 1997; and World Bank, 1999. The model is intended to test as independent variables the conditions that existed when the epidemics began. After reaching prevalence of 5 percent or more, as many African epidemics have, the stage is already set for extensive spread.

analysis rather than reduce the sample size due to missing data for those variables. I also used a variable for the proportion of the population without access to health services, anticipating that countries where a large proportion of the population did not have access to health services would have a high prevalence of HIV, but no significant statistical correlation was found. Nevertheless, caution should be exercised in interpreting that result. Access to health services reported by national governments can be exaggerated for political purposes. Also, access to health services means only that a person can go to a clinic, but it does not mean that the clinic will have any medicine to offer, such as antibiotics for curable STDs. As noted above, access to medicines fell sharply during the period in which HIV flourished. Another reason that access to health care may not correlate with lower HIV is suggested by the data on HIV infections attributable to medical injections in articles by David Gisselquist et al. (2003) (see chapter 2). While health care obviously offers many benefits, it could increase HIV transmission through unsafe injections.

The expectation was that changes in the consumption of calories and protein would be inversely correlated with the prevalence of HIV, whereas the Gini coefficient and the change in the urban population would be positively correlated. I expected the Gini coefficient to be more significant than either GDP per capita or change in GDP per capita because the Gini tells us more about the conditions of life for poor and very poor people in countries of roughly the same level of income. Urbanization would be expected to increase viral traffic, exposing larger populations to new viruses. It is difficult to predict whether HIV prevalence will have a positive or negative correlation with either the level of or the change in per capita income. Based on the analysis presented above, one might expect low and declining per capita income to be associated with increased vulnerability to HIV and thus higher prevalence rates. Alternatively, high and rising per capita income could be associated with internal and external migration, social disruption, and increasing inequality and poverty. Consequently, we might find that the level of and the rate of change in per capita income are positively correlated with HIV prevalence. Data for some of the variables were missing for some countries, so the sample size was reduced to 44 Asian, African, and Latin American countries.

Several bivariate and multivariate ordinary least squares regressions were estimated in order to establish the presence of statistical correlation among the variables. The two measures of the dependent variable (HIV prevalence among urban low-risk populations and estimates of national adult prevalence from UNAIDS) produced remarkably similar results in terms of signs of the coefficients and *t* statistics.

As expected, increases in the consumption of calories and protein were significantly (at the 99.9 percent confidence level) and negatively correlated with the prevalence of HIV. The two variables, however, were highly collinear, and the *t* statistics on the regression coefficients fell sharply when the two variables were included in the same regression. In subsequent multivariate regressions, therefore, the change in protein consumption was dropped from the analysis because of its correlation with the change in calorie consumption. There was a very strong positive correlation between unequal income distribution and prevalence of HIV. Also as expected, the percentage of change in urbanization was strongly and positively correlated with the prevalence of HIV. Change in real GDP per capita was the only variable to perform inconsistently; it was not significant in the regression using the UNAIDS measure of HIV prevalence, but was significant and positively correlated with HIV prevalence as measured by urban low-risk data. It is not surprising that economic growth (rising GDP per capita) with consequent labor mobility and social dislocation would lead to increasing transmission, especially since in some higher-growth countries conditions for the poorest 20 percent worsened. It was expected that poorer countries (with low real GDP per capita) would have a higher prevalence of HIV, but this variable fell far below the standard of statistical significance, even though more direct measures of nutritional status (change in calories) and relative income of the very poor (Gini coefficient) are strongly correlated with HIV prevalence.

A multivariate regression using these independent variables (omitting the decline in protein consumption because of multicollinearity) was computed, and the results are presented in Table 4.2. The multiple regression confirms the results of the bivariate regressions. Depending on which dependent variable is used, the *R*-squared is .545 or .517. The two regression

Table 4.2
Regression results

	Independent variable				
Dependent variable	Change in calories, 1970–1995	Gini coefficient	Change in urban population, 1970–1995	Real GDP per capita, 1995	Change in per capita GDP, 1960–1995
HIV prevalence among urban low risk populations: $R^2 = .545$					
Regression coefficient	−28.232	44.506	1.502	0.0001	1.988
t statistic	−3.36	3.236	2.269	0.102	2.426
Significance	0.002	0.002	0.029	0.919	0.02
β coefficient	−0.421	0.386	0.271	0.014	0.321
National HIV prevalence (UNAIDS): $R^2 = .517$					
Regression coefficient	−18.965	22.45	1.011	0.0003	0.763
t statistic	−3.573	2.584	2.417	0.406	1.475
Significance	0.001	0.014	0.02	0.687	0.148
β coefficient	−0.462	0.317	0.297	0.056	0.201

coefficients that are most significant (change in calories and Gini coefficients) are significant at a 99.8 percent level of confidence for the census data and at the 99.9 percent and 98.6 percent levels, respectively, for the UNAIDS data. The change in urban population is significant at the 97 and 98 percent levels for the two dependent variables.

5

Dualism in Latin America and the Caribbean

HIV/AIDS has developed under diverse conditions globally and with variations in the modes and rates of transmission. Latin America represents a composite of the industrial and developing worlds, both in its economic performance and in its HIV epidemics. This chapter draws lessons from epidemiology and from the experience of sub-Saharan Africa in examining some of the economic and biomedical determinants of HIV transmission in Latin America and the Caribbean.

Most Latin American and Caribbean countries are ranked as middle-income and of medium human development. That ranking does not represent an intermediate stage between the developing and industrialized countries, however. Instead, it is the result of averaging the affluence of Latin America's modern sector and the extreme poverty and economic and political instability on which it uneasily rests. Latin America has the most unequal distribution of income of any world region, a fact that influences every aspect of its society and economy. That inequality has contributed to the stagnation of Latin American economies and the volatility of its politics. It also produces a health profile that has been termed an epidemiological accumulation, rather than an epidemiological transition (Franco Agudelo, 1988). Diseases of the poor (infectious and parasitic diseases) continue to claim a large percentage of lives, while the so-called diseases of affluence (chronic and degenerative diseases) contribute increasingly to morbidity and mortality, at higher age-adjusted rates among the poor than among the rich.

Latin America and the Caribbean also have a dual HIV profile. The region mirrors the industrialized world in HIV epidemics among men who have sex with men and people who share needles, and it has a rapidly spreading heterosexual epidemic, as is the case in sub-Saharan Africa and South Asia (UNAIDS, 2004).

In this chapter, I apply what we have learned about a generalized heterosexual epidemic of HIV/AIDS in Africa to Latin America. A dangerous situation exists in "exceptionalizing" the African case. If we assume that HIV levels are so high in some African countries because African behavior is so different from that of Latin America and Asia, then we can conclude that we will not see an African-level AIDS epidemic elsewhere in the developing world. If we look at the wider range of host factors contributing to AIDS in Africa, however, then we must conclude that the possibility exists for much more serious epidemics in Latin America and Asia than we have seen so far because those same factors are present among poor populations in other world regions. Neither the international donors nor Latin American governments and individuals are prepared for the heterosexual epidemic in Latin America because Africa is considered a special case.

The AIDS literature in the social and biomedical sciences clearly demonstrates the importance of a broad array of factors in the spread of HIV, including gender relations, labor migration, and poor access to hygiene and curative care for STDs. As chapters 2 through 4 have shown, malnutrition and parasitosis provide the context of susceptibility in sub-Saharan Africa for the epidemic spread of HIV. Almost all the factors seen in Africa are also present in the economic and health conditions in Latin America and contribute to the AIDS epidemics there.

Additional factors in Latin America include the large number of street children and the use of injected drugs in some countries. This chapter includes the results of statistical analysis showing the correlation of economic factors and levels of HIV in Latin America and a discussion of the path that the epidemic can be expected to take in the region. The results are not meant to show an exclusive correlation of economic variables and HIV transmission. Rather, they suggest some of the economic and health interactions that have been overlooked. Better preventive policy will arise from a better understanding of the multiple causes of the spread of HIV.

The preceding chapter showed that HIV prevalence was highly correlated with falling calorie consumption, falling protein consumption, unequal distribution of income, and other variables conventionally associated with susceptibility to infectious disease, however transmitted. Those characteristics that most markedly distinguish the lives of the poor from those of the rich in economic studies are also the factors that contribute to higher rates of morbidity and mortality from infectious and noninfectious diseases for the poor. HIV and other sexually transmitted diseases do not constitute a special case in that regard.

It is clear that prevalence of malnutrition and parasitosis comparable to that in much of sub-Saharan Africa exists in Latin America among a significant minority of the population. Furthermore, rates of HIV found in some African countries are already appearing in large cities and segments of the populations of Latin America. The widespread notion that a high prevalence of HIV was a peculiarly African problem had a dangerous effect on the pace of prevention in Latin America and other parts of the developing world.

Context of HIV transmission in Latin America

In Africa, deteriorating economies led to increased labor migration, increased economic insecurity for women (already precarious in patriarchal land tenure systems), worsening nutritional status, and high rates of parasitosis aggravating chronically compromised immune status. Together, those factors produced epidemic levels of HIV/AIDS. How does the African situation compare with that of Latin America and the Caribbean? To what extent have we seen, and will we see, AIDS epidemics in the Americas that are generated by the same factors as in Africa: malnutrition, declining economies, unequal distribution of income, urbanization, and labor migration?

Latin America is economically diverse, and the HIV/AIDS epidemics that are emerging in Latin America are also varied. Argentina, Brazil, and Mexico are middle-income countries but have levels of poverty ranging from 22 to 30 percent of their populations[1] (World Bank, 2004). By the late 1990s, Argentina and Brazil already had HIV rates in the major cities at levels seen in Zambia and Malawi only a decade earlier (World Bank, 1997). Among the poorest Latin American and Caribbean countries are Haiti, Dominican Republic, and Honduras, all with very serious epidemics, and Ecuador, Bolivia, and Nicaragua, countries that have recently endured serious economic crises, with nascent or concentrated epidemics.

Some countries in Latin America have HIV epidemics fed partly by needle-sharing for injecting drug use. Successful interdiction of some supply lines to the United States has sharply increased the supply of drugs in South America since it is more profitable to dump drugs there, even at very low prices, than to ship them to the United States (Faiola, 1999). HIV infection from injecting drug use increased rapidly in Brazil from 2.5 percent of all people living with HIV and AIDS in 1985 to 25 percent in 1998 (UNAIDS, 1998), but heterosexual transmission also increased from 25 percent of infections in 1993 to 40 percent in 1989/1999. In Argentina, 40 percent of people with AIDS by 2000 were infected from injecting drug

1. Extent of poverty is measured as percent of the population living on less than US$2 a day or below the national poverty line, depending on availability of data.

use (PAHO, 2002). In other countries, injecting drugs is not a significant factor in the HIV epidemic, including Ecuador; only 10 of the nearly 2,500 cumulative reported infections resulted from drug use (Ministerio de Salud Pública del Ecuador, 2000), and Mexico, where HIV transmission from injecting drugs is less than 1 percent of reported infections (Izazola-Licea et al., 2000).

Another important factor in the Latin American epidemics is homosexuality and bisexuality, but with great variation between richer and poorer countries. Homosexual transmission accounted for 5 to 7 percent of infections in Suriname, Dominican Republic, and Guyana, but 67 percent in Chile, 73 percent in Costa Rica, and 83 percent in Colombia (UNAIDS, 1998). In Mexico, 60 percent of men with sexually acquired HIV classified themselves as homosexual, 25 percent as bisexual, and only 15 percent as heterosexual. Reports from all over Latin America indicate that a large proportion of men who have sex with men also maintain heterosexual relationships, often in marriage (Izazola-Licea et al., 2000).

Most HIV/AIDS in Latin America and the Caribbean reportedly results from sexual contact. Data on sexual behavior reported in the appendix to chapter 1 indicate high rates of early initiation into sexual activity and high rates of multipartnering; a high proportion of men in stable relationships who also have relations with sex workers; low rates of condom use, including in high-risk situations; high levels of prostitution, including child prostitution of both sexes; and significant numbers of men in heterosexual relationships who also have relations with men. Corroborating evidence comes from the levels of sexually transmitted diseases (including in children) and the proportion of births to adolescents. Except for child prostitution and perhaps bisexuality, Latin America and the Caribbean do not seem very different from North America or Europe. But the data show that the sexual preconditions for the rapid spread of HIV are present in Latin America, along with other social, economic, and epidemiological factors discussed below.

The focus here is the influence of economic variables on the risk of HIV transmission in Latin America among heterosexuals who do not inject drugs, a population comparable to the HIV-affected population of Africa. The most important characteristics that Latin America shares with Africa and Asia are poverty, malnutrition, high rates of parasitosis, and high rates of internal and international labor migration. A feature distinguishing Latin America is the presence of 40 million children who live and work on the street. Child prostitution is increasingly a problem in Latin America, attracting sex tourists from the United States and Europe. What also sets Latin America apart from Africa is its greater integration with the world economy. Many more Latin Americans than Africans can afford to travel frequently to industrialized countries, and a much higher proportion of Latin Americans use drugs, although tourism to Africa and the mobility of a small affluent class also contributed to the spread of HIV in Africa. Both the wealth and the poverty of Latin America still shape the AIDS epidemics there.

Economic determinants of heterosexual HIV in Latin America

The HIV epidemics in Latin America are fueled by two sets of forces: wealth and poverty. The region is relatively affluent compared to sub-Saharan Africa. The first reports of AIDS in the higher-income Latin American countries were men returning from travel to the United States, giving HIV a foothold in the region. AIDS was first reported in the region in Argentina in 1982, but it is the poverty of the majority (or a significant minority) that keeps AIDS going. Since the focus here is the continuation of the epidemic, rather than its origins, the discussion below focuses on poverty, malnutrition, parasitosis, prostitution, street children, and lack of access to health care and health information. Those characteristics that proved statistically significant in analyzing African AIDS (poverty, inequality, malnutrition, and migration) also affect health in the Americas.

Poverty

A few Latin American countries have GDP per capita (adjusted for differences in purchasing power) roughly equivalent to the moderately successful transition economies of central and eastern Europe. Almost all Latin American and Caribbean countries are middle-income, but that represents a broad range of GDP per capita from Nicaragua (US$2,523), roughly equivalent to Vietnam or Zimbabwe, to Argentina and Chile, which have incomes similar to those of South Africa and Poland. All Latin American and Caribbean countries except Barbados and Argentina have incomes lower than South Africa, and almost half of the countries rank below China in GDP per capita. The poorest country in the Americas is Haiti, which has a Human Development Index rank of 150 out of 175 countries, below that of Kenya. As Table 5.1 shows, Latin American and Caribbean countries intermingle with African, Asian, and Eastern European countries in the rankings by GDP per capita (WDI, 2004).

The average income, however, does not give a very clear impression of the extent of poverty in the hemisphere because Latin American countries have the most unequal distribution of income in the world. In fact, all countries in the Americas except Canada, Jamaica, and Trinidad and Tobago have Gini coefficients greater than the world average (approximately 0.41). There is generally a negative correlation between income and Gini coefficient, but all Latin American and Caribbean countries, with the exception of Jamaica and Uruguay, have Ginis even higher than would be predicted

Table 5.1
Latin American, Caribbean, and Sub-Saharan African GDP per capita

Country	GDP per capita US$ (PPP) 2003	Country	GDP per capita US$ (PPP) 2003
Barbados	15,714	El Salvador	4,994
Argentina	11,586	Venezuela	4,909
South Africa	10,492	Paraguay	4,724
Chile	10,206	Swaziland	4,719
Trinidad and Tobago	9,975	Guyana	4,194
Costa Rica	9,490	Jamaica	4,184
Mexico	9,136	Guatemala	4,122
Botswana	8,359	Ecuador	3,684
Uruguay	8,280	India	2,909
Brazil	7,767	Honduras	2,658
Grenada	7,337	Lesotho	2,645
Colombia	6,784	Bolivia	2,546
Dominican Republic	6,703	Nicaragua	2,523
Belize (2002)	6538	Vietnam	2,490
Panama	6,475	Zimbabwe (2001)	2,370
Namibia	6,375	Senegal	1,682
Peru	5,267	Haiti	1,635
China	4,995	Uganda	1,471

Note: PPP, purchasing power parity, indicates that monetary variables have been adjusted for the cost of living in each country, reflecting the value in local terms.

Source: WDI, 2004.

on the basis of per capita GDP. One characteristic of inequality in Latin America that is not fully reflected in the Gini coefficient is the extent to which income is concentrated in the top decile. As seen in Table 5.2, in some countries—including Brazil, Chile, Ecuador, Mexico, and Paraguay—the top 10 percent receives almost three times the income of the next decile (IDB, 1998). Consequently, the middle-income GDP per capita of the Americas conceals the absence of a sizable middle class. The two countries that historically had the most equal distributions of income and the largest middle classes, Argentina and Venezuela, have suffered economic and political upheaval in recent years that have increased poverty and inequality.

Another aspect of Latin American income distribution is the extreme poverty of the bottom 20 to 40 percent of the population. In Ecuador, the bottom decile of the population receives only 0.6 percent of the country's income, and the bottom quintile receives only 2.3 percent. Other countries in which the bottom 20 percent receives less than 3 percent of the national income are Brazil, Panama, and Paraguay. In all four of those countries the top quintile receives 60 percent or more of national income (see Table 5.2 and IDB, 1998). Latin America exhibits a veneer of affluence to visitors

Table 5.2
Income inequality in Latin America: share of total household income (%)

Country	Poorest 20%	Top 20%	Ninth decile	Top decile
Argentina[a]	4.3	52.9	17.0	35.9
Bolivia[b]	4.1	57.7	15.6	42.1
Brazil	2.5	63.4	16.4	47.0
Chile	3.5	61.1	15.3	45.8
Costa Rica	4.3	50.6	16.4	34.2
Ecuador	2.3	59.6	15.6	44.0
El Salvador	3.4	55.6	16.2	39.4
Honduras[c]	3.5	57.2	16.3	40.9
Mexico	3.3	60.0	15.6	44.4
Panama	2.3	59.6	16.9	42.7
Paraguay	2.3	62.3	15.8	46.5
Peru	4.4	51.3	15.9	35.4
Uruguay	5.0	48.7	16.4	32.3
Venezuela	4.5	52.0	16.2	35.8

[a]Greater Buenos Aires only.
[b]Urban areas only.
[c]Labor income only.
Source: Derived from IDB, 1998, appendix table 1.2.1, page 25.

and in statistical summaries of economic activity. But a large minority of Latin Americans and Caribbeans lives on less than US$1 a day: nine countries in the region report more than 14 percent of the population living on less than that amount (World Bank, 2004). No data were reported for Haiti, but with income per capita of US$380 (US$1,635 adjusted for purchasing power), it is very likely that Haiti should be added to that group.

Several Latin American countries have sizable indigenous populations that are either geographically or economically isolated from the rest of the country. There are large disparities in income, education, and health status between indigenous and nonindigenous people. For Bolivia nationally, the child mortality rate (0–5 years) is 102 per 1,000 live births, but for indigenous children it is nearly double that figure. In Mexico, the under-5 mortality rate among indigenous people (139 per 1000) is more than twice as high as for nonindigenous children. Education levels for indigenous women in all countries are extremely low. In the five Latin American countries with large indigenous populations, the proportion of indigenous women with more than primary education ranges from 2.4 percent in Guatemala, 7.3 percent in Mexico, and 14 percent in Peru and Bolivia to a high of almost 25 percent in Ecuador (Terborgh et al., 1995). Although the social isolation of the indigenous population has tended to protect them from HIV, all other factors promote their vulnerability, including poverty and lack of education, health services, and access to land, which stimulates temporary labor migration.

Malnutrition

Considering the importance of nutrition in overall health, there are surprisingly few national data on macro- and micronutrition levels. The Pan American Health Organization estimated in 1995 that among the region's children younger than 5 years old, 11 percent were suffering from protein-energy malnutrition. In the subsequent 7 years, there was little improvement: 10 countries were still reporting more than 10 percent of children younger than 5 years old to be underweight for their age, and in Honduras and Guatemala, one-fourth of children were underweight for age. In the region as a whole, 11 percent of the total population was reported to be undernourished in 2001, a very slight improvement from 1990 (UNDP, 2004). In shantytowns throughout Latin America, however, rates of stunting, wasting, and psychomotor problems in children are not only much higher than official data indicate but are even more severe in children between the ages of 5 and 12 years, an age group that is often overlooked (Stillwaggon, 1998).

Micronutrient deficiencies persist throughout the region. Goiter and cretinism are serious conditions that result from iodine deficiency in Dominican Republic, Haiti, and Guatemala. This is not an insurmountable problem, as successful programs in the Andean region have recently demonstrated (PAHO, 2002). Vitamin-A deficiency varies by socioeconomic class. Overall prevalence of vitamin-A deficiency in Nicaragua is over 31 percent, but higher among poor children (PAHO, 1998). Vitamin-A deficiency is three times higher among children of illiterate mothers in Ecuador than among children of educated mothers, and twice as high (22 percent) in rural areas as in urban areas. Periurban shantytown children in Lima have five times the prevalence of vitamin-A deficiency as children from urban Lima (PAHO, 1998). Subclinical vitamin-A deficiency affects an estimated one-fourth of the children under 5 years of age in the region, including 15 percent or more of preschoolers in Dominican Republic, Ecuador, and Mexico. Lack of data in several countries, including Brazil and Bolivia, obscures the extent of this critical micronutrient deficiency (PAHO, 2002).

Iron-deficiency anemia affects more than 50 percent of the population in some countries in the region, affecting work capacity, resistance to disease, and maternal and fetal survival (PAHO, 1998). More than 77 million children and women in Latin America and the Caribbean are anemic, and the proportion of infants and young children who are iron-deficient ranges from 9 percent in Chile to 33 percent in Mexico and Argentina. Hookworm and other parasites contribute to the causes of anemia in the population (PAHO, 2002).

Food security refers to the ability of a population to acquire adequate nutrition. It depends not only on food supply but also on distribution capacity and effective demand, or the purchasing power of the population. Almost all the countries of Latin America and the Caribbean have insecure food systems so that even when supply is adequate, undernutrition is still widespread. In Colombia, Ecuador, and Paraguay, even when food supplies have been 10 percent or more above the FAO minimum, there has still been high prevalence of malnutrition. In Latin America as a whole, 46 percent of the population is poor, and over half of those are indigent, which means that even if the entire family income were spent on food, it would not secure 80 percent of the minimum food requirement (Barraclough, 1997).

Parasitosis

Safe supply of drinking water is still lacking for rural and periurban populations throughout the region; 15 percent of the total population and 40 percent of rural households have no easy access to safe water supplies. Half of rural households and 10 percent of urban households (21 percent overall) have neither a connection to a sewer system nor even on-site sanitation, such as septic tanks or latrines (PAHO, 2002, 217). Half of all houses are connected to a sewer system, but 86 percent of sewage in Latin America is dumped untreated directly into streams and rivers (PAHO, 2002). Intestinal helminths affect 20 to 30 percent of the general population of all the countries in the region and 60 to 80 percent of people in highly endemic regions (PAHO, 1998). If the data were collected by income, it would show that virtually 100 percent of children in poor neighborhoods have intestinal helminths because they lack clean water and sanitary services. The heavy parasite load in children and adults plays a dual role in disease susceptibility. First, diarrheal infections are the most important cause of malnutrition and, hence, immune suppression. Second, parasite infestation chronically activates the immune system, as described in chapters 2 and 3. In both ways, parasitosis weakens the immune response.

Malaria infection plays an important role in immune suppression in Latin America, as it does in Africa. Malaria is endemic in 21 American countries, and 20 percent of the people in the region live in areas of moderate or high malarial risk (PAHO, 2002, 253). Malaria is the single most important cause of anemia in endemic zones. In Latin America, 30 percent of pregnant women are anemic, leading to greater susceptibility to infection and increased likelihood of delivering an underweight baby who will face a life-long disadvantage due to immune system weakness (Brundtland, 2000).

Labor migration and dislocation of populations

Among the results of rural poverty and the concentration of land ownership are urbanization and short-term labor migration, both internal and international. The pace of urbanization in Latin America over the past 30 years, although not as rapid as in Africa, has been substantial. Several countries also have steady streams of international labor migrants, among them Dominican Republic, Ecuador, El Salvador, Guyana, Haiti, Jamaica, and Trinidad and Tobago. Temporary migration is very common; migrants, mostly men, spend a few years in the United States or Europe, sending money home to build houses or start small businesses.

Ecuador is an illustrative example. By 2000 there were an estimated 500,000 Ecuadorians in New York alone, approximately 4 percent of Ecuadorians. There are also large numbers in Miami, Chicago, Madrid, and agricultural areas of Spain. Laborers from the area around Cuenca, Ecuador, have worked on a temporary basis in New York since the late 1960s. A study in Cuenca in the early 1990s found that over 80 percent of the people who had contracted HIV were economic migrants who had returned from the United States or their partners (Centro Cultural "La Pájara Pinta," 1996). Ecuador's worsening economic crisis is swelling the migrant stream. From records of the migration authorities at the Quito and Guayaquil airports, in 2000 there were 15,000 Ecuadorians a month leaving for Europe and the United States. The official figures tell only part of the story, since there were thousands more people leaving by small boat for Central America to make their way to the United States. Data on temporary internal migration are scant, but in the central highlands of Ecuador, over 80 percent of men between the ages of 20 and 35 migrate, mostly to Quito, for work. They apparently bring home STDs, according to data from women's gynecological exams (visit to hospital in Zumbahua, Ecuador, 2000).[2]

A factor in the spread of AIDS in Africa that merits greater attention in the Americas is the dislocation of populations due to war and natural disasters with attendant effects on health status and social cohesion. Colombia alone has more than 1 million people internally displaced by the guerrilla-paramilitary war, the fourth-largest internally displaced population in the world (Deng, 1999). Guatemala, El Salvador, and Nicaragua also have a large number of internally displaced persons (PAHO, 2002). In Peru, poverty in the countryside and the disruption caused by Sendero Luminoso (Shining Path) have driven hundreds of thousands of people into the *pueblos jóvenes*, the shantytowns that crowd around Lima. El Niño hit Ecuador very hard between 1997 and 1999. Landslides caused enormous destruction of homes and agricultural areas, resulting in the migration of over 300,000 people to Guayaquil alone. In 1999, eruptions of two volcanoes in Ecuador forced the evacuation and permanent dislocation of thousands of people.

2. The hospital has had a very successful program in gynecology and has much better data on STDs than exist for the country as a whole (visit, Zumbahua, Ecuador, 2000).

Lack of access to health care and medicines

As in Africa, an important cofactor for HIV is untreated STDs due to lack of access to health care and lack of medicines. Some countries had good public health systems in the past, but have let them deteriorate. In Argentina, for example, decades of economic decline and policies of the military government (1976–1983) and the administration of Carlos Saúl Menem (1989–1999) left the public health sector in disarray and the population burdened with infectious and parasitic disease. Health centers and public hospitals lack medicines, sterilizing equipment, sinks for washing hands, and reagents for testing blood. In a shantytown within the federal capital of Buenos Aires that has one of the country's highest rates of drug use and HIV, the health center does not even have running water, let alone gloves or disposable syringes (Stillwaggon, 1998). Other countries never had adequate public health facilities, especially in the rural areas, and so STDs that can act as cofactors of HIV remain undiagnosed and untreated. Even where there are facilities for gynecological exams, there are no laboratories. In cities, most hospitals do not follow an accepted set of norms. In Ecuador, for example, only two private hospitals in the capital, Quito, Hospital Metropolitano and Hospital Voz Andes, follow accepted norms for infection control (source in Ecuadorian military, 2000).

Prostitution

As in Africa, Asia, and the transition countries, poverty, abuse, and lack of alternatives drive people into prostitution. The economic vulnerability of the sex worker makes negotiating safe sex extremely difficult, especially since most sex workers in Latin America and the Caribbean work on the street; child sex workers in particular are at risk. There are an estimated 60,000 sex workers in Peru (population, 26 million), and more than half of the sex workers in Lima have HIV or other STDs. In the Dominican Republic (population, 8.5 million), the Health Ministry estimates that more than 200,000 women and men engage in sex work, especially in the tourist trade (Abel, 1999). Supporting the prostitution economy in Latin America is the still dominant force of machismo. The custom of fathers bringing their sons to prostitutes for initiation continues to contribute to the incidence of HIV (interview, Hospital Voz Andes, Quito, May 2000).

Trafficking of women and children, although difficult to document, is reported by the Pan American Health Organization to involve tens of thousands people involuntarily transported. Traffickers work in concert with organized crime groups and sex tour operators. The number of women trafficked from Latin America and the Caribbean is very high. It is estimated that 50,000 women from the Dominican Republic, 75,000 women from Brazil, and 35,000 from Colombia work in the sex industry abroad, primarily in Europe (PAHO, 2003).

Street children

There are an estimated 40 million children in Latin America who work and live on the street, beginning on average at age 9. Street children often engage in "survival sex" with adults to secure food, clothing, and shelter. Surveys in Honduras found that 85 percent of sexually active street children had been treated for a sexually transmitted disease and that 6 percent of street children were infected with HIV (Scanlon et al., 1998). Over 70 percent of the street girls in Guatemala are prostitutes. A study of 143 Guatemalan street children found that 93 percent of the children had STDs, and none used condoms (Seitles, 1997/1998). There are 600 brothels in Guatemala City, with 2,000 children in sex work. San Jose, Costa Rica, has an estimated 2,000 girls working in prostitution, and in the Dominican Republic there are 25,000 child prostitutes (PAHO, 2003). In Brazil, over 500,000 prostitutes under the age of 17 work the streets. In Mexico City, as a result of child prostitution and sexual abuse, 5 percent of the children served by the street children's advocates, Casa Alianza, are infected with HIV, and none of the children has access to state health services (Seitles, 1997/1998).

Central America has become the new destination for sex tourism, especially for child prostitution, promoted on the Internet to men from North America, Europe, and Latin America (Kovaleski, 2000). Costa Rica and the Dominican Republic are the main destinations for child-sex tourism, but it is also increasing in Brazil, Guatemala, Haiti, Honduras, Nicaragua, and other countries (UNAIDS, 1999b). Governments are doing little to protect the children. Sex tourism generates an increasing amount of revenue and foreign exchange in Latin America (Seitles, 1997/1998). It is difficult to estimate the extent of sexual transmission of HIV among children aged 10 to 14 because 0 to 14 years is the data grouping on child infections. In Brazil, however, almost 10 percent of AIDS infections in children aged 12 or younger in 1998 were not the result of mother-to-child transmission (UNAIDS, 1999b).

Lack of awareness

Although not entirely an economic factor, lack of AIDS consciousness plays an important role in the spread of HIV in Latin America. In Brazil, 80 percent of women and 85 percent of men believe they are not at risk of contracting HIV. Sterilization is the contraceptive method chosen by 40 percent of married women, making it very unlikely that they would use condoms with their husbands (McDaniels, 1998). In a 1995 survey in Guatemala of over 12,000 women, 71 percent of women surveyed had heard of AIDS, but only 36 percent of indigenous women, 41 percent of women without education, and 57 percent of rural women surveyed had (Remez, 1997). According to a 1994 Haitian Survey of Mortality, Morbidity and Utilization of Services, 98 percent of men and women knew of

AIDS, but 69 percent of women and 74 percent of men who knew about AIDS considered themselves at no risk of contracting HIV ("In Haiti,", 1996). Those data could signal greater risk, or they could indicate the high proportion of men and women who are in stable relationships in which the high confidence of fidelity is warranted. It is important to remember that the extent of multipartnering can be overestimated if the impact of cofactor diseases and conditions is ignored. Cofactor conditions and diseases increase the likelihood of transmission with each sexual contact. On a population level, given the prevalence or incidence of HIV, we cannot validly derive the number of partners unless we know the actual probability of transmission, based on cofactor infections (see chapter 8).

Statistical analysis of economic factors in Latin American HIV/AIDS

As in chapter 4, I used statistical methods to estimate the effect of social, economic, and nutritional factors on HIV transmission. The statistical analysis shows very clearly the duality of the AIDS epidemics in Latin America and the Caribbean. HIV is strongly correlated at a high level of significance with higher real GDP per capita and at the same time with variables that represent the vulnerability of Latin American economies: urbanization, labor migration, and low calorie intake all reflect the poverty of the bottom half of the population. The positive correlation with GDP per capita is not as anomalous as it might seem, although for most diseases, income and morbidity are inversely related. The HIV epidemics in Latin America are complex. It is the argument of this chapter that the future spread of HIV in Latin America and the Caribbean will be most influenced by the poverty of the majority, but the initial opportunity for infection in the region came primarily from international contact afforded by affluence.

HIV is very highly correlated with migration because migrants bring back HIV from places where rates are higher (for example, Ecuadorians and Dominicans returning from New York). Urbanization has the same effect of mixing populations as migration, but on a domestic scale, and is also highly correlated with HIV. Finally, the level of calorie supply is highly correlated with HIV levels. That is the other face of a complex HIV epidemic, the face that mirrors the African experience, and the one that presages the future course of HIV in the Americas. Malnutrition compromises immune response, and it is also a proxy for the poverty that fuels the adult prostitution and the abandonment and prostitution of children in Latin America and the Caribbean.

There are a few outliers. Honduras has a much higher level of AIDS than predicted. In fact, Honduras—specifically its business center, San Pedro Sula—is the epicenter of Central American AIDS. Honduras has an exceptionally large population of street children, many of whom sell sex to live and to pay for drugs. With a population of fewer than 1 million, San Pedro Sula had 500 deaths a month from AIDS by 2000 (Varney, 2000). Honduras has a Gini coefficient of 0.59. The richest 10 percent of Hondurans capture more than 44 percent of national income, and the poorest 10 percent receive 0.5 percent. One-fourth of the population of Honduras lives on less than US$1 per day (UNDP, 2004).

Another consistent outlier is Ecuador. With its high level of migration (considerably higher than the official data used in the regression) and its high levels of malnutrition, the model predicted high levels of HIV. The UNDP data (for 1997 for most countries) used here listed a rate of 5.2 cases per 100,000 for Ecuador, about 650 persons, or the cumulative number reported in Ecuador in 1993. For 1997, what the model predicts—97 cases per 100,000 (about 12,000 persons)—is very close to the actual prevalence for 1997 estimated by AIDS experts I interviewed in Ecuador (about 10 times the reported prevalence) (interviews, Hospital Voz Andes and Cruz Roja, Quito, 2000).

What can we expect in the HIV epidemics in Latin America and the Caribbean?

The HIV epidemics in Latin America and the Caribbean reflect the region's mix of economic and social factors: wealth and international mobility that rival the industrialized countries' for a minority, as well as vast numbers of poor, as in other developing countries. In North America and Western Europe, HIV first spread among men who have sex with men and among needle-sharing drug users without disproportionately affecting the poor. Now transmission in developed countries is predominantly among poor and marginalized people and increasingly through heterosexual contact. Soon after AIDS was recognized in the United States, it was reported in Argentina and Brazil, both countries with relatively high GDP per capita and a high volume of two-way tourist traffic with the United States and Western Europe. As in the latter regions, HIV emerged first among men who have sex with men and then among needle-sharing drug users. In Latin America generally, HIV was reported earlier in those countries with higher GDP per capita (Haiti and Dominican Republic being notable exceptions because of tourism and circular labor migration). Increasingly, however, it has been the countries with higher levels of poverty, greater inequality, and lower levels of nutrition and access to health care that have had higher incidence of HIV.

In Africa, transmission of HIV is primarily heterosexual and mother-to-child and from unsafe blood and medical instruments and is highly correlated with malnutrition, unequal distribution of income, and urbanization. The conditions that promote heterosexual, vertical, and medical HIV transmission in Africa are also evident in the transition of Latin American

AIDS from an epidemic that mirrors the United States to one that mirrors Africa. The proportion of men and women infected has already shifted dramatically in the Americas, and in some countries the ratio is approaching 1:1.

It is generally in the poorest countries, and among poor people in middle-income countries, that heterosexual, vertical, and medical transmissions are greatest. We can expect that characteristic to become more pronounced in the future. Since the middle-income countries comprise an affluent minority and a poor majority, semi-generalized epidemics—that is, generalized among the poor—are likely. In very poor countries, such as Haiti, Dominican Republic, and Honduras, we may see fully generalized epidemics for the same reasons they have occurred in sub-Saharan Africa: because of the high percentage of people whose malnutrition, parasite load, and lack of access to hygiene and health care are devastating to their overall health. Now that prevalence exceeds 1 percent of the general population in several Latin American countries and HIV is reported in rural and urban areas throughout the region, it is clear that HIV will continue to spread among poor people. Exceptions to the pattern of a "poor-only" epidemic could be countries such as Ecuador, where poverty is severe and there are no significant preventive programs, so that even affluent people with access to education are still uninformed and at risk (interviews in Quito, Esmeraldas, and Zumbahua, Ecuador, 2000). Misconceptions about the African AIDS epidemic as a "special case" and about HIV transmission have contributed to a complacency in Latin America and some Caribbean countries regarding AIDS.

The pattern of HIV epidemics suggests several useful lessons for AIDS policy. In some industrialized countries in which transmission has been greatest among men who have sex with men and among drug users, incidence has leveled off. In Africa, where there is a heterosexual epidemic, only a few countries have seen falling incidence. In Latin America, there has been a marked shift in the proportion of new infections to women and children and from higher to lower income levels. That suggests that preventive policies that emphasize behavior modification are effective among identifiable or self-identifiable groups where behavioral factors are most important in the rate of transmission. Promoting safe sex among men who have sex with men and providing clean needles to drug users are effective policies for those kinds of epidemics.

The epidemic is not leveling off in most developing countries with heterosexual epidemics. Where protein-energy malnutrition, micronutrient deficiency, parasitosis, lack of hygiene, lack of health care and medicines, and child abandonment are important factors in HIV epidemics, behavior-based preventive policies are not enough. HIV has become a part of poor people's lives, and the solution to HIV will have to include an assault on poverty and its effects on survival strategies and on general health. In the developing world, behavior-modification programs are useful but are not substitutes for economic policies that promote equitable development and health programs that provide preventive and curative care.

Appendix: Regression Analysis

To investigate the factors that correlate with HIV prevalence, I estimated a multivariate ordinary least squares regression using the number of persons reported living with AIDS (per 100,000 population) as the dependent variable and several factors suggested by the foregoing discussion as independent variables. The independent variables are per capita GDP (measured on a PPP basis for 1995), a measure of urbanization (the percentage change in the urban population between 1970 and 1995), a measure of international migration (the percentage of national population living outside the country, 1991), and a measure of nutritional status (per capita daily supply of calories as a percentage of the average in industrialized countries in 1995). The regression was computed for all Latin American and Caribbean countries for which data were available, producing a sample size of 20. The *R*-squared for this regression is .828; the complete results are presented in Table 5.3. All of the regression coefficients are significant at the 99 percent level of confidence or better except for the coefficient on calorie supply, which is significant at the 96 percent level.

Further tests (possibly combining behavioral and nonbehavioral variables) would be useful, but data on behavior are not generally available on a national basis. Time-series studies and intranational studies focusing on socioeconomic class would also be useful, since disaggregated national AIDS

Table 5.3
People living with AIDS and real GDP per capita, urbanization, migration, and calorie supply in Latin America and the Caribbean

Independent variable	Regression coefficient	*t* statistic	Significance
Constant	−113.8	−0.40	.70
Real per capita GDP	0.059	8.15	.00
Urbanization	86.83	2.92	.01
International migration	18.41	3.62	.00
Calorie supply	−6.04	−2.20	.04

Note: Dependent variable was people living with AIDS per 100,000 population in each country ($N = 20$).

Sources: GDP, urbanization, and calorie data (UNDP, 1998); migration data (PAHO, 1998); AIDS data (UNDP, 1999).

data are rarely adequate. Additional tests for interaction among variables could also be carried out. The findings above suggest the importance of malnutrition and other factors associated with poverty that need to be explored to understand HIV transmission in poor countries.

6

The Context of HIV/AIDS in Eastern Europe and the Former Soviet Union

The world region with the fastest reported rate of increase in HIV infection comprises several of the former Soviet republics. Neighboring countries in Eastern Europe, also in transition from centrally planned to market economies, are not as seriously affected, but they have some of the same economic and social conditions that are fueling the epidemics in the former Soviet Union. The Central Asian republics have relatively low reported prevalence of HIV infection at present, but very rapid rates of increase have been reported in Kazakhstan, Kyrgyzstan, and Uzbekistan since 2001 (UNAIDS, 2004).

The transition countries with the most serious epidemics at present are the Russian Federation, Ukraine, and Estonia, with prevalence of more than 1 percent of the adult population at the end of 2003 (WHO, 2004). In Russia, HIV infections among pregnant women increased tenfold from 1998 to 2002. Throughout the region, surveillance is inadequate and so the data could seriously underestimate the extent of the epidemic, particularly among men who have sex with men (UNAIDS, 2004).

The HIV epidemics in Eastern Europe and the countries of the former Soviet Union are often seen as vastly different from those in sub-Saharan Africa. In many ways that is true. The epidemics in the former socialist countries appear to be driven primarily by injecting drug use (IDU) and commercial sex, although infections among drug users are decreasing as a percentage of new infections and heterosexual infection is increasing

(UNAIDS, 2002). There is almost universal agreement that drug use is not a significant cause of HIV transmission in sub-Saharan Africa. While there are those who assert that transactional sex is an important element in the African epidemics (see chapter 7), the literature does not generally maintain that strictly commercial sex work is a key factor in Africa, whereas it is reported to be in the formerly socialist countries. The emphasis on drug and sex behaviors in the transition economies, however, may be masking the important role played by falling living standards and the collapse of public health services in promoting the spread of HIV, as well as other infectious diseases. This chapter broadens the analysis of declining health in the former socialist economies and situates the study of HIV epidemics in that region within the context of economic decline and disease vulnerability.

While it is commonly stated that AIDS is a development issue for Africa, Asia, and Latin America, the policies to address the epidemic do not follow upon that observation (see chapter 9). Similarly, the AIDS literature acknowledges that the breakdown of the economic and social fabric of the former socialist societies contributes to the epidemics of drug use and sex work. Yet the economic collapse is not otherwise integrated into the analysis of the HIV epidemic nor into policies that protect the population in the face of economic and social crisis.

The portrayal of the HIV epidemic in the transition economies in behavioral terms has the effect of emphasizing individual choices, rather than the causes of those behaviors or the context of poverty that not only produces the behavior but also makes it more dangerous. There are two important effects of the focus on individual behavior in the epidemics in the transition economies: first, the solutions proposed are, as in Africa, Latin America, and Asia, exceedingly late; second, it is politically very easy to write off those affected because they are members of marginalized, denigrated groups. An epidemic among sex workers and needle sharers is a problem that many government officials and citizens think they can ignore.

To understand the HIV/AIDS epidemics in the former Soviet Union and Eastern Europe, we have to understand the other epidemics visited upon the people there, in the context of weak economies with declining income, consumption, and provision of social services. Hence, this chapter surveys the economic, social, and health situation in the transition economies into which HIV has entered.

Economic decline

All of the former socialist countries experienced decreases in production (gross domestic product, or GDP) and GDP per capita during the first 5 years of transition, some of them quite dramatic. The shock of transition was borne in economies that were already struggling.

Low and falling incomes

The former socialist countries of Central and Eastern Europe and the USSR were industrialized, but they were not, for the most part, affluent. In 1989, average income in those planned economies included in World Bank reports was comparable to that of middle-income developing countries (see Table 6.1). The abrupt change from party-led, planned economies to open, market economies at first precipitated sharp declines in output. By 1994, when most of the economies had reached the end of their decline, all but three of the 25 transition countries had GDP per capita (adjusted for purchasing power) below that of South Africa (see Table 6.1), and all but six were below the average for Latin America and the Caribbean, US$6,057 (WDI). Per capita GDP in the United States was four times that of all but five countries (Slovenia, Czech Republic, Hungary, Slovakia, and the Russian Federation). Most of the transition countries began to recover after 1994, both absolutely and relative to other regions. Even with the recovery, by 2002, only seven countries had achieved the level of output of 1989, while eight countries were still at less than 70 percent of 1989 output (see Table 6.2). The shrinking national output occurred at the same time that inequality increased, so that the burden of the decline fell most heavily on the poor. In all of the countries, Gini coefficients show a worsening of earnings distribution, and in all but Turkmenistan, inequality increased substantially (see Table 6.2).[1]

Failing economies and a dismal record in civil and human rights made economic and political transition necessary, and the economic and social costs of the reforms have to be considered in light of the suffering that the population would have experienced sooner or later. The process of transition, however, also imposed costs on the economy and the population, but most of those costs were avoidable. Just as in the structurally adjusting countries of Africa and Latin America, the way in which reforms were administered imposed the burden on the poor and middle classes, rather than on the well positioned. The corruption of the former regime does not excuse the inequity of the reforms, nor does that inequity excuse the earlier abuse of the people's trust.

Pillaged assets

In the former Soviet Union and in some of the countries of Eastern Europe, well-placed government employees used their positions to strip the state enterprises of assets and secure the gains of privatization for themselves. As a result, those countries had to finance the economic transition with few

1. An increase in the Gini coefficient (index greater than 100) indicates a worsening of income distribution.

Table 6.1
GDP per capita, 1989 and 1994: transition countries and others, ranked by 1994 data

Country	GDP per capita US$ PPP 1989	GDP per capita US$ PPP 1994
Barbados	11,124	11,502
Slovenia	n/a	11,489
Czech Republic	n/a	10,806
Argentina	7,497	10,501
Hungary	9,018	8,761
South Africa	8,035	8,275
Slovak Republic	8,913	8,090
Chile	4,528	6,669
Malaysia	4,132	6,481
Poland	n/a	6,417
Costa Rica	5,160	6,395
Estonia	8,341	6,333
Brazil	5,394	6,081
Russian Federation	8,289	6,024
Croatia	n/a	5,941
Lithuania	n/a	5,698
Colombia	4,523	5,639
Bulgaria	5,874	5,464
Venezuela	4,452	5,462
Botswana	4,564	5,441
Macedonia	n/a	5,370
Thailand	3,200	5,336
Namibia	4,615	5,151
Romania	n/a	5,097
Latvia	8,308	4,967
Paraguay	3,737	4,401
Ukraine	7,176	4,321
El Salvador	2,772	3,787
Belarus	n/a	3,475
Kazakhstan	n/a	3,452
Guatemala	2,677	3,254
Turkmenistan	4,538	3,025
Ecuador	2,748	3,019
Albania	2,748	2,304
Honduras	1,975	2,273
China	1,233	2,213
Azerbaijan	n/a	1,865
India	1,283	1,706
Haiti	1,871	1,570
Bosnia and Herzegovina	n/a	1,527
Armenia	n/a	1,498
Georgia	4,595	1,283

Source: WDI, 2004.

Table 6.2
Change in GDP per capita and change in Gini coefficient, 1989 to 2001–2002.

	Change in GDP per capita 1989=100		Change in Gini coefficient 1989=100
Country	1995	2002	2001
Albania	81	114	n/a
Armenia	49	78	188 (2000)
Azerbaijan	37	63	182
Belarus	63	93	146
Bosnia-Herzegovina	n/a	n/a	n/a
Bulgaria	77	80	137 (1996)
Croatia	67	86	n/a
Czech Republic	94	106	134
Estonia	65	91	149 (2000)
Georgia	26	38	165 (1997)
Hungary	86	112	144
Kazakhstan	61	86	n/a
Kyrgyzstan	50	69	197
Latvia	52	76	132
Lithuania	55	73	147
Macedonia	68	76	128
Moldova	38	38	157
Poland	99	130	147 (1999)
Romania	85	85	250
Russia	56	64	193
Serbia and Montenegro	44	51	n/a
Slovakia	84	110	n/a
Slovenia	93	121	142
Tajikistan	41	57	n/a
Turkmenistan	64	89	104 (1999)
Ukraine	45	47	185
Uzbekistan	83	107	n/a

Note: Hungary: Gini 1988 = 100; Bulgaria, Macedonia: Gini 1990 = 100.
Source: TransMONEE Data Base, 2003, UNICEF IRC.

public resources. The opportunity for political reform and economic reconstruction was blunted because the gains were captured by party and government leaders and the substantial mafias that had profited from the restrictions of the old regime. After privatization, few resources were left to provide a social safety net of nutrition, health services, and education for displaced workers and their families.

Not only did cuts in spending affect the current provision of services in most countries, but infrastructure deteriorated due to the lack of maintenance. The depreciation of physical capital was matched by a deterioration in human capital as well. In myriad ways, the institutions that had maintained human capital in the socialist era (albeit not well) vanished.

Unemployment and real wages

The closure of some state enterprises, the privatization of others, and cutbacks in state spending contributed to increases in unemployment that are unevenly distributed across the transition economies. In 11 countries, official unemployment rates were in excess of 10 percent in 2001 (see Table 6.3). Official unemployment rates were especially high in Macedonia (41.7 percent in 1997), in Bosnia-Herzegovina (39.8 percent), and in Serbia and

Table 6.3
Unemployment rates, official and labor force survey, 2001

Country	Official rate (%)	Labor force survey rate (%)
Albania	14.5	17.0 (1998)
Armenia	10.4	n/a
Azerbaijan	1.3	12.8
Belarus	2.3	n/a
Bosnia-Herzegovina	39.8	n/a
Bulgaria	17.5	19.7
Croatia	22.0	16.3
Czech Republic	8.5	8.1
Estonia	6.5	12.6
Georgia	5.0	11.1
Hungary	8.0	5.7
Kazakhstan	3.7 (2000)	10.4
Kyrgyzstan	3.2	13.9 (1999)
Latvia	7.8	13.1
Lithuania	12.5	17.0
Macedonia	41.7 (1997)	30.5
Moldova	2.0	7.3
Poland	16.2	18.5
Romania	8.6	6.6
Russia	1.6	9.1
Serbia and Montenegro	27.5	17.4
Slovakia	18.2	19.3
Slovenia	11.6	5.9
Tajikistan	2.3	n/a
Turkmenistan	n/a	4.9 (1999)
Ukraine	3.7	11.1
Uzbekistan	0.4	n/a

Source: TransMONEE Database, 2003. UNICEF IRC.

Montenegro (27.5 percent) (TransMONEE Data Base, 2003). Unemployment rates calculated from Labor Force Surveys (LFS) are much higher than the official rates in some countries. According to household surveys, the unemployment rate in Estonia is 12.6 percent, not the 6.5 percent officially recorded. The other Baltic states show similar discrepancies: in Latvia the official rate is 7.8 percent, but by the LFS, the unemployment rate is 13.1 percent; in Lithuania, the official register shows 12.5 percent unemployed, but the LFS lists 17 percent unemployed. The largest discrepancies between the two measures of unemployment occurred in Azerbaijan, Kyrgyzstan, and Russia (see Table 6.3).

In Russia, the largest group among the unemployed is of people 20 to 24 years of age; they constitute 17 percent of the unemployed. Almost 40 percent of the unemployed are under the age of 30 (Zbarskaya, 2002). In Central and Eastern Europe by 1999, there were 18 million people between 15 and 24 years of age who were neither in school nor employed (CEEHRN, 2002).

The impact of the economic transition on real wages has been especially harsh. In only three countries were average real wages in 2001 higher than in 1989. In all of the other countries for which data were available for 1989 to 2000, real wages fell. While real wages recovered from their lowest values of the mid-1990s in most countries, in 11 of 22 countries reporting for the decade, real wages in 2001 were still less than 60 percent of what they were in 1989 (see Table 6.4).

Table 6.4
Change in average real wages, 1989–2001

Country	1989 = 100	Country	1989 = 100
Albania	154.6	Lithuania	44.5
Armenia	46.2	Macedonia	51.1
Azerbaijan	49.9	Moldova	64.6
Belarus (2000) (1993=100)	97.8	Poland	114.3
Bosnia-Herzegovina (1997=100)	120.2	Romania	77.1
		Russia	52.7
Bulgaria	50.3	Serbia and Montenegro (1994=100)	147.4
Croatia (1995=100)	133.2		
Czech Republic	118.5	Slovakia	82.0
Estonia	74.7	Slovenia	89.5
Georgia	95.7	Tajikistan	18.9
Hungary	90.6	Turkmenistan (1999) (1993=100)	34.7
Kazakhstan (1991=100)	52.8		
Kyrgyzstan (1990=100)	29.3	Ukraine	59.1
Latvia	71.1	Uzbekistan	24.9

Source: TransMONEE Database, 2003. UNICEF IRC.

These figures may still overstate wage recoveries because a large number of services had been provided free, even housing at times. In addition, most private employers do not offer the same fringe benefits as had the state, and they reduced vacation time and increased working hours. The change to the European norm shifted working hours later, making it impossible to hold a second job. Working six A.M. to two P.M. in the formal sector and then a second shift for cash was once the norm. The loss of the second salary is not recorded since it had been informal.

Food security

Food production fell in all but two of the transition countries from the 1989–1991 average to 1994, and continued to fall in 12 of the countries in the second half of the 1990s. By 2002, four countries—Estonia, Moldova, Ukraine, and Latvia—were producing less than 55 percent of the food they had produced in 1989. This change does not represent a rapid adjustment to world markets for the sake of comparative advantage because none of these economies has improved so dramatically that it can afford to import the food it needs (WDI, 2004). Table 6.5 shows food production in 2002 compared to each country's average for 1989–1991 for the transition countries and a selection of others.

Food Balance Sheets produced by the Food and Agriculture Organization of the United Nations show the impact of declining food production

Table 6.5
Change in food production, selected countries, 1989–2002

Country	1989–1991 = 100	Country	1989–1991 = 100
Angola	177	Macedonia	84
Argentina	144	Moldova	55
Armenia	83	Poland	84
Azerbaijan	90	Romania	86
Belarus	64	Russian Federation	69
Bulgaria	71	Serbia and Montenegro	n/a
Croatia	67	Slovak Republic	n/a
Czech Republic	77	Slovenia	102
Estonia	41	Tajikistan	63
Georgia	75	Turkey	116
Hungary	75	Turkmenistan	132
Kazakhstan	80	Ukraine	54
Kyrgyz Republic	137	Uzbekistan	126
Latvia	45	Vietnam	181
Lithuania	66	Zimbabwe	96

Source: WDI, 2004.

on availability of food for consumption. These are imperfect measures of food security, but they attempt to estimate availability of calories and protein, based on production, imports, exports, and wastage. Food balances declined in eight countries in the region to dangerously low levels. (Ten countries had declining balances, but two of those had more than adequate calorie availability even with the decrease.) Three countries (Armenia, Azerbaijan, and Tajikistan) had total calorie availability less than the average caloric supply for Africa for 1996 to 2000, and Croatia and Georgia had slightly more than that (FAO, 2003b).

One group that usually enjoys privileged access to food is the military. Yet Human Rights Watch reported in 2003 that food shortages were so severe in Russia that there were deaths from starvation and from malnutrition-related infectious diseases among military conscripts. The organization also reported that half of pregnant women in Russia are undernourished and that only one-third of children can be categorized as healthy (HRW, 2003).

Disintegration of social infrastructure

During the socialist era, the state provided most, if not all, of the physical and organizational infrastructure that integrated people into society. From infancy to old age, educational, cultural, sports, leisure, and transportation facilities were state-provided. When the state collapsed or withdrew in those countries, it left a vacuum for the provision of services. The absence of civil society groups has been amply noted in discussions of governance for transition economies, but the impact is also felt in the everyday functioning of social life.

The proportion of children attending preschool has shrunk, leaving many children, especially those from poor and marginalized groups (ethnic minorities in particular), ill prepared to enter school. Also, the deterioration of public transit makes it more difficult for children to attend school, especially in rural areas (Meurs and Ranasinghe, 2003). The lack of resources makes each day spent in school less productive. Even elite schools have few resources, from preschool through graduate programs at the universities. Sports teams, dance groups, and all the other organizations for the enjoyment of daily activities are sorely lacking.

Human capital in the form of healthy students and workers also deteriorated. When income, employment, and access to food were shrinking, the population needed more government spending on health to compensate. World Development Indicators (World Bank) and Human Development Indicators (UNDP) report public health spending as a proportion of GDP, which is generally a useful indicator if countries are growing, even modestly. Most of the countries maintained that proportion over the first decade of transition. But GDP fell so greatly in the 1990s that reporting health spending as a share of GDP obscures the dramatic decreases in spending on

Table 6.6
Public spending on health per capita, 2000

Country	Spending on health US$ PPP	Country	Spending on health US$ PPP
Albania	89	Lithuania	382
Armenia	78	Macedonia	335
Azerbaijan	17	Moldova	37
Belarus	221	Poland	417
Bosnia and Herzegovina	164	Romania	297
Bulgaria	247	Russian Federation	268
Croatia	708	Serbia and Montenegro	0
Czech Republic	910	Slovak Republic	584
Estonia	462	Slovenia	1,013
Georgia	21	Tajikistan	7
Hungary	644	Turkey	272
Kazakhstan	95	Turkmenistan	107
Kyrgyz Republic	32	Ukraine	119
Latvia	267	Uzbekistan	42

Source: Derived from WDI, 2004.

health, both in total and per capita. Some of the countries did not even maintain public health spending as a share of the shrinking GDP. In Bulgaria, public health spending shrank to 49 percent of the 1991 share of GDP. The Central Asian republics and the Caucasus region had the lowest indices of health spending as a share of GDP compared to pretransition times (TransMONEE Data Base, 2003). Since public spending in real terms fell so dramatically in many countries, people were compelled to finance health care themselves. Public spending on health in 2000 is reported in Table 6.6.

Ethnic and linguistic minorities

Ethnic minorities were especially hard hit during the crisis. Roma people[2] are a significant minority in Ukraine, Kaliningrad (Russia), Czech Republic, Slovakia, Hungary, Bulgaria, and Romania. Unemployment rates are very high among the Roma, and education levels are low. Many Roma children are seriously malnourished, with half of Roma children in Bulgaria and more than 40 percent in Romania estimated to be "constantly starving" (UNDP, 2003b, graph 22). Infant and maternal mortality rates are also high.

The transition has also been especially harsh for people of Russian

2. Roma people are referred to as "gypsies," but that term is considered derogatory.

descent in the non-Russian republics of the former Soviet Union. Amid the nationalist revival of the transition era, many non-Russians see their Russian minority as enemies of independence and economic reform. For a large minority of people in the Baltics, Russian is their primary language, and many thousands of people speak only Russian. In Soviet times that was not an economic disadvantage, but now Russian-only speakers are among the long-term unemployed. Poverty, drug use, and alcoholism are concentrated more heavily in the Russian populations of the Baltic republics. Moreover, many Russians became "forced migrants"; half a million ethnic Russians left the newly independent states and settled in Russia by 2001 (UNICEF, 2003).

Migration

In the face of collapsing economies and shrinking opportunities, many people are migrating for work, permanently or temporarily. Remittances of earnings are an increasingly important contributor to GDP in the former socialist economies, just as in Latin American and Caribbean countries. Migration is an important factor in health and in social abuse, undermining long-term unions and increasing the possibility of exposure to sexually transmitted diseases.

Social fabric

Economic crisis has exacerbated social problems and contributed new sources of stress for populations accustomed to at least some social protection. The impact of the crisis is reflected in rates of marriage, divorce, suicide, homicide, prostitution, and drug use.

Marriages, divorce, births, and despair

The first decade of transition saw numerous symptoms of a stressed social fabric. The number of marriages decreased, and the number of divorces increased. Some of the change probably reflects young people choosing their own form of unions in a new political environment with reduced incentives to marriage, such as access to housing. Births to unmarried women under the age of 20, however, are considered a good indicator of a vulnerable population. In every country, the share of births to unmarried women under age 20 increased substantially (TransMONEE Data Base, 2003). An increase in the number of divorces is not an unequivocal sign of a strained social fabric, but a society in which there are 70 divorces for every 100 marriages, as in Lithuania in 2001, is not dealing well with economic and social stress.

The most unambiguous indicators of a shredding social fabric are the increasing rates of homicide, suicide, and accidents (often the result of alcohol) in almost all of the countries of Eastern Europe and the former Soviet Union. Table 6.7 shows the extremely high suicide rate for young men in many of the transition countries. In Lithuania, suicide is the leading cause of death for people between 15 and 24 years of age. (In general, the proportion of deaths from suicide can loom large for this age group because there are few deaths from heart disease, cancers, and the other leading causes of death for older persons. Even adjusting for the lower likelihood of death of young people from other causes, youth suicide is an extremely serious problem in the region.)

The countries with the highest incidence of young male suicide are the northern cluster of the former USSR and Kazakhstan. Belarus, Estonia, Kazakhstan, Lithuania, and Russia have suicide rates more than twice those of other transition countries. Kyrgyzstan and the Ukraine also have high rates. Except for Estonia, those countries have also seen some of the highest rates of increase of suicide in the region, with incidence more than doubling in Russia and Belarus (see Table 6.7). By 2000, there had been some improvement from the high rates of the mid 1990s, but they still exceeded suicide incidence in Western Europe and other world regions by a significant margin (WHO, www.who.int). Table 6.8 shows male and female suicide rates (all ages) for countries reporting suicide data to the World Health Organization. The former socialist countries are among the populations with the highest rates of suicide for all ages, including for females.

Table 6.7
Male suicides, age 15–19, per 100,000 in 2001 and change since 1989

Country	Male suicides per 100,000	Index (1989 = 100)	Country	Male suicides per 100,000	Index (1989 = 100)
Albania	n/a	n/a	Lithuania	36.6	195
Armenia	1	22	Macedonia	2.3	92
Azerbaijan	0.9	37[a]	Moldova	8.3	110[a]
Belarus	23.6	204[a]	Poland	14.2	134
Bosnia-Herzegovina	n/a	n/a	Romania	7.5	119
Bulgaria	6.4	60	Russia	39.3	213
Croatia	13.1	91	Serbia and Montenegro	6.9	128
Czech Republic	9.5	105			
Estonia	22.4	72	Slovakia	5.8	68
Georgia	2.1	65	Slovenia	11.6	94
Hungary	10.1	61	Tajikistan	n/a	n/a
Kazakhstan	30.1	139	Turkmenistan	8.8	119
Kyrgyzstan	18.7	146	Ukraine	18.7	157
Latvia	14	79	Uzbekistan (2000)	12.5	153[a]

[a]1990 = 100
Source: TransMONEE Database, 2003. UNICEF IRC.

Table 6.8
Suicides per 100,000 by country, year, and sex (most recent year available, as of June 2004)

Country	Year	Males	Females
Albania	2001	5.5	2.3
Argentina	1996	9.9	3.0
Armenia	2002	4.0	0.7
Austria	2002	30.5	8.7
Azerbaijan	2002	1.8	0.5
Belarus	2001	60.3	9.3
Belgium	1997	31.2	11.4
Bosnia and Herzegovina	1991	20.3	3.3
Brazil	1995	6.6	1.8
Bulgaria	2002	25.6	8.3
Croatia	2002	30.2	10.0
Czech Republic	2001	26.0	6.3
Denmark	1999	21.4	7.4
Estonia	2002	47.7	9.8
Finland	2002	32.3	10.2
Georgia	2000	4.8	1.2
Hungary	2002	45.5	12.2
India	1998	12.2	9.1
Jamaica	1985	0.5	0.2
Japan	2000	35.2	13.4
Kazakhstan	2002	50.2	8.8
Korea, Republic of	2001	20.3	8.6
Kyrgyzstan	2002	19.1	4.0
Latvia	2002	48.4	11.8
Lithuania	2002	80.7	13.1
Macedonia	2000	10.3	4.5
Mexico	1995	5.4	1.0
Moldova	2002	27.9	5.2
Netherlands	2000	12.7	6.2
New Zealand	2000	19.8	4.2
Poland	2001	26.7	4.3
Romania	2002	23.9	4.7
Russian Federation	2002	69.3	11.9
Slovakia	2001	22.2	4.0
Slovenia	2002	44.4	10.5
Tajikistan	1999	4.2	1.6
Turkmenistan	1998	13.8	3.5
Ukraine	2000	52.1	10.0
United Kingdom	1999	11.8	3.3
United States of America	2000	17.1	4.0
Uzbekistan	2000	11.8	3.8

Source: WHO, 2004. http://www.who.int.

The extent of multipartnered sexual activity in the region is comparable to other parts of the world, as are longstanding patriarchal relations that influence male behavior in many ways. But the economic crisis and the dissolution of marital relationships may also be contributing to an increase in partner change and the spreading epidemics of STDs (see below). As indicated in the appendix to chapter 1, the extent of casual sex, sex with commercial sex workers, and multipartnered sex provides adequate opportunity for the spread of HIV and other diseases.

Prostitution

Opening the borders has allowed an influx of tourism into Eastern Europe and the former Soviet Union. While it may increase incomes and foreign exchange reserves, a significant proportion of the inflow is sex tourism, promoted in a variety of ways. The Internet provides hundreds of opportunities for sex shopping prior to arrival in the Baltics and other Eastern European countries and Russia. Sex magazines in Western European and Nordic countries promote sex tours in the region. City guides available free at all hotels—such as *Exploring Vilnius, Riga This Week, What Where When Warszawa,* and *Safe St. Petersburg: Welcome*—devote a significant number of pages to ads for massage and escort services that also explicitly sell sex. In *Riga This Week,* for example, 14 of the 98 pages are devoted to sexual services (March/April 2003 and others). Business-card advertisements for masseuses and prostitutes litter the ground like confetti in Warsaw and other cities. Rural areas that border more affluent countries are affected as well. Sex workers line Czech roads near the German and Austrian borders. Entire towns, such as Dubi, have been converted into sex markets, with scores of brothels, along the German border in the Czech Republic. Women and young girls by the hundreds dance in the large windows of converted houses and stores or stand out in the parking lots in skimpy clothes in all weather. (When I was there, it was snowing.) Long lines of cars bearing German license plates with only male passengers form at the border crossings (visit, 18 April 2003).

Trafficking women and girls

In this context of fragmenting economies and social fabric, we can better examine the epidemic of commercial sex work and trafficking in women and children that has engulfed the region. The poverty at home creates pressure to tolerate the migration of family members for commercial sex work. Increasing stress, alcoholism, and drug use in these countries are also producing more dysfunctional families that permit, and even promote, the trafficking of their daughters for commercial sex work (IOM, 2002).

Prostitution certainly existed in the Soviet era and was reportedly even run in the Intourist hotels by Intourist itself, possibly as an arm of the

KGB. During the Soviet era, prostitution was more discreet, without the blatant advertisements for escort services and sex clubs that are now common in the Baltic states and Eastern Europe.

Trafficking is new because the borders were effectively sealed by the Soviet regime. Now, organized crime plays a major role in prostitution, both within the former Soviet republics and in the external trafficking of women and girls to Western Europe and Scandinavia. It is a bitter irony of the independence era, however, that the freedom to leave the country and the inflow of tourists have permitted the explosive growth of prostitution in the region and the trafficking, forced and voluntary, of women for prostitution in Western Europe and beyond. It is also a bitter aspect of independence that, freed of Nazi aggression and then Soviet occupation, young women are still being transported from the Baltics to Germany, and other countries as well, as new captives.

An accurate estimate of trafficking from Russia and the Baltics is impeded, of course, by the illegal nature of the trade. It is difficult to coordinate the information from police forces in Western Europe with the inquiries of families in search of missing girls and women in Eastern Europe. Some women agree to be trafficked knowing that they are going to work in prostitution, although they may not be aware of the conditions in which they will be held. Perhaps as many as 50 percent of women are trafficked by force or by trickery, thinking that they will be working as au pairs or in the restaurant trade (Audra Sipaviciene, interview, 19 March 2003). Child pornography and trafficking are increasingly serious problems in Russia because there are no laws restricting either. The legal age of consent in Russia is 14, making policing of trafficking and child pornography more difficult (Zbarskaya, 2002).

The ultimate destination of trafficked girls and women from Eastern Europe is often Germany, although it is also a wholesale location from which they are then shipped to other countries. The Nordic countries are also a principal destination, but some of the women are transported as far as Japan. According to a report published by Danish police in 2001, "Denmark and Sweden are the main destinations in the Nordic countries for organised prostitution from the Baltic countries" (Moustgaard, 2002, 6). In the Nordic countries as well, some villages have been converted into sex clubs, and there are reports of prostitution concentration camps in Poland, Albania, and Italy where women from Baltic countries are kept imprisoned behind barbed wire and subjected to abysmal conditions. Large-scale criminal networks control 60 percent of prostitution in Western Europe, as well as drug trafficking. They have solid political and financial contacts in the countries of origin, destination, and transit (Moustgaard, 2002).

The Baltics are particularly vulnerable as front-line states to the Western market. For Baltic women: "The United Kingdom and Germany are the absolute leaders among the countries comprising trafficking destinations, followed by the Nordic countries and the Netherlands" (Sipaviciene, 2002,

13).[3] Organized crime and the sex trade are well established in the Baltics, giving a solid foundation for those who are trafficking women out of the region. In Tallinn, the capital of Estonia and a city of 400,000 people, there are 70 to 80 brothels. Poverty, family dissolution, and substance abuse have precipitated an epidemic of child neglect and filled the streets of Tallinn with street children. They are extremely vulnerable to sexual abuse, depending at times on survival sex (Lopez, 2001). There are an estimated 10,000 women in prostitution in Latvia, of whom 75 percent are of Russian ethnicity (Lynggard, 2002). The population of Latvia is 2.3 million, of which 750,000 are women between 15 and 60 years of age (derived from UN, 2000), indicating the magnitude of the situation. The largest number of women reported trafficked are from Lithuania, and the flow from rural regions is especially serious. It is not clear if the largest number trafficked are in fact from Lithuania, or if more Lithuanian women have lodged formal reports with police.

The situation is made worse by the conventional networks women use to look for work. Especially in Lithuania and Estonia, women rely on family and friends for references or to find work instead of legal employment agencies. Family connections are one of the most important means of recruiting women for trafficking in the Baltic states (IOM, 2002). The impact of trafficking in the Baltics is apparent. In Lithuania, 12 percent of 15–24-year-olds know someone who has been trafficked, 6 percent of young Latvians, and 9 percent of young Estonians (IOM, 2002).

Drug use

The epidemic of injecting drug use (IDU) should also be viewed within this context of economic and social distress. Drug use is a new face on an old problem of alcoholism in the Soviet Union. Supply of drugs, part of the legacy of the Soviet war in Afghanistan, and partly the result of increasingly powerful organized crime groups, is one aspect of the problem, but a social crisis has produced the demand. These are not happy, optimistic young people injecting drugs, and the IDU epidemic has parallels in the suicide epidemic in the region.

The increase in sex work in the 1990s in Eastern Europe has been accompanied by an epidemic of injecting drug use among prostitutes. Moscow has up to 70,000 sex workers: "It is estimated that between 25 to 35 percent of sex workers in the Russian cities of Moscow and Volgograd, the Belarus capital of Minsk, and the Ukrainian cities of Odessa and Donetsk

3. Because of the criminal nature of trafficking, the true destination of all the trafficked women and girls is not known. Hence, there is a discrepancy between the estimate of the Danish police and the head of the International Office for Migration in Vilnius in the two paragraphs above.

inject drugs. . . . In Kaliningrad, Russia, anywhere from 40 to 80 percent of the sex workers are thought to be HIV positive" (OSI, 2001, 15). The epidemics in those countries have received more attention than in the smaller countries, but Lithuania also reports a fivefold increase in drug use in recent years (Eidukiene, 2002).

Much of the drug use is among prisoners. A study by Médecins Sans Frontières found that, in seven Russian prisons, 43 percent of the inmates had injected drugs and, of those, 14 percent had started in prison. About one-fifth of Latvia's known HIV-infected persons are prisoners (OSI, 2001). In Lithuania, it was the discovery of a dramatic increase of HIV in Alytus Prison that alerted the country to a growing threat, although it has been little heeded by the general public. The epidemic of drug use is not confined to prisoners, however. A recent study, based on survey results, estimated that one-half of Russian college students had injected drugs (CEEHRN, 2002). In Vilnius, Lithuania, a beautiful new mall opened (the largest in the Baltics) with a skating rink, a bowling alley, shops, and restaurants. All the bathrooms in the mall have blue lights only, to prevent drug users from finding their veins, indicating the level of concern about the prevalence of drug injecting there.

Commercial sex workers and drug users are considered outcasts by the majority of the population in the region, as in the West. Thus, the epidemics of sex work and drug use, HIV, hepatitis, and other blood-borne and sexually transmitted diseases, and the explosion in TB rates, in part due to the increase in HIV, are easy for politicians and citizens to dismiss. But people with risky behaviors are part of, not apart from, these societies. Sharply increasing rates over a short period of time should make that even more apparent. Perhaps, during a time of economic collapse and social disintegration, it is easier to see that epidemic increases in the numbers of injecting drug users and commercial sex workers certainly signal that they are members of a crumbling society and their situation arises from the crisis in that society. It is not just the elimination of barriers to the drug trade and sex work (the failure of police systems) and the rapid rise in gangsterism in the drug and sex trade that fuel the epidemic. The wretched condition of people in failing economies gives rise to the situation as well. We have no reason to assume that the demand side of the Western European market for commercial sex is a new phenomena. What is new is the desperate lack of security on the part of young people in the transition economies that sucks them into the Western European sex market, both in the west and for Western clients who travel to Eastern Europe.

Health impact

Economic decline and resulting social disruption are creating serious health impacts in most of the countries in transition. As with the economic distress, many of the health problems have their origins in the era before transition but have been exacerbated by the falling incomes and declining health services as the transition proceeds.

Nutrition

Food supply was an important political variable in the pretransition era. For political stability, governments subsidized food prices, especially for meats, fats, and sugar. Low prices undermined any attempt that government nutritionists made to promote healthy nutrition. The impact of poor diet, cigarettes, and alcohol was visible in declining life expectancy in Russia (Shkolnikov et al., 1998) and in Bulgaria, Hungary, Poland, and Romania, even before the transition, due to increasing rates of heart disease and cancers (Sekula et al., 1997).

Other nutritional problems afflict many of the countries in the region; some of them were of long standing, and others are the result of sudden impoverishment. In Bulgaria, intake of essential micronutrients is 30 to 40 percent below reference levels for some groups. Since 1988 the infant mortality rate in Bulgaria has been increasing, as is the proportion of newborns of low birth weight. Moderate to severe iodine deficiency affects one-third of population, and goiter prevalence has doubled since 1974 to 23 percent of Bulgarians. Early in the transition era, the Bulgarian government abandoned iodine-supplementation programs because of lack of funds and inadequate production of iodized salt. Nutritional deficiencies were exacerbated by the decreasing proportion of children eating school meals, from 49 percent in 1991 to 28 percent nationally, and to only 10 percent in Sofia in 1994 (Sekula et al., 1997).

In Romania there is a high prevalence of anemia in children, as with poor children everywhere. In the 1990s in Romania, 50 percent of children younger than 2 years old and 30 percent of children 3–5 years old were anemic. Calcium deficiency with clinically expressed rickets was also prevalent. There was high prevalence of iodine deficiency, even in areas where it was not thought to be endemic. Iron-deficiency anemia among pregnant women ranged from 12 to 42 percent by region (Sekula et al., 1997). In Lithuania, 30 percent of pregnant women were anemic in 2000, which reflected some improvement from 1996 (Eidukiene, 2002).

Toxic exposure

A serious health problem, the magnitude of which is unknown, in the transition countries is the exposure to toxins from a seriously contaminated environment. Industrial pollutants and inadequate treatment make tap water unsafe even in some capital cities, including the beautiful city of Riga. Fishing in streams and lakes provides a source of food for the population, but the fish come from dangerously contaminated sources.

The best-known environmental catastrophe in the former Soviet Union occurred in 1986 in Chornobyl (Chernobyl, in Russian), Ukraine. Over 260,000 square kilometers of Ukraine, Belarus, and Russia were contaminated, with a population of 2.6 million. In addition to the immediate impact of radiation poisoning among workers during the explosion and cleanup, there have been long-term consequences. Thyroid cancer in Ukrainian children has increased 10-fold since 1986. Members of the cleanup crew experienced a new medical syndrome, including fatigue, apathy, and a decreased number of natural killer (NK) cells, that doctors called Chornobyl AIDS (Shcherbak, 1996).

Reproductive health

Reproductive health is worsening, with dramatic increases in sexually transmitted diseases in some countries. Genital infection is one of two main problems for pregnant women in Lithuania, along with anemia. Incidence of spontaneous miscarriage doubled between 1991 and 2000 (Eidukiene, 2002). In Russia, the incidence of syphilis in 2000 was 31 times higher than in 1990, and congenital syphilis contributed to that increase (Zbarskaya, 2002). In the Baltics, the incidence of syphilis and gonorrhea was reduced to pre-1989 levels by 2000, although the incidence had doubled or tripled in those countries in the mid-1990s. In the rest of the former Soviet Union, the incidence of syphilis and gonorrhea in 2000 was still higher than in 1989, and in some countries it was two or three times as high (TransMONEE Data Base, 2003).

Child health

While infant mortality rates have not increased substantially in most of the countries in transition, there are ominous signs for the future health of children and adolescents. The proportion of low birth weight infants to all live births increased in 18 of the 26 countries reporting (TransMONEE Data Base, 2003). In Lithuania, the share of low birth weight infants tripled from 1991 to 2001, five percent of babies are born prematurely, and congenital anomalies increased from 0.3 percent in 1991 to 4.5 percent of births in 2000 (Eidukiene, 2002).

Sicknesses in children increased 2.8 times from 1990 to 2000, mostly in respiratory diseases. Even in well visits, doctors are finding that children suffer from numerous maladies. In Lithuanian children under the age of 16 seen for health checkups, the share of absolutely healthy children was 59 percent in 1991 and by 2000 had fallen to 46 percent. Tuberculosis in children stopped increasing at 17 infections per 100,000 in 2000, but that is almost twice the 1990 rate (Eidukiene, 2002). In Russia, as well, doctors noted a serious deterioration in mental and physical development of children. In 1999, almost 20 percent of children were observed to have some kind of physical defect, in hearing, sight, speech, or posture (Zbarskaya, 2002).

In the late 1990s, deteriorating health trends were most pronounced among adolescents 15 to 17 years of age. Increases of 80 to 100 percent in virtually all classes of disease were recorded for Russian adolescents (Zbarskaya, 2002). Considering that health services were declining, these trends suggest that even higher rates of morbidity would be observed if the youths without access to health care were included. Tuberculosis prevalence among children and adolescents in Russia is especially high, and it is twice as high in adolescents (36 cases per 100,000) as in children under 14. Alcoholism, drug addiction, and syphilis are also increasing among children and adolescents. Incidence of syphilis is 60 percent higher among adolescent girls in Russia than in the population as a whole (Zbarskaya, 2002). In Belarus, as well, there has been a substantial increase in child morbidity, including an increase in tuberculosis among adolescents. Incidence of thyroid cancer continues to be high among young people as a result of the Chornobyl accident, and infant mortality is still high in areas contaminated by the accident. (Belarus was immediately downwind of the accident.) In the 1990s, the proportion of children born with some defect or illness increased over 150 percent to almost 20 percent of all births (Gasyuk, 2002).

Tuberculosis

One of the most troubling aspects of worsening health indicators in the former socialist countries is the very high and increasing prevalence of tuberculosis. Tuberculosis has a synergistic effect with HIV; people with HIV readily succumb to tuberculosis, and in people with TB, HIV progresses more rapidly to AIDS. Nearly two-thirds of the people living with HIV or AIDS are living in the countries with the highest tuberculosis burden in the world (OSI quoting Peter Piot of UNAIDS, 2001, 15).

In all the transition countries, prevalence of TB is at least four times the level in the United States and Sweden, but most worrisome are the 14 countries with prevalence in 2002 more than 20 times that (WDI, 2004). In Russia, TB prevalence is 45 times that of the United States. Many cases of TB in Russia and Estonia are multidrug resistant (OSI, 2001). Not only is TB prevalence very high in most of the countries (especially the northern cluster), but TB incidence is increasing rapidly. Since 1992, prevalence of tuberculosis has increased 10 to 15 percent per year in Russia (Zbarskaya, 2002). In 13 countries, TB incidence has increased more than 50 percent (index greater than 150) since 1989 (see Table 6.9). Some of the increase can be attributed to the HIV epidemics already occurring in the region, but most of it merely reflects the weakening health and health service situation in these countries. As such, the TB epidemic constitutes a pump for accelerated HIV transmission in a population whose health is already severely compromised.

Table 6.9
New tuberculosis infections per 100,000 people in 2001, and change from 1989

Country	2001	Index (1989 = 100)
Albania	21.6	101 (2000)
Armenia	39.9	221
Azerbaijan	60.1	147
Belarus	47.5	156
Bosnia-Herzegovina	n/a	n/a
Bulgaria	48.2	186
Croatia	34.3	57
Czech Republic	13.1	69
Estonia	42.0	182
Georgia	80.1	287
Hungary	32.6	91
Kazakhstan	155.5	210
Kyrgyzstan	127.3	257
Latvia	73.4	273
Lithuania	63.9	196
Macedonia	34.3	85
Moldova	83.1	183
Poland	27.6	65
Romania	115.3	198
Russia	88.1	234
Serbia and Montenegro	38.9	81 (2000)
Slovakia	20.0	74
Slovenia	18.9	61 (2000)
Tajikistan	127.3	118
Turkmenistan	55.6	135
Ukraine	69.2	201
Uzbekistan	64.6	140 (1999)

Source: TransMONEE Database, 2003. UNICEF IRC.

During Gorbachev's antialcohol campaign of the 1980s, rates of all causes of death decreased. The campaign was abandoned after Gorbachev was replaced, and the price of alcohol fell relative to the price of foods. Not only did deaths directly related to alcohol increase, but so too did deaths from infectious and parasitic diseases, which is not surprising since alcohol consumption depresses immune function, and the risk of tuberculosis is associated with alcohol consumption as well (Leon et al., 1997).

Malnutrition and poor living conditions also increase activation of latent tuberculosis infection, while the lack of essential antituberculosis drugs results in inadequate treatment. Consequently, TB mortality increased steadily in Armenia, Kyrgyzstan, Latvia, Lithuania, Moldova, Romania, and

Turkmenistan, whereas other countries saw no improvement, especially in the early years of the transition (Raviglione et al., 1994).

The failure to maintain public health services, sanitation, and heating provoked a resurgence of other diseases, including diphtheria and increasing lice infestation. Lice transmit typhus, a disease which had caused several million deaths in Russia in the twentieth century, probably more than any other disease. Hospitals without heat for extended periods of time saw outbreaks of typhus in the 1990s (Tarasevich et al., 1998).

Sickness, death, and transition

One of the most dramatic events of the 1990s was the rapid deterioration of health in the transition economies, especially in Russia, with rising mortality rates and falling life expectancy. In 15 transition countries, male life expectancy at birth in 2002 was lower than in 1989, and in eight of those life expectancy was still falling from 2000 to 2002. Russian men are expected to live as many years as men from Nepal and have a life expectancy shorter than men in Bangladesh and Bolivia (WDI, 2004).

How did it happen so fast? A population that is essentially healthy can weather a few years of economic disruption without massive increases in mortality and morbidity. The rapid decline suggests that the population was already at the margins of adequate nutrition and good health. Just as the state and the economy collapsed from prior weaknesses, the health of the people in the 1990s reflected frailties that had developed in earlier decades.

There is a low-grade ideological debate behind the explanations for the health crisis in the former socialist countries. Some people with loyalty to a socialist tradition are inclined to blame the transition for the rapid decline in the health of the population. In contrast, supporters of transition, deflecting criticism from the clumsiness and corruption of the reforms, attribute rising mortality to unhealthy lifestyles and, hence, individual behaviors. Both sides are a bit off the mark, and the implications of both arguments are somewhat dangerous.

For critics of reform, it is important to distinguish between the aspirations of socialists and social democrats around the world and the actual operation of the socialist economies in the Soviet era. The Soviet Union and its allies, in spite of some remarkable achievements in economic growth and some social indices, left ruined economies, contaminated environments, and dispirited peoples. It will take more than a lifetime to rebuild the soul of those communities, suspicious and fearful of anyone, even sometimes family members. Production and distribution depended on a web of legal and illegal institutions that, with the withdrawal of the state, left the economy to organized crime, already apprenticed in the Soviet era. The socialist governments did offer national health programs, and official data suggest good access to health care services, but bribes were often necessary to obtain prompt and adequate care (Cockerham, 1997).

Ignoring the conditions that precipitated transition makes it harder now to identify a path that is both workable and just. Even mortality data show a class gradient before transition, and the effect of educational advantages carries over into the transition era. Educational differences in mortality are at least as great in Russia as in Western countries and were so even during Soviet era. During transition, there is evidence of widening of socioeconomic differences in mortality, including a large increase in alcohol-related deaths. Alcohol consumption varies significantly with educational level, and that difference widened during the 1990s. The larger differences in mortality rates between classes are not only in directly alcohol-related causes, such as injuries and violence, but also for infectious and parasitic diseases. Census data from the mid-1990s indicate that educational differences in mortality widened by 15 to 20 percent (Shkolnikov et al., 1998).

Economic reform, even with political reform, is not a panacea, however, especially if it is conducted in such a way as to worsen the condition of poor people. As in sub-Saharan Africa and Latin America, structural adjustment carried out at the expense of the working population is mean-spirited and short-sighted. The success of economic reform itself is hobbled by inequities in the process, evident in countries like Argentina that were hailed as economic miracles but later collapsed. In the context of our study of the epidemics of HIV in the transition economies, it is especially problematic that defenders of the transition have emphasized individual lifestyle choices in assessing the mortality impact of the transition, as though the increasing mortality were not directly related to the economic, political, and social processes before and during transition.

It is a peculiar aspect of the health crisis in the region that the burden of morbidity and mortality seems to be falling more on adult males. Populations in crisis usually see a rise, or at least slower improvement, in infant and child mortality rates. Child and maternal health are most immediately affected by declining health services, but children and women have fared better than men in the transition economies (Suhrcke, 2000). The most dramatic declines in life expectancy for men were in Russia and the Ukraine, which were accelerations of the trend during the Soviet era (Adeyi et al., 1997).

Adult male mortality risk, which is the likelihood of dying before the age of 65 for a boy who has reached the age of 15, is much higher in most of the former socialist economies than in the established market economies, which have an adult male mortality risk of 20 percent. In Russia, a 15-year-old male has a 55 percent chance of dying before age 65; in the Ukraine, 46 percent; in Latvia, 52 percent; in Lithuania, 46 percent; and in Estonia, 47 percent (Adeyi et al., 1997). The causes of high male mortality, particularly in the northern cluster of the former Soviet Union (the

Baltic countries, Russia, and Belarus) include alcohol, smoking, diet, pollution, and occupational hazards. A national health policy, rather than specific interventions, is probably more important in reversing negative trends in those causes (Murray and Bobadilla, 1995).

Some of the literature hints that the health crisis in the transition economies is simply the result of poor choices—bad behavior—not the consequence of transition. Even though men's health suffers from conditions precipitated through behavioral modes, that does not mean that those are not serious problems, not only for the individuals but also for society. Adult males are at least partial providers for households and have traditionally been the backbone of heavy industry, construction, and certain trades. Unhealthy men are a grave burden on their families, whether that ill health is physical or mental. Alcoholic and drug-addicted men abuse their wives and children and pass on tuberculosis and STDs, including HIV, to them. In a more sympathetic sense, too, it must be recognized that the unhealthy behaviors of men are the symptoms of a crushing and collapsing social and economic system. The same patriarchal system that afforded men advantages in the past retards their ability to adapt their attitudes and be flexible in the face of changing circumstances. Their prior advantages do not obviate the need to remedy the situation for them and for their families.

There has been so much emphasis in international health, and rightly so, on the health of the most vulnerable—women and children—that there is some danger of overlooking the importance of health problems of adult males. It is compounded by the assignment of individual blame for poor health. The increases in accidents, homicide, suicide, alcohol-, fat-, and tobacco-related morbidity and mortality are "all occurring within the context of a ravaged healthcare system" (Shaw et al., 1999, 220). The increase in mortality slowed in 1995 to 1998, but since 1999, the rate is again rising for almost all the main causes of death. Four times as many men die during the working years as women, which should have serious implications for the return to investment in human capital. The excess mortality of working-age males is a long-standing problem. Life expectancy for men reached its highest level in Russia in 1986/1987 when it was 70 years (Zbarskaya, 2002).

The emphasis on alcohol puts the focus on behavior and on the individual rather than on a social crisis of enormous proportions. It is essential to ask what is causing suicidal levels of drinking behavior. In the case of the transition economies, stereotypes of the rough, hard-drinking Russian male are as dangerous as the stereotype of the lusty African. We lose sight of the people in the throes of a health crisis. The emphasis on behaviors carries over to the HIV/AIDS epidemics. Is this an epidemic we can dismiss as behavior-related, with stereotypes about sex workers and drug users and alcoholics, and address with last-minute behavior modification? Or is the exponentially increasing HIV epidemic an indicator of profound needs to be addressed throughout the transition societies?

The threats to health caused or exacerbated by the transition in Eastern Europe and the former Soviet Union are not generally the same as those in Africa, Asia, and Latin America. But those regions are not homogeneous either. There is as much difference between Haiti and Costa Rica or Chile as there is between Belarus and Hungary. Between world regions there are both similarities and differences. Poor and declining nutrition, lack of access to health care and medications, and exposure to infectious diseases are elements common to some countries in all the regions. Parasites are not ubiquitous in the northern latitude countries as they are in the tropical and subtropical countries of the developing world. But in their place are the health-damaging effects of alcohol and drug abuse, TB, and trafficking of women and children. As in the developing world, HIV interventions limited to clean needles and condoms abandon millions of people to increasingly unhealthy lives.

III

Derailment of HIV/AIDS Research

7

Racial Metaphors

Interpreting Sex and AIDS in Africa

Over 50 years ago, Gunnar Myrdal observed that cultural influences "pose the questions we ask; influence the facts we seek; [and] determine the interpretation we give these facts" (Myrdal, 1944, 92). He continued: "Biases in research . . . are not valuations *attached* to research but rather they *permeate* research . . . [and] insinuate themselves into research in all stages, from its planning to its final presentation" (Myrdal, 1944, 1043). By the 1980s it was widely recognized that science "is a socially embedded activity" and that culture "influences what we see and how we see it" (Gould, 1981, 21–22), and by the 1990s, postmodernists would challenge even the possibility of social explanation (Bonnell and Hunt, 1999). Although that cultural debate has raged for half a century, it has been absent in most of the AIDS literature of the past 20 years.

The AIDS-in-Africa discourse in most scholarly journals and books and also in policy documents has not examined its assumptions and sources critically, and the explicit or implicit depiction has often been indistinguishable from popular notions of "what everyone knows" about Africans. This chapter examines widely cited works that framed the discussion of AIDS in Africa and the cultural influences that permeate that research. It also examines some later examples of the Western portrayal of an exotic and exceptional "Africa." A methodology that constructs dissimilarity between peoples has dominated social science research on Africa and imbues AIDS policy for poor countries.

Why has mainstream epidemiology had so little influence on AIDS discourse?

As discussed in chapters 2 and 3, mainstream epidemiology has long acknowledged the role of host factors, including poverty, in promoting disease transmission. Like other infectious diseases, HIV is more easily transmitted to persons whose immune systems are compromised by the effects of poverty. The characteristic that most readily and visibly distinguishes sub-Saharan Africa from Europe and North America is widespread poverty. When an explanation was sought for the rapid spread of HIV in sub-Saharan Africa, however, the standard epidemiological cofactors in disease transmission (malnutrition, parasite load, access to health care, etc.) were generally overlooked.

The implicit, and often explicit, assumption of AIDS policy is that differences in behavior adequately determine differences in HIV prevalence between populations. Given that HIV is sexually transmitted, some emphasis on behavior was appropriate, and there were some valid reasons why early policy focused on sexual behavior. First, in industrialized countries, behavior-modification programs were quite successful in slowing the spread of HIV. Second, early in the epidemic, population-control groups—whose focus and method are behavioral—were among the few organizations to address the emerging AIDS crisis. Third, a behavioral emphasis seemed to offer a quick solution. Concerned and compassionate policy makers and analysts saw distribution of condoms and AIDS education as the quickest barriers they could place between people who were infected with HIV and those who were not.

An explanation of the huge difference in HIV prevalence between North America or Europe and Africa that centers on the difference in sexual behavior, however, depends on epic rates of sexual partner change in Africa for which empirical support is lacking. Numerous books from reputable publishers, articles in established academic journals, and publications of international organizations replayed the same theme, without evaluating the reasonableness of a model that attributed rates of HIV in Africa that were 25 to 1,000 times those in the rest of the world to differences in behavior. Not all of the AIDS literature explicitly claimed that higher rates of HIV could be attributed to higher rates of sexual activity and partner change. Some did (see Caldwell et al., 1989; Ford, 1994; Rushing, 1995; UNFPA, 1999—discussed below), but others merely left that impression by the minimal attention paid to other factors. This chapter tells the meta-story of those works. The behavioral paradigm not only distorts an understanding of the causes of high rates of HIV in poor populations, but it also limits policy options to end-game behavior modification. That is the only option that remains when all other factors are ignored.

The dominance of the behavioral paradigm in spite of the absence of empirical support derives to a great extent from the overwhelming influence of long-standing Western stereotypes of Africans as a special case. Persistent notions of racial difference suffused the social science literature on AIDS in Africa, especially in the first 15 years of the epidemic. No one used the word *race*, but it entered into the discourse as *culture*. HIV prevalence is attributed to cultural characteristics that are assumed to be common to 700 million people from hundreds of language and ethnic groups. That supposedly homogeneous cultural zone is coincident in its boundaries with a region identified with blackness in the Western view. No other mapping of language, religion, agricultural systems, genetics, economic systems, or systems of land tenure fits. Notions of race and racial difference cannot be separated from any Western discourse that treats African culture as a "seamless whole" (Caldwell and Caldwell, 1987, 410), as it has been portrayed in the behavioral literature.

Centuries-old stereotypes that emphasize exotic and exceptional sexuality encumber the attempt to understand the intensity of the HIV/AIDS epidemic in sub-Saharan Africa. The explanation for African AIDS emerged from a characterization of Africans as the social "Other," vastly different from Europeans in culture and social norms. That was aggravated by the tendency for writings about Africa, academic and journalistic, to consist of a "repertoire of amazing facts" (Coetzee, 1988, 13). The portrayal of Africans as a special case contributed to the emphasis in research and policy on individual behavior instead of on the ecology of disease in poor populations.[1]

Here we examine some key works on fertility preference and on AIDS in Africa that influenced much subsequent research and policy. The intellectual and cultural legacy imbedded in those works determined the questions they asked and the facts they sought, as well as the interpretation they gave to the facts. In critiquing those works, I address in particular the use of metaphor in filtering and distorting observations and the use of suggestive language to make implied comparisons that are not supported with data. The legacy of those works is evident in current social science research. Recent works and the impact of the behavioral paradigm on policy are addressed in subsequent sections.

1. An important exception in the social science literature is an article by Packard and Epstein (1991). The authors do an excellent job of critiquing racist influence on AIDS research. Citations to the article do not appear elsewhere in this chapter or in the book because I had finished writing the book when I first saw the article. In the same issue, in fact beginning on the same page on which their article ended, *Social Science and Medicine* published five sets of lengthy comments. The first, and most vituperative, was written by someone who was himself engaged in the kind of anthropological research Packard and Epstein were criticizing. I checked over a decade of all issues of *Social Science and Medicine* and I found no other article that had such a barrage of comment appearing in the same issue.

Foundations of the behavioral model of AIDS in Africa

The assurance with which social scientists and policy makers, as well as the general public, have referred to the impact of high rates of sexual partner change on AIDS in Africa would suggest a wealth of data from a broad array of sources. In fact, most assertions about African sexuality cite the same sources, which are based on ethnographic reports of varying reliability, many of which date from the early twentieth century. The articles cited most widely in the social science and policy literature on the African AIDS epidemic were published in 1987 and 1989 by John Caldwell and Pat Caldwell of the Australian National University (the latter article with Pat Quiggin). These two articles were cited by other authors over 200 times from 1988 to 2001 in the journals surveyed by *Social Science Citation Index* and many more times in influential books and policy documents of international organizations. Of the numerous books, book chapters, field reports, and articles written by the Caldwells, alone or with others, these two articles play a central role in the AIDS-in-Africa literature and thus warrant extended analysis. The influence of that ethnographic approach pervades the AIDS discourse.

The Caldwells spent many years in fertility research in Africa. The stated objective of the 1987 article was to explain how "African" religious views impede the aims of population-control programs.[2] They write: "It is the argument of this essay that these lineage-based systems are so coherent that they will offer greater resistance to the success of family planning programs than has been encountered elsewhere" (Caldwell and Caldwell, 1987, 410). Their 1989 article with Quiggin uses the arguments developed in the Caldwells's 1987 work on African fertility to explain "The Social Context of AIDS in Sub-Saharan Africa." In the 1989 article, Caldwell et al. repeatedly offer the caution that their data are very limited, scattered, or pertain only to a limited region (pp. 194 twice, 195, 198, 199, 206, 210, 212, 214, 215, and others).[3] Nevertheless, they propose a very sweeping

2. According to the authors, much of the financial support for their 1987 article came from the Population Council: "The present essay draws more heavily on the authors' own research experience, especially in research projects conducted in Ghana in 1962–64, Nigeria in 1969, Kenya in 1969–70, Nigeria in 1971–72, and on the Changing African Family Project's field work carried out in Nigeria during 1973 and in other parts of Africa in subsequent years (all funded by the Population Council), and on the Nigerian Family Study of 1974–75 and 1977 (funded by the Population Council and the Australian National University)" (Caldwell and Caldwell, 1987, 434, Notes). Between 1968 and 2000, 35 articles by one or both of the Caldwells were published in journals produced by the Population Council—20 in *Population and Development Review* and 15 in *Studies in Family Planning*.

3. The 1987 and 1989 articles are based on their 1985 report for the World Bank (Caldwell and Caldwell, 1985). The 1987 article states: "The full range of evidence that

view of the whole of Africa as an "alternative civilization—very different in its workings, including its patterns of sexual behaviour" (Caldwell et al., 1989, 185).[4]

The underlying theme of the 1987 and 1989 articles, repeated in later works as well, is that African sexuality is a special case. Essentially, Caldwell et al. argue that a religious world view dominates the choices that African people make regarding fertility, that this world view is almost universal in sub-Saharan Africa, that it weakens conjugal bonds in favor of lineage (because of ancestor worship), and thus it accounts for high rates of partner change and the consequent higher rates of HIV transmission in the region.

Caldwell and Caldwell employ a foundational metaphor to convey their idea that modern-day African fertility choices derive from a religious world view that harks back to the dawn of humankind. They propose "a focus on Africa as the domain of *Homo Ancestralis* . . . [to] explain many African anomalies" (Caldwell and Caldwell, 1987, 410). Whatever their intent in employing the separate species classification of *Homo ancestralis* to refer to Africans, the metaphor inescapably brings with it the intellectual baggage of nineteenth-century racial science.[5] The metaphor is especially effective in a discussion of sexual behavior because so much of the racial difference literature of the nineteenth and early twentieth centuries focused on the sexuality of Africans (see Gould, 1981; Stepan, 1982; Stepan, 1990; Dubow,

supports the more theoretical argument developed in this essay is presented in a report prepared by the authors for the World Bank" (1987, 434, Notes), a caution repeated in two endnotes. The 1985 report, however, contains essentially the same material.

4. "Such social research [to contain AIDS] is likely to reveal a coherent society—indeed, an alternative civilization—very different in its workings, including its patterns of sexual behaviour, than outsiders prescribing cures and even offering sympathy and support often realize" (Caldwell et al., 1989, 185).

5. The metaphor is a take-off from Louis Dumont's *Homo hierarchichus* (Dumont, 1966/1980) to characterize Eurasian patriarchy. Such an approach was criticized by Montagu (1952, 7n), quoting Weidenreich: "[R]aising the differences between racial groups to the rank of specific differences by giving those groups specific names is nothing but an attempt to exaggerate the dissimilarities by the application of a taxonomic trick" (Weidenreich, 1946, 2). Though perhaps unwittingly, the Caldwell metaphor sets them apart not only from the biblical and Christian view, in which all people are recognized as children of Adam—that is, of one creation (Stepan, 1982)—but also from Linnaeus's taxonomy, in which all races are subsets of the one species, *Homo sapiens*. Linnaeus did think that the differences among peoples merited some codification and observed that *Homo sapiens europaeus* is sagacious, inventive, and ruled by customs, while *Homo sapiens afer* is negligent and ruled by caprice (Linné, 1758/1956, 21–22; my translation). The Caldwell construction makes the specific break at *Homo*. Modern biologists distinguish *Homo habilis* and *Homo neanderthalensis* from *Homo sapiens* and from modern humans, *Homo sapiens sapiens*.

1995).[6] Racial science and popular racial stereotypes stressed sexual differences between the races, and the representation of physiological differences in the portrayal of Africans in art was an important pillar maintaining the popular view of Africans as exotic, strange, and even disturbing (see Gilman, 1985; Gilman, 1990; Gilman, 1992). Notions of African sexuality are still very evident in European advertisements for the sex trade, in which women of color are categorized as exotic or "wild" (Keeler and Jyrkinen, 2002; Jacobson, 2002; Spanger, 2002).

Both the 1987 and 1989 Caldwell articles begin with the *Homo ancestralis* metaphor. Although they do not dwell on the *Homo ancestralis* theme, they have introduced the image of the primitive as the framework for everything that follows. They repeat the metaphor at the beginning of the 1989 article, thus situating their analysis of African AIDS in a social context already characterized as primeval. The premise of their interpretation of both fertility preference (1987) and HIV prevalence (1989) is that Africans are so different, their belief system so ancient, that they are inscrutable to the Western (read "modern") mind. The hundreds of works that cite Caldwell and Caldwell (1987) and Caldwell et al. (1989) do not generally repeat the metaphor explicitly, but the theme of an African sexuality that is universal (pan-African), ahistorical, and exotic carries over.

Use of metaphor in science

The use of metaphor and analogy is common in science, and not completely inappropriate. The metaphor, however, is not merely an image that summarizes facts; it acts as a filter to choose facts. It is the metaphor that helps us see similarities that the metaphor helps constitute, and it also excludes contradictory evidence: "Similarity is not something one finds but something one must establish" (Fish, 1983, 277). In the same way, I argue that Caldwell et al. construct dissimilarity between Africa and the rest of the world, by omitting commonalities among people and overlooking universalities. In order to construct a fundamental dissimilarity between peoples of different world regions, the metaphor must exclude most facts (common human traits).

Because the nuances of language are so important, the role of metaphor in science and social science merits special attention. Max Black argues that

6. Manet's *Olympia* (1863) is one example, of many, of the inclusion of a black woman servant to represent eroticism and thereby indicate that the main subject is a prostitute. The use of Africans to symbolize sexuality in art is not merely a historical artifact found in museums. The 1995 movie version of *The Scarlet Letter* by Hollywood Pictures has an extended scene that is supposed to represent Hester and Rev. Dimmesdale's tryst. The lovers slip away, and the script introduces into Nathaniel Hawthorne's story an African-American servant girl in a sensual bath scene.

metaphors are not just figurative statements (unemphatic), and he proposes the interaction view in which the metaphor "selects, emphasizes, suppresses, and organizes" data to confirm the metaphor (Black, 1979, 28–29). With the *Homo ancestralis* metaphor, information from the context of early hominids is projected onto modern Africans by implication. That projection interacts with or acts upon one's conception of modern Africans.

Black's notion of emphatic or strong metaphors is similar to Schön's (1979) "generative metaphor."[7] Generative metaphors simplify complex social situations, often reducing such complexities to normative dualisms, such as health/disease. Schön argues that metaphors define problem setting and consequently limit the directions of problem solving. Metaphor is effective because "everything one knows about [the metaphorical subject] has the potential of being brought into play. . . . There is, in this sense, great economy and high leverage in this particular kind of redescription" (Schön, 1979, 259).

Because the metaphor is metaphysical, or meta-fact, one of its most important characteristics is its nonfalsifiability. The metaphor suggests an African culture so different from that of Eurasia that it warrants a separate species classification. Like Schön's generative metaphor, "everything one knows" (or imagines) about early humans can be brought to play, if subconsciously, although the Caldwells are discussing Africans in the 1980s. Undoubtedly, they saw it as a stylistic device and would insist (rightly) that they never *said* that Africans are a different species, nor did they explicitly state the view that Africans exhibit arrested development in their fertility preference. Hence, the metaphor is nonfalsifiable, but it has accomplished the task of characterizing Africans as dramatically different, antediluvian, and sexually exceptional. Because it is nonfalsifiable, contradictory evidence (which is abundant in their articles) does not alter the image, or their conclusions.

Legacy of racial science

The *Homo ancestralis* metaphor is, indeed, economical in the multiple ways it evokes constructs of nineteenth- and early-twentieth-century racial science.[8] It is useful to review some of the notions of racial sci-

7. Not all metaphors are generative; they can be merely more interesting ways of describing subjects according to the comparison view. "She wore a mask of indifference" is suggestive but not necessarily generative. Schön would say that referring to poor neighborhoods as blighted is a generative metaphor because it presumes the nature of the problem and suggests solutions.

8. Although the Caldwells employ the constructs of racial science, I am not asserting that they do so in conscious imitation of racial science, but they should certainly have been aware of the rhetoric and categories of racial science. John Caldwell joined the

ence,[9] because its methods and concepts influence the social science mainstream today (Dubow, 1995). The grip of racist intellectual history affects the direction of social science research and the range of policy alternatives that can be considered. The weight of past theories in the popular mind and in the imagery of science is insidious and difficult to counter because so much of racial stereotyping is in the "unstated assumptions and unthinking responses" (Dubow, 1995, 7), rather than in explicit postulates. Scholars who would unequivocally reject the validity of racial science unconsciously use metaphors and suggestive language that evoke those stereotypes. This section offers a brief survey of some of the earlier constructions of race that reappeared in the AIDS literature, in constructs and concepts of taxonomy, recapitulation, arrested development, prelogical and group mentality, and sexual exceptionalism. To appreciate the impact of the *Homo ancestralis* metaphor and the portrayal of Africans as unique, which is so common in both scholarly work and journalism, it is necessary to show the parallels between this very effective image and the history of Western ideas about Africans. Precisely because of that history, the *Homo ancestralis* image is both evocative and easily accepted by the hundreds of scholars who cite these Caldwell works.

In the nineteenth century, race theorists—including mainstream scientists—broke from the accepted view of one creation and maintained that Africans were a genetically distinct species from Europeans. Scores of scientists attempted to prove genetic differences between the races by measuring cranial capacity, jaw length, and other physical characteristics. When craniometry and other physical measurement proved fruitless, they attempted to establish qualitative differences in cognitive and perceptual processes. Even many who accepted that Africans and Europeans descended from a common ancestor maintained that differentiation of the races occurred at a time before human intelligence had fully evolved. Hence the races would exhibit differences in intelligence determined by their separate evolutions. The lesser precision of this theory proved to be an advantage since, although less verifiable, it was also less falsifiable (Dubow, 1995). The *Homo ancestralis* metaphor posits an African society isolated from Eurasia from the dawn of human development and evolving, albeit slowly, according to a separate cultural model.

An early-twentieth-century notion in racial science, called recapitulation, contended that the different races represent stages of human evolution. Recapitulationists used both physical and psychological characteristics as evidence that Europeans were the highest stage of the development process

Society for the Study of Social Biology in 1974, the year after it changed its name from the American Eugenics Society (http://www.africa2000.com/ENDX/aemema.htm).

9. I refer to science, rather than pseudoscience, which might seem preferable, because racial science was considered mainstream at the time.

and Africans were an early, ancestral form of human development. Dudley Kidd, for example, in *Savage Childhood* (1906) and *Kafir Socialism* (1908), drew heavily on the eugenics literature to derive his notion of "arrested development" of Africans (Dubow, 1995, 199). In *The Essential Kafir*, Kidd assesses the "Mental Characteristics" of Africans: "The whole mental furniture of a Kafir's mind differs from that of a European. . . . The most incompatible things seem to be able to dwell together in harmony and peace in the muddy and turbid stream of his thoughts. . . . His conceptions of cause and effect are hopelessly at sea, and . . . his religion is a confused mass of ancestor-worship coupled with dread of magic" (Kidd, 1904, 277).

The Caldwells employ a recapitulationist conception of the development of cultures, arguing that "[t]he cult of the ancestors is not unique to sub-Saharan Africa. It may well have been the original religion of most of mankind" (Caldwell and Caldwell, 1987, 409). The portrayal of African society is starkly ahistorical; modern Africans appear in the narrative as adherents to a culture that has been superseded elsewhere by Eurasian patriarchy obsessed with controlling female sexuality.[10] They assert that, across the continent, Africans preserve a view of sex lost in the Eurasian world from which Africa was isolated by geography and time.

In the early twentieth century, as the fields of anthropology and psychology increasingly found common ground, the measurement of racial differences focused on understanding "the primitive mentality." Lévy-Bruhl argued, in *How Natives Think* (1926), that the ideas of "natives" had to be understood as collective representations: that is, their thinking could only be analyzed at the level of the group rather than as independent thought of individuals. He described the mental processes of Africans as "fundamentally mystical, emotional or 'prelogical' " (Dubow, 1995, 203). Although Lévy-Bruhl has been discredited on a number of grounds, his ideas find expression in the AIDS-in-Africa literature. Caldwell et al. (1989, 195) cite Little (1973) as having "concluded that Africa has a different view of sexual relations." This borderless, personless "Africa" (rather than individual Africans) is strikingly like Lévy-Bruhl's conception of native mentality that could be understood only at the level of the group.

The image of African-Americans that prevailed in the United States mirrored the contemporary European view of Africans. Robert Bennett Bean, then chair of the department of anatomy at the University of Virginia (1916–1942), wrote: "The Negro [possesses] . . . an instability of character incident to lack of self-control, especially in connection with the sexual relation" (Bean, 1906, cited in Gould, 1981, 70). The same kind of racist

10. The Caldwells repeatedly use the reference to Eurasian patriarchy as a preemptive attack on criticism (1989, 185, 186, 193, 194). In a 1991 article, Caldwell et al. respond to measured criticism of their work by Le Blanc et al. (1991) by misconstruing what the critics say and asserting that any critics are in the thrall of Eurasian patriarchy.

exceptionalizing of Africans that characterized nineteenth- and twentieth-century theories of racial difference continues to crop up in the 1980s to the present in the literature on African AIDS.

Racial science, social Darwinism, eugenics, and social hygiene theories had political as well as academic functions and were espoused by both conservatives and reformers. Conservatives argued for harsh poor laws, and reformers relied on social hygiene theories to promote population control among the poor. Similarly, the *Homo ancestralis* metaphor, as with all metaphors in science, defines the parameters of research and policy options (Schön's problem setting). By framing AIDS in Africa as something that results from an exotic and exceptional sexuality, it has restricted the scope of acceptable research to sexual behavior (and social phenomena that influence partner change, such as migration and gender relations) and circumscribed the actions taken to address the epidemic (problem solving). Consequently, AIDS policy does not reflect the extensive research findings linking HIV transmission and parasite infection, malnutrition, and other biological conditions explained here in chapters 2 and 3.

The metaphor versus data: Homo ancestralis *and modern Africans*

A metaphor has suggestive power and is more flexible than a factual statement in that it begins with an image but relies on "conceptual displacement" for maintaining the analogy. The difference between African and European cultures is "first taken to be *like* distinctions among biological species" (Lang, 1997, 19) and then it assumes the power of a literal statement.[11] The use of the word *ancestralis* in the *Homo ancestralis* metaphor imbues the two articles with an inescapable image of an early human or hominid, although Caldwell et al. are writing about modern Africans. Since it is meta-fact, variations among African societies and changes over time are rendered unimportant.

Furedi (1997) ably critiques the ahistorical nature of the Caldwell analysis, but the *Homo ancestralis* trope is more than ahistorical. The metaphor achieves what Turbayne calls sort-crossing, when "the use of a metaphor involves the pretense that something is the case when it is not" (Turbayne, 1962, 13). Clearly, the very power of this metaphor is in its suggestiveness; it conjures the image of twentieth-century Africans operating in a cultural

11. Lang was not referring to the Caldwell metaphor, but applying Lang's designation of metaphysical racism seems appropriate. Lang characterizes metaphysical racism as not based on genetic traits or even cultural homogeneity, which would be falsifiable, and uses another very evocative metaphor, "biological warfare by other means," to describe such works (Lang, 1997, 17).

world that Europeans and Asians had left in the far recesses of our common past, so long ago that we have to refer to it in italics and in Latin.

Another aspect of this portrayal of "African" fertility and sexuality is its polarity or dichotomy, as is common with generative metaphors (Schön, 1979, 266). Nineteenth-century racialism consistently posed Africans as antithetical to Europeans and specifically applied that dichotomization to sexuality (Stepan, 1990; Gilman, 1992). Caldwell and Caldwell assert that Africa alone defies the developmental model of fertility change employed in World Bank and United Nations studies (Caldwell and Caldwell, 1987, 414). In that model, a demographic transition toward lower death rates and lower birth rates accompanies economic growth, a pattern that has been observed in many parts of the world. Caldwell and Caldwell (1985; 1987) pose the fertility issue instead as a dichotomy between Africa and the rest of the world. As proof of Africa's anomalous behavior, they argue that several African countries had incomes and levels of education and urbanization higher than India and yet did not achieve the rates of fertility decline that India did in the 1970s. They fail to mention, however, that the Indian government carried out a campaign of forced sterilization.[12]

To support their hypothesis that an ancient religious view determines modern Africans' decisions regarding fertility and sexual partnering, Caldwell et al. offer evidence from the economic and social context of modern Africa. To do this, they have to adapt and distort data and to reject other data to fit the *Homo ancestralis* metaphor (see Stepan, 1990, for the use of metaphor to create new knowledge and suppress knowledge.)

Adapting data

The Caldwells begin from the position that African fertility preference is anomalous (Caldwell and Caldwell, 1987) and determined by a religious belief system of ancestor worship. Yet their examples repeatedly show pragmatic, economic reasons for high African fertility, including high infant mortality, the importance of family size in the reallocation of village land, the economic insecurity of childless women, and upward intergenerational flow of wealth. Nevertheless, they dismiss the rational economic choices people make in the face of those factors and attribute higher fertility to ancestor worship.

12. While acknowledging the role of economic factors in fertility transition, the Caldwells reiterate the dichotomous view of Africa versus the rest of the world in a 2002 article. Referring to Asian countries that experienced a fertility decline before African countries with similar human development indices, they comment: "This finding merely adds another item to the list of those that set sub-Saharan Africa apart" (Caldwell and Caldwell, 2002, 77).

Distorting data

Their characterization of Africans as driven by fear of ancestral spirits prevents the Caldwells from acknowledging important health concerns voiced by the women they interviewed. Like Lévy-Bruhl, they maintain that the women's mental processes are prelogical. They report that the women complained of excessive bleeding with IUDs, a particularly serious problem for women in poor countries where many, if not most, are already anemic. But the Caldwells conclude: "There can be little doubt that the dominant element in these reactions is a general apprehension of contraception rather than the specific case against any individual method: the fears are related to the taint of evil that attaches to innovative fertility control" (Caldwell and Caldwell, 1987, 425). They distort the women's reasonable concerns to fit their image of a primitive people ruled by "ancestor-worship coupled with a dread of magic," as Kidd described "Kafir" religion (Kidd, 1904, 277).[13]

To support their argument that peculiarly high rates of premarital sexual activity are among the elements of "the social context of AIDS in sub-Saharan Africa," they quote Laughlin and Laughlin (1973) regarding "the Ugandan So: "A man is allowed to have as many premarital sexual contacts as he desires; however, the upward limit among our informants was six, with the more frequent number being one or two" (Caldwell et al., 1989, 211). A modal frequency of one or two premarital sexual contacts cannot explain a heterosexual epidemic such as Uganda's. Yet the sequence of clauses in the quoted sentence emphasizes the notion of limitlessness, rather than the reality of few contacts among those surveyed, and conveys the image of sexual license.

Rejecting data

The construction of Africans as completely different from non-Africans requires one to reject information about the rest of the world that demonstrates the commonalities among peoples, including the similarities of people's responses to issues of fertility. For example, family pressure on young wives to bear children and a double standard regarding sex (Caldwell and Caldwell, 1987) are not peculiar to Africa. To show that an overpowering, religious conception of fertility sets Africans apart, the Caldwells (1985; 1987) report at length that Africans refer to children as a blessing from God. But even a very cursory survey of greeting cards for the birth of a child in other world regions would find that a large proportion refer to the child as God's blessing. In most cultures—perhaps all—children are seen as a blessing, and infertility is seen as a misfortune.

13. *Kafir* is not a polite word but a racial slur.

In their 1985 report to the World Bank, Caldwell and Caldwell give an example that is supposed to show how exceptionally (quoting Martin Southwold, they say "hysterically," p. 15) preoccupied with fertility Africans are. They quote Fortes (1959): " 'If, as happens only too often, a young wife loses her babies one after another by miscarriage or in early infancy, she becomes chronically miserable and dejected, and her husband too, for that matter' " (Caldwell and Caldwell, 1985, 14–15). Is there any society where a woman is not likely to become depressed under such circumstances, and her husband too?

One would think the Caldwells are writing tongue-in-cheek, as in Horace Miner's classic satire of anthropology, "Body Ritual among the Nacirema" (1956), in which he describes common U.S. hygiene practices (such as brushing teeth) as though they were truly exotic. But it is clear that the Caldwells and others who follow in their footsteps are quite serious when they report practices and emotions that span the globe as though they were uniquely African and then attribute the African AIDS epidemic to African cultural idiosyncrasy. These examples are part of the construction of Africans as the "Other" and maintain the myth of hypersexualized Africans with an illogical fertility preference whose anomalous behavior can only be transformed by outside agents. They are portrayed as "timeless societies" for which all sources of change are exogenous (Lutz and Collins, 1993, 108), as well as ritual performers, "living in the sacred (some would say superstitious) world" (Lutz and Collins, 1993, 90).[14]

In a 1993 article, the Caldwells radically alter their methodology and their conclusions. Building on the work of Bongaarts et al. (1989) and Moses et al. (1990) and others, and without recanting their own earlier works, they conclude that differences in sexual behavior alone cannot adequately explain differentials in rates of HIV and AIDS in Africa. Rather, HIV transmission in high-prevalence areas of sub-Saharan Africa is fueled to a great extent by lack of male circumcision and the high prevalence of ulcerative genital disease, which is promoted by lack of male circumcision, lack of access to health care services, and limited access to water for personal hygiene (Caldwell and Caldwell, 1993). In a later article, however, John Caldwell returns to his 1987 and 1989 formula. He asks, "Just how different is Africa?" (Caldwell, 2000, 119) and seeks to explain why behavior-change

14. Lutz and Collins were critiquing *National Geographic*'s portrayal of world cultures. It is an unfortunate result of an anthropological approach that, in the study of humans, what are emphasized are differences rather than commonalities. As an economist, I am aware that my discipline's greatest strength is also its greatest flaw. Economists generalize about the choices that people make when faced with the problem of scarcity. We assume that all people are essentially the same, and that is a good starting point. In making those generalizations, however, economics has often been guilty of overlooking the differences in power that constrain choices for some people.

approaches have been so little tried and so unsuccessful there. He lists (1) higher levels of extramarital sexual activity, (2) high levels of prostitution, (3) resulting levels of STDs, (4) lack of treatment for STDs, and (5) low level of condom use as the reasons for high prevalence of HIV in Africa. For East and Southern Africa, he adds lack of male circumcision. Unfortunately, the work most referred to in the policy literature is not the Caldwells' useful 1993 contribution, but their assertions of African sexual exceptionalism, grounded in their *Homo ancestralis* construction in the 1987 and 1989 articles that was motivated by their intent to explain "African resistance" to population-control projects.

The Caldwells (1985; 1987; 1989; and others) offer copious ethnographic data. Although they make for absorbing stories, they do not make a case for a pan-African culture of fertility so distinct from everywhere else that it explains the prevalence of HIV in sub-Saharan Africa as is claimed by the hundreds of scholars and policy makers who cite the Caldwells in the AIDS literature.

Once HIV prevalence in Africa had been "explained" with such hypothetical models—that is, once the metaphor had been accepted—the work of dealing with the pandemic seemed straightforward. Subsequent analyses began from the assumption that, in Africa, "having multiple sexual partners is a common cultural practice" (Rushing, 1995, 60). The task of social science then was investigating the economic, legal, and other factors that interacted with that presumed cultural norm. The lack of comparative data correlating HIV prevalence with rates of sexual partner change was apparently overlooked. The use of suggestive language conveyed the desired message without having to provide evidence.

◣ *Reflections of the sexuality paradigm in AIDS discourse*

The construction of exceptional African behavior, particularly with respect to sexuality, continues to the present day in AIDS discourse. Some works are heavily influenced by the Caldwell/Quiggin metaphor and explicitly repeat the assertion that extraordinary levels of multipartnered sex are the primary cause of the severity of the AIDS epidemic in Africa. Other works often cite the Caldwells and use a similar methodology that filters and interprets facts to suggest fundamental differences between Africans and others. Even recent works perpetuate the construction of primordial dissimilarity between Africa and the rest of the world by describing common attitudes, behaviors, and events as though they were peculiarly African. Finally, policy documents of international and bilateral aid organizations might not explicitly state that behavior is the primary factor, but they promote only behavior modification for HIV prevention and therefore must be seen as implicitly accepting the primacy of differences in sexual activity in explaining differences in rates of HIV. A few examples of each category are examined below.

Works that assert higher rates of multipartnered sex in Africa

William Rushing provides a good illustration of the way the Caldwell/Quiggin hypothetical argument can be used in a pyramid scheme of African-sexuality studies. In *The AIDS Epidemic: Social Dimensions of an Infectious Disease* (1995), Rushing cites Caldwell et al. (1989) as proof that "[e]thnographic studies leave no doubt that having multiple sexual partners is a common cultural practice in many groups in Africa (Caldwell et al., 1989, 205–16; . . .)" (Rushing, 1995, 60), thereby converting their hypothesis into proven fact. Rushing relies heavily on Caldwell et al. (1989), but he strips it of all qualifying phrases, and he makes selective, almost surgical, use of other works to support his portrayal of a pan-African culture of sex as a commodity.

Rushing argues that "a major reason for the pattern of HIV-AIDS in Africa" is the way that "sexual expression is structured . . . in African societies, or 'tribes' "[15] (Rushing, 1995, 60). Rushing adopts the Caldwell construction of a pan-African sexuality: "Certain cultural features are common to most African tribal groups, including the social meaning of sex and the way it is expressed" (Rushing, 1995, 61), again citing Caldwell et al., 1989. The first common cultural feature Rushing asserts is that polygyny produces weak conjugal bonds (cites Caldwell et al., 1989) and so extramarital sex is common, normal, and even expected (again citing Caldwell et al., 1989).

The second pan-African cultural trait, according to Rushing, is that "most Africans . . . enter into sex more casually and have more sexual partners than Westerners do" (Rushing, 1995, 62), although that statement is made without data or citations. He continues: "The cultural beliefs and norms that do bear most directly on sex are the transactional element in sexual relations, a masculine sexual ideology, and sex-positive beliefs" (Rushing, 1995, 62) and argues, "Traditional sexual ethics are similar to those that regulate other services, namely, the ethics of exchange (Caldwell et al., 1989, 194, 209, 218). Sexual relations are characterized by a 'transactional element' (Caldwell et al., 1989, 202–205), which is especially explicit in the traditional marriage" (Rushing, 1995, 63). Rushing does not present this as a universal human trait, as transactional psychologists or microeconomists might, or as a universal feature of heterosexual relations as some radical feminists might; rather, he presents it as an African trait. In essence, Rushing makes the very bald claim that all sex in Africa, but not elsewhere, is prostitution.

Many of Rushing's unconditional assertions have no citations. Others

15. The designation "tribe" is considered an inappropriate term by many Africans.

are blanket statements, such as, "[b]y all accounts, prostitution is widespread in African cities" (Rushing, 1995, 71) with citations to the same few sources, including Little (1973) and Caldwell et al. (1989). He concludes that transmission of HIV in Africa and among gays in the West depends on "sex in which multiple partners are common. In each instance, therefore, the environment—the behavior of the host population—is largely responsible for the high prevalence of HIV-AIDS and its distribution between males and females" (Rushing, 1995, 85).

Rushing and others who emphasize a "transactional element" see it as an aspect of an "African" culture that includes pan-African sexual attitudes. They seem unaware, however, of similar messages in non-African cultures. One feature of "African culture" listed in many works as contributing to the spread of HIV is the dependence of young women on "sugar daddies," which no doubt occurs. But to purport that the commoditization of sex is peculiar to Africa is naive. Transactional sex is not the norm anywhere, but its existence in rich countries is overlooked even though it is discussed openly. The U.S. beauty magazine, *Allure*, marketed to teenagers and young women, ran a feature article entitled "Tricks for Treats" that was an instruction manual for securing expensive gifts from wealthy men through sex (Bachrach, 2002). Does *Allure*'s monthly circulation of 1 million copies signal that transactional sex is the norm in the United States? Teens', women's, and men's magazines in the United States frequently publish articles about nonmonogamous and nonmarital sex. Very often the title is a come-on, and the article conveys a mixed message, in much the same way that many Africans signal a mixture of bravado and conservatism in their statements about sex and sexuality.

Another "African" cultural view reported by Rushing, but also by the Caldwells and many others, is "a masculine sexual ideology"—the notion that men must have many sexual partners to be satisfied. Yet, they miss in their own countries the ubiquitous messages in that regard. Advertising and the cinema often perpetuate the notion that men have or need virtually limitless premarital or extramarital sexual pairings. One U.S. beer commercial shows the numbers on an odometer spinning in a man's mind as he tries to count up his previous sexual contacts. It is the sort of message that would easily be overlooked because it is just background noise in one's own culture, but it seems so blatant (and exotic) when expressed in the cultural context of another land. Cultural artifacts, such as the American blues song, "You Got to Have More Than One Woman (If You're Gonna Get Along)," recorded by Tim Hardin in 1967, are insufficient evidence that polygyny is widespread in the United States. Anyone looking for limitless multipartnered sex will find "data" in sub-Saharan Africa, just as any foreign censor of American or French advertising, movies, magazines, and music can find ample proof of generalized "Western decadence," if that is what is sought. With those data, however, we are no closer to understanding a generalized epidemic of HIV in one region than in the other.

The Caldwell works are standard references for African sexuality studies, and their uncritical use is common, as in an article by Philipson and Posner (1995). The authors admit that they are not African specialists, but rational-choice theorists who had applied their method to the AIDS epidemic in the United States. Their methodology is interesting, and some of their policy recommendations for Africa are appropriate, such as educating women and targeting STDs. But on the basis of very little information about Africa, they declare: "We now explain the course of the disease in Africa and the differences from the experience in the United States" (Philipson and Posner, 1995, 836). As rational-choice economists whose work focuses on the United States, where did they get their information about the course of HIV in Africa? Of the 37 footnotes (excluding purely explanatory notes or references to data sets), nine refer to the Caldwell/Quiggin works and eight to themselves. It would be comforting to think that nobody pays attention to unsupported broadsides about African sexuality, but the authors express their appreciation for the helpful comments of "participants in a seminar at the World Bank, where an earlier version of this paper was presented" (Philipson and Posner, 1995, 845).

As in so many other works on this subject, the use of language is very important in conveying an impression about African sexuality, rather than quantifying its contribution to HIV transmission. One way is to use a categorical statement in the text that is modified in an endnote. Philipson and Posner state: "Another factor contributing to the later peak of the disease in Africa is the greater prevalence of female prostitution there than in Europe and North America" (Philipson and Posner, 1995, 838). This statement is followed by an endnote that reads in part: "We are not aware of any reliable worldwide census of prostitutes. The statement in the text is therefore conjectural, but it appears to be well supported. See especially Caldwell and Caldwell, . . ." (Philipson and Posner, 1995, 846 n22).

Moving from formal prostitution to other forms of sexual interaction, the authors state: "The frequency of nonmarital sex in Africa appears to be very high by world standards" (Philipson and Posner, 1995, 840). The citation for that is Caldwell et al. (1989). "The frequency appears to be high" is not a phrase commonly used in statistical analyses about other parts of the world, at least not in ones that get a hearing at the World Bank and get published in prominent academic journals. And the authors build from there. Having "established" the prevalence of prostitution, they use it to explain the male–female ratio and the overall prevalence of HIV, considering only behavioral factors. A wider reading of the literature would have uncovered the biological reasons why women are more vulnerable to transmission than men in heterosexual relations, which is certainly an important variable in explaining the male–female ratio.

The intention of these authors is surely not to perpetuate racial stereotypes. Many Westerners have little correct information about Africa, and they rely on experts whose views seem plausible because they resonate in the Western mind. By conventional standards, the Caldwells qualify as experts because they have published scores of articles, and the large number of citations in each article makes their argument seem well founded, or at least daunting. Citing the Caldwells has become pro forma in the 1990s and the 2000s, although some of their evidence is anecdotal and some of it dates from the 1920s. The same ethnographic reports appear in many of their articles, many of the works they cite date from the colonial era, some are of dubious scholarly value, and many do not provide data relevant to their hypothesis.[16] In spite of the plethora of citations, subsequent authors should critically examine the claim of African exceptionalism.

Nicholas Ford is another author who has argued explicitly that the difference in rates of multipartnered sex is the crucial variable in explaining the "global pattern of the transmission of HIV/AIDS" (Ford, 1994, 84). He asserts that "HIV transmission has been much faster in societies where there are high levels of unprotected sexual interaction with prostitutes, who have very many sexual partners, than in societies where the majority of people have few or moderate numbers of partners in their lifetime" (Ford, 1994, 88). Such a statement could be a hypothesis with a ceteris paribus condition: all other things being equal, two countries otherwise identical (in income distribution, gender relations, migration patterns, nutrition, access to health care, etc.) will differ in their rates of HIV according to difference in their rates of sexual partner change. As a hypothesis to be tested, the statement works. But Ford does not offer any data to show that countries with higher rates of HIV have higher levels of unprotected multipartnered sex. Instead of data, he offers speculation and generalizations, such as, "in parts of Africa, Asia and Latin America rapid social change may be expected to have had an impact upon patterns of sexual interaction" and "[i]t is often held that one of the effects of modernization in Africa has been the dismantling of many of the traditional constraints on pre-marital sexual activity" (Ford, 1994, 88). Those statements could be true, although he offers no evidence, but are hardly a basis for health policy, since the dismantling of many of the traditional constraints on premarital sexual activity in the United States and Europe has not led to a heterosexual epidemic of HIV. Finally, Ford offers Thailand as a case study of HIV/AIDS in all of the developing world. He fails to mention that Thailand is a highly

16. The 1985 report for the World Bank provides the "full range of evidence" (Caldwell and Caldwell, 1987, 434, Notes) for the 1987 article, which they, in turn, cite as the foundation of the 1989 work (Caldwell et al., 1989, 185). The works cited in the 1985 report include approximately 25 from 1920 to 1960, 17 from the 1960s, 30 from the 1970s and 25 more from a 1973 collection of earlier works, 30 from the 1980s, and 42 citations of their own works. In 1985, when the Caldwells cited field reports from the early 1970s, they were roughly contemporary. Authors who cite the Caldwells in the late 1990s or now are using data that are at least 30 years old.

idiosyncratic case. The extent of injecting drug use and the existence of an export-oriented sex industry make Thailand quite irrelevant for drawing conclusions about AIDS in Africa or Latin America.[17]

The United Nations Population Fund published an *AIDS Update 1999* in which the largest of several text boxes was entitled "Promiscuity, and the Primacy of Cultural Factors: A Lethal Mixture in Africa" (UNFPA, 1999, 6). UNFPA was promoting the "promiscuity" paradigm in spite of the 1995 WHO report and the 1999 UNAIDS study that rejected any empirical basis for that argument (Cleland and Ferry, 1995; UNAIDS, 1999a). Discussion of those works appears in the appendix to chapter 1.

The media also continue to perpetuate an unsubstantiated but potent image of a lusty, ancestral African careening headlong into doom propelled by sexual behavior. An article about AIDS in South Africa in the *Economist* exhibits the sleight-of-hand so common in writing about Africa, perhaps not realized by its author. The article opens with a brief vignette about a truck driver at the Zimbabwe–South Africa border. Border delays compel the truckers to stay overnight, and it is cheaper to stay with a prostitute than pay for a hotel room. One trucker is reported to say, in front of his buddies (introducing possible bias in his estimate), that he sleeps with 30 women a month. Then the article reports on the extent of the AIDS epidemic in South Africa. At no point does it provide data on sexual practices of the people who are not truck drivers, their wives, or their commercial sex partners. It makes no further mention of why HIV is so prevalent, so it does not explicitly make the argument that higher rates of multipartnering are adequate to explain the HIV epidemic in sub-Saharan Africa. But it certainly leaves the impression that having 360 partners a year is the real South Africa, and the article concludes that, besides antiretrovirals, "[t]he other way to curb AIDS is to persuade people to sleep around less and to use condoms more" ("South Africa's President and the Plague," 2000, n.p.).

Constructing dissimilarity

The writing of ethnographies often has the unfortunate result of inventing differences between people around the world. Although the works can be merely descriptive snapshots of a people, by implication they are comparative in nature because what they describe is represented as noteworthy. Perhaps unintentionally, they reinforce the notion that there is something idiosyncratic and exotic about the people, even when they report on events,

17. Latin America may indeed begin to resemble the Thai case. Intervention by the Thai government has resulted in some shift in sex tourism, in particular with children, to Latin America. When I was in Thailand in 2004, however, I still saw Western sex tourists with their child victims. Drug use is also more common in some Latin American countries than in Africa and provides another source of risk for the region.

attitudes, or practices that are common in many parts of the world. In special issues on AIDS in *African Studies* in 2001 and 2002, several of the articles fit the model of portraying the most mundane and ubiquitous events as though they were peculiarly African.

An article entitled "Sexual Socialisation in South Africa: A Historical Perspective" reports that "[t]his research has revealed an alarming failure of communication between parents and children on sexual issues. Parents find it very difficult to broach the issue of sex with their children who, as a result, have little option but to seek information elsewhere—normally from their peers" (Delius and Glaser, 2002, 27). That is certainly a relevant observation and one that impinges on the AIDS crisis, but it does not distinguish South Africa from almost every other society. The article attempts to find a cultural and historical explanation for this "awkward intergenerational silence on issues of sexuality" (Delius and Glaser, 2002, 30), without ever noting that this is common in many other societies, Western and non-Western alike. As evidence of a cultural and historical origin for this behavior, they quote Pitje, an anthropologist who studied Sekhukhuneland in the 1940s, who found that children sometimes listened to adults' " 'quarrels in which whole lists of sexual obscenities and technicalities are recited.' (Pitje 1948: 65–66)" (Delius and Glaser, 2002, 30). Indeed, we can all be shocked along with Pitje that children should be exposed to such things, but it is reported in 2002 as though it tells us something about South African culture that is different from what can be seen in U.S. television sitcoms.

The lives of African children seemed to be equally puzzling to Pitje and to the twenty-first-century authors who cite him. They report that after the age of 6, African boys and girls tended to be occupied in different activities, and "[w]hen pre-pubescent boys and girls *did* meet they often mocked and taunted each other, leading Pitje to note 'there is thus apparent antagonism between the sexes' " (Delius and Glaser, 2002, 30). Around the world, of course, children commonly group in same-sex play activities, and in a visit to any middle-school playground, skating rink, or swimming pool in the United States, one would see nothing but taunting between prepubescent boys and girls. Thus although there is important information in the Delius and Glaser article, it is lost in the ethnographicizing of gender and intergenerational issues. Gender roles may differ by degrees between populations, but the situation in Sekhukhuneland is not differentiated from any other place with these observations.

In his article, "AIDS in Malawi: Contemporary Discourse and Cultural Continuities," Peter Forster reports on research to test his hypothesis that "a link existed between indigenous cultural background and current response to the issue of AIDS and AIDS control" (Forster, 2001, 245). The author's ethnographic research method was to record "informal comments, gossip and off-the-cuff remarks" (Forster, 2001, 245) overheard in bars in

Zomba Town, the site of Malawi's main university campus. Some of the findings of the Zomba research are the following:

- "Like beer, casual sexual activity is widely seen as an essential expression of masculine enjoyment. Comments of such a nature were widespread in all-male groups" (Forster, 2002, 247–248).
- "Others in all-male groups also commented that a woman's enticing appearance could make them lose self-control" (Forster, 2001, 248).
- "In view of the AIDS threat, some would recognise the need for self-control, but this could easily be diminished when drunk; this was a very relevant factor, since casual sex and drinking tend to take place in the same establishments" (Forster, 2001, 248).

It would be entirely appropriate to report this barroom talk if the objective were to show the near universality of young male conversations about sexual relations or the similarities in college life around the world. By not making that point, however, the account encourages the view that there is something extraordinary that is revealed by the research. Moreover, the bar talk is offered as evidence of an insight into indigenous Malawian culture captured in a real-life situation.

I did a bit of ethnographic research of my own, and I asked the male students in my seminar to report on locker-room conversations. They confirmed my hypothesis that in all-male groups in the eastern United States they had heard men comment that a woman's enticing ("hot") appearance had caused them to feel a loss of self-control. My participant-observer team was unable to corroborate the statements of many of the men regarding their behavior subsequent to the loss of self-control. In fact, that corresponded to the experience of the Zomba research team: "Comments about what goes on in private cannot always be regarded as a true record of actual practice" (Forster, 2001, 246).

The article also reports having found that "[a] further element, again associated with all-male groups, was bravado or a willingness to take risks" (Forster, 2001, 248). As the higher mortality rates around the world for adolescent and young adult males clearly demonstrate, this too is not peculiar to the indigenous cultural background of Malawi. Forster promises a follow-up article on the "considerable material" (Forster, 2001, 248) he collected on bargirls.

A third article in *African Studies* credits John and Pat Caldwell and their collaborators (1989, 1992, 1993, 2000) with being the only other researchers to have dealt with the problem of witchcraft in Africa. The author reargues his case from earlier works that witchcraft is ubiquitous in modern South Africa and then poses the hypothetical question of what it would mean for the government "[i]f the AIDS pandemic becomes widely interpreted in terms of witchcraft" (Ashforth, 2002, 136). The argument, in brief, is that belief in witchcraft is widespread in South Africa; many people attribute the AIDS epidemic to witchcraft; if people get upset enough about AIDS/witchcraft and they feel that the government is not doing enough about AIDS/witchcraft, then they will overthrow the government.

Ashforth maintains that the reason people have not rallied to demand that the government address matters of witchcraft is that they do not have enough experience with democracy and so lack a sense that government should respond to popular demands. The lack of agitation does not, therefore, contradict the author's hypothesis. It is difficult to see what this exercise accomplishes besides adding fuel to the notion that "Africa" is not only rife with superstition but is also a political time bomb, even when progress in democracy is apparent.

Stories about witchcraft and sex rituals are very catchy and reaffirm many readers' notions of an exotic Africa. The *New York Times Magazine*, on October 26, 2003, ran a six-page article about cannibalism in African military groups. The practice of cannibalism and belief in witchcraft might even be true for a small number of people, and much-publicized criminal cases in the United States and England indicate that they exist in those countries as well. But they do not convey to readers in the West any notion of everyday life in Africa: a life of hauling water, catching buses, and studying for exams; running corporations, hospitals, or universities; needing mosquito nets, designing road systems and dams, gathering aquatic plants, teaching children to farm or play field hockey, and working on construction sites or in offices. There are no real people in those stories, just sweeping images of a strange and pretty scary place. It is then very difficult for Westerners to imagine how they can help resolve a health crisis when they are up against not worms, but witches. It is hard to get Congress behind nutritional supplements for cannibals.

Even for situations that are fairly common in all societies, journalistic representations suggest that there is something quite different about Africans or African-Americans. In 2003, both the *New York Times* (August 3) and the *Washington Post* (August 4) ran feature articles on African-American men on the "Down Low," which means having sex with men while maintaining relationships with women who are unaware of the men's bisexuality. Bisexuality is an important consideration in epidemics of sexually transmitted diseases, but the articles would have one believe that it is peculiar to African-Americans. There are certainly plenty of white men on the "Down Low" because the social climate that is hostile to homosexuality and bisexuality is not unique to the African-American community.

Blatantly racial arguments in scholarly literature are relatively few, and bald statements that differences in rates of multipartnered sex adequately explain differences in rates of HIV are becoming less common. Much more common are works that begin from a tacit behavioral assumption that is comparative in nature, without providing comparative data to support that paradigm and without addressing other possible explanations for the intensity of the African AIDS epidemic, for which we have better data. That is actually the main problem with the AIDS-in-Africa discourse from a pragmatic standpoint. The works contain too many broad, unsupported assertions that draw attention to presumed differences in behavior that resonate with Western stereotypes of Africans. They draw attention away from the glaring differences between rich and poor countries in nutrition, clean water, waste disposal, and access to health care that are important factors in disease transmission but are less sexy and lack the culturally confirming ring of racial stereotypes.

Translating a paradigm into policy

A final category of works within the behavioral paradigm comprises policy documents that, while they might acknowledge social and economic factors, offer only behavioral solutions. As Schön (1979) explained, the critical role of the generative metaphor is problem setting. This step precedes and defines problem solving within the parameters set by the paradigm.

One of the most important policy documents of the 1990s on HIV/AIDS is the World Bank's *Confronting AIDS: Public Priorities in a Global Epidemic* (1997). Although the book mentions numerous factors that influence HIV transmission, its overall plan derives from the behavioral paradigm. In discussing sexual behavior as a determinant of HIV prevalence, *Confronting AIDS* cites Caldwell et al. (1989). It also mentions the WHO survey of behavioral risk factors, without mentioning that it resoundingly refuted the behavioral explanation of differentials in HIV spread (Cleland and Ferry, 1995). *Confronting AIDS* bases its policy recommendations on 31 cost-effectiveness studies for HIV prevention. Of the 22 studies reported in appendix A of *Confronting AIDS*, 18 are about condom use, one is about needle exchange, and three pertain to STD treatment. Of nine trial interventions reported in appendix B, five deal with sex workers and needle sharers; three are population-level interventions for treatment of symptomatic STDs, social marketing of condoms, and safe blood supply. Only one is a model of antiretroviral treatment of mothers to prevent vertical transmission, and that study, unlike the others, is only hypothetical. None of the cost-effectiveness studies deals with general health, nutrition, or other variables associated with infectious disease transmission, although the body of the report makes reference to those factors. The resulting focus of *Confronting AIDS*—adapting the behavior of sex workers and injecting drug users—should be very useful for middle-income or transition-economy countries with nascent or concentrated epidemics. In fact, *Confronting AIDS* is a good resource for many aspects of AIDS-related economic issues. But its approach and conclusions are inadequate for most of Africa and other regions with extreme poverty and generalized epidemics.

The United Nations organizations and bilateral aid agencies whose stated purpose is human development and poverty reduction have yet to address the socioeconomic context in which AIDS has arisen. The International Labour Organization and a number of other organizations promote workplace interventions to prevent HIV. But those interventions go little beyond end-game strategies of condom distribution in the workplace. Changing the workplace, the work itself, who gets the jobs, and the pay for work are all possible components of a workplace strategy for HIV prevention, but they are not considered in a policy that narrowly focuses on the last possible moment to prevent HIV. Scores of reports from international organizations and consulting firms rework cost estimates for little more than condom-distribution and peer-education programs because the behavioral paradigm does not permit policy makers to think beyond sex. Chapters 9 and 10 examine the limitations of a behavioral paradigm for global AIDS policy.

Conclusion

This chapter has given a few examples of racial metaphors and other evocative language that framed the AIDS-in-Africa discourse and established the behavioral paradigm as the basis of AIDS policy. Discredited racial science reared its ugly head in the form of a metaphor with formidable generative powers, carried along by deeply imbedded Western racial views that presume exceptional sexual behavior by Africans. A narrowly behavioral explanation for differences in rates of HIV prevalence dominates the AIDS literature, sometimes explicitly but more often implicitly by failing to consider other factors generally included in epidemiological studies.

The acceptance of the behavioral paradigm is facilitated by the fact that Western research on Africa, especially with respect to sexuality and other aspects of cultural and social life, is not required to conform to conventional standards for evidence in scholarly work. It seems that assertions that would require documentation in scholarly work about people in other parts of the world can be published without support when made about Africans. Racial bias in standards of evidence is a problem of long standing that has lethal consequences in AIDS discourse.

What distinguishes most Africans, Asians, and Latin Americans from most Europeans and North Americans is not extraordinary behavior but poverty. Effective prevention depends on recognizing the real commonalities among people, as well as the real differences. The behavioral paradigm and its assumption of African exceptionalism largely determine the questions that can be asked and the solutions that can be proposed in AIDS research and AIDS-prevention policy for Africa and other profoundly poor populations. As Kuhn pointed out, "one of the things a scientific community acquires with a paradigm is a criterion for choosing problems that, while the paradigm is taken for granted, can be assumed to have solutions. To a great extent these are the only problems that the community will admit as scientific or encourage its members to undertake" (Kuhn, 1970, 37). By accepting the wrong paradigm, the AIDS discourse has failed to ask the right questions, and we have lost well over a decade in understanding the complexity of AIDS, especially among poor, malnourished people.

8

Individual Bias in Methodology

This chapter continues the discussion of flaws in the AIDS discourse that steer the participants away from obvious clues to understanding the epidemic. The previous chapter showed how Western misconceptions of Africans led to a misunderstanding of the AIDS epidemic in Africa and derailed AIDS policy. This chapter demonstrates how the current practice of public health and the methodologies of the health and social sciences also confound the effort to understand AIDS and to design effective preventive policies.

The question, Why does a person contract HIV? gives rise to an answer about an individual and to policies that address individual-level, generally behavioral variables. It is a very different question to ask, Why do nearly 40 percent of the adult population in one country and only 1 percent in another country contract HIV? Widely divergent rates of infection suggest different underlying causes of epidemics among populations and even different contributing causes of individual infection. Abundant evidence supports the inclusion of nonbehavioral characteristics (for both infecting and infected persons in each transmission) and group-level variables, such as the prevalence and the intensity of other diseases that increase transmission of HIV.

The standard methodologies employed by most health scientists and social scientists prevent them from seeing ubiquitous host factors and their interactions that produce epidemic spread of HIV, from measuring those interactions, and from using that knowledge in prevention. Neither epidemiology nor health economics uses tools that adequately incorporate interactions or group-level variables, and so neither discipline can incorporate disease synergies and spillover effects in a model of HIV transmission.

This chapter examines the methodological limitations in the fields of public health, epidemiology, and economics that undermine the ability to understand health problems in the developing world and that have specifically impeded the understanding and prevention of HIV/AIDS.

Epidemiology and public health

Epidemiology—the study of health conditions affecting populations—has split into opposing camps in the past 30 years over the issue of whether the appropriate level of analysis is the individual or the group and, consequently, over the appropriate tools of research. Epidemiology began as an interdisciplinary investigation integrating the knowledge of biological mechanisms and the insights of social science, and it employed both controlled experiments and ecologic studies. Controlled experiments attempt to measure interindividual differences and abstract from environmental factors. *Ecologic* is the term epidemiologists use for studies of correlation, but the term is meant to suggest analyses that recognize interactions between the individual and the environment, as well as characteristics of the environment, which includes other individuals in the population.

What distinguishes epidemiology from medicine is the analysis of characteristics of populations and of individuals interacting with the population. In recent years, the controlled experiment, addressing only individual-level effects, has become the dominant tool in epidemiology. The focus has shifted from the health of populations, which implies interactive effects, to the health of individuals in large numbers. This is one manifestation of a broader epistemological transformation that permeates contemporary thinking in fields as diverse as economics, political science, sociology, and medicine. That shift means that important data about groups, and about interactions between groups and individuals, are overlooked.[1]

Biology can ask the question of why individuals (even in large numbers) are affected by exposures to infectious and noninfectious agents. Epidemiology can ask both the question of why some populations are exposed to greater risk and why there can be a difference in level of injury between two populations with similar exposures. The case of lead poisoning illus-

1. For background on epidemiology and the debate over the appropriate level of analysis, see Cassel, 1976; Susser, 1977; Rifkin and Walt, 1986; Renton, 1993; Cohen, 1994; Greenland and Robins, 1994; Krieger, 1994; Fairchild and Oppenheimer, 1998; and Young, 1998.

trates the differences among the three questions. The first question would generate a study of interindividual differences in neurological variables between children exposed to lead paint dust and children not exposed. It aggregates information about a large number of individuals. The second question would focus on the fact that children living in poverty in older, unrenovated housing have higher exposure to lead paint dust. The third question would ask why African-American and Hispanic children have higher blood lead levels than white children in comparable housing. Are there nutritional or other factors that interact with lead that result in greater harm from similar exposures? In recent years, the first question, which is about differences between individual exposures, has received more attention than the population-health questions for most diseases. Epidemiologists have thoroughly debated the issue of individual versus group or population variables, or what has been called the "causes of cases and causes of incidence" (Rose, 1985, 34). That debate, however, has rarely addressed HIV/AIDS, although the methodological questions of individual or group analysis are crucial to a correct understanding of the AIDS epidemics.

The choice of the experimental model does not just limit the understanding of population events. The abstraction from environmental and population variables can even distort the understanding of causes of cases (causes of individual illness) because the relevant data surrounding the event are lost (Young, 1998). Use of the experimental model to study HIV necessitates abstraction from host factors, such as nutrition or parasite load; the role of cofactor infections; the heterogeneous immune system reactions, such as depressed immune response, inflammatory effects of cofactor infections, and the specific interactions of endemic conditions (parasite infection) and $CD4^+$ cells; the synergistic effects of HIV and TB; and the numerous other individual and group factors discussed in earlier chapters. The appropriate discipline for studying epidemics such as HIV/AIDS is population health, which is concerned with the entire distribution of risk factors in a population and the effect that has on individual infection and epidemic spread. The difference is important because interventions that derive from a population-health perspective attempt to remedy environmental factors, as well as focusing on "risk groups."

Lesson from early epidemiology

In the nineteenth century, the approach of epidemiologists went hand-in-hand with public health interventions of the day. Individual behavior and other individual risk factors were considered in the context of an environment of risk. The public health measures consisted of providing piped water, enclosing sewage systems, draining swamps, moving residences to higher ground, and covering the decaying vegetable and animal waste in streets with cobblestones. Such sanitary interventions, incidentally, have the desired effect without requiring the active cooperation of the public (Litsios, 2002).

They bring about the needed change in the environment directly. Consequently, as public goods, they are more efficient targets for public investment than expenditures for which the government cannot control the final outcome, such as behavior-change communication. Such environmental interventions also eliminate root causes of disease.

Along with the epidemiological analysis of those days went a rough cost-benefit analysis. A government's expenditures were expected to reap a return in healthy workers that would compensate for the effort and investment. In the 1880s cities like New York, Montreal, and Buenos Aires were competing for European immigrants. News of a 12 percent mortality rate in some years due to yellow fever epidemics, or high mortality from recurrent cholera epidemics, would reach Italy or Ireland and influence the choice of destination for the emigrants (Escudé, 1989). The public health measures, such as building sewers, resulted in rapid declines in mortality, as expected, without justification through individual-level analysis, such as randomized controlled trials.

The epidemiology of infectious disease was based on scientific analysis that incorporated individual and ecologic variables, leading to public health interventions that accommodated human behavior by addressing environmental causes. In 1854 John Snow observed that residents in the vicinity of the Broad Street pump in London had a much higher mortality rate from cholera than did residents in other areas. It was clear to Snow that an individual behavior—drinking from the pump—was leading to the deaths of many people in that neighborhood. But he also observed that the population near the Broad Street pump had a higher mortality rate than populations with similar behavior in the vicinity of other pumps. He recognized the risk of individual behavior in the context of proximity to a particular water source. Not everyone in the Broad Street population got sick or died, nor was everyone in other neighborhoods spared, but the correlation of location and mortality suggested a risky environment, as well as a risky behavior in the vicinity of the Broad Street pump.

Snow's framing of the problem, as an environmental one, led to his choice of policy intervention. He did not go door to door, recruiting volunteers to be trained as peer educators who would advise their neighbors to cease drinking from the pump. Nor did he recruit businesses to train their managers to talk to the workers about their drinking problem and distribute water purification tablets in the workplace to be used when the workers got home. Snow presented his results to the authorities of the parish, and the next day they dismantled the pump. He altered a significant part of the risk environment, and mortality in the neighborhood dropped quickly, even without enlisting the active cooperation of residents. As we saw in chapters 2 and 3, simple, known interventions, such as safe water supply and antihelminthic treatment, are capable of altering the environment of risk and dramatically reducing the prevalence of diseases that promote the transmission of HIV in poor populations.

As the twentieth century progressed, greater mastery of research tools, vaccines, and antibiotics shifted the focus from ecologic factors to the individual. In spite of a recognition of group-level factors, such as herd immunity, most pathogen–host relationships could be studied more easily at the level of the individual. That accorded well with the germ theory of disease, even though it was still recognized that it took the interaction of pathogen, host, and environment to fully explain disease in an individual and certainly to explain population events such as epidemics. Increasingly, the lure of the methods of medical research attracted epidemiologists, although as late as 1985, Mervyn Susser wrote in a retrospective on the field that epidemiologists still rarely used randomized controlled experiments, perhaps because they were "reluctant to sacrifice generalizability and representativeness for specificity and internal validity" (Susser, 1985, 167).

Individual and ecologic analysis in modern epidemiology

The new emphasis on individual-level effects mirrored a shift in public health policy toward individual interventions, aided in part by the availability of new therapies such as antibiotics. Diseases with a well-defined social context and an effective remedy afford us the opportunity to examine individual- and group-level interventions. Tuberculosis had been the single most lethal infectious killer of all time. TB treatment, along with sanitation, better housing, and better nutrition appeared finally to have conquered that terrible disease around the mid–twentieth century. Cutbacks in government spending in the 1960s and the spreading epidemics of drug abuse and AIDS of the 1980s contributed to the reemergence of tuberculosis. Today, Directly Observed Therapy (DOTS) is having excellent success in diverse settings and represents a very significant advance for public health. In the current environment that focuses on individual solutions, however, enthusiasm for DOTS can obscure the fact that increasing waves of people are still becoming infected because of environmental factors such as poverty and its attendant poor nutrition, crowded housing, and poor access to health care. Even in the age of effective DOTS treatment, TB prevalence continues to increase. Moreover, an ecologic consequence of larger numbers of new infections is that drug resistance is more likely to develop as more and more people are brought into treatment. The implications for drug resistance should also be included in any comparative study of the cost-effectiveness of prevention versus treatment for tuberculosis. As the number of people with HIV-induced TB increases, we can expect an acceleration of drug resistance.

Since Susser's retrospective in 1985, the randomized controlled trial (RCT) has frequently been called the "gold standard" by epidemiologists and even by some economists for evaluating social investments (Schultz, 1997). But RCTs, precisely because they abstract from population characteristics, are unlikely to have external validity—that is, to provide results that can be applied in other contexts. To understand the development of disease in different populations, to evaluate investment decisions between groups, or to determine the relative benefits of investments in alternative fields—they are not valid for any of these.

For its part, the use of ecologic analysis has generated considerable criticism because of the potential for ecologic fallacy, which is a valid concern. Drawing inferences from statistical correlations can be completely unwarranted, if the underlying theory is incorrect. For example, an ecologic study might show a correlation of cancer rates with "race" or "ethnicity." An inappropriate conclusion could be that African-Americans are more susceptible as a "race" to certain cancers. More useful, however, would be a geographical mapping of toxic-waste dumps in African-American residential areas, along with a demonstration of a biological mechanism of the carcinogenic effects of exposure to toxic waste, to explain the high prevalence of certain cancers among African-Americans in a particular region. Ecologic models can be useful to suggest associations for which the correct theory can be sought, as in this case of mapping the effects of environmental racism.[2]

Within the AIDS-in-Africa discourse, the behavioral paradigm incorporates an ecologic fallacy. Many analysts observed the high prevalence of HIV/AIDS in sub-Saharan Africa and skipped right to applying models based on behavioral differences, which they had assumed underlay the prevalence. The assumption that differences in rates of HIV could be explained entirely by differences in sexual behavior had no plausible basis, and no empirical support was offered.

Individual effects and multilevel causes

Ecologic models are useful when there are interactions between group-level variables and individual vulnerability. Since multilevel interactions often occur, it is important not to neglect them by using only individual-level modeling. An excellent example of the importance of multilevel models is a study of dengue transmission in villages in Mexico. Within each village, the researchers found no significant correlation between living in a house infested with mosquitoes and dengue infection. A logical policy conclusion based only on that information would be that there is no appreciable benefit from mosquito eradication. In examining results from numerous villages, however, it was shown that villages with a higher prevalence of mosquito-infested houses had higher prevalence of dengue. But "transmission from infected individuals with household mosquitoes to individuals without

2. The scenario is hypothetical. There are, however, genetic predispositions to certain diseases. Biologists have explored apparent genetic immunity to HIV among some people (Altschuler, 2000), a possibility that should be explored further.

household mosquitoes raises the rate of infection in [apparently] unexposed individuals. . . . The more exposed individuals there are in a community, the more the rate of infection in the unexposed population will be raised by this secondary transmission and the smaller the individual-level association will be" (Koopman and Longini, 1994, 838). The likelihood of *individual infection* is determined either by the individual risk of living in an infested house or the environmental risk of living in a village with many infested houses and thus a high proportion of infected neighbors. *Prevalence* of dengue, however, is determined by village characteristics, not by individual characteristics.

The individual risk model, therefore, misses certain factors that are very important in transmission. Another example is the Salk vaccine, the greatest benefit of which is not that it decreases the rate of infection in vaccinated persons but that vaccinated persons who become infected excrete fewer polio virus organisms, and thus the circulation of the virus is slowed (Koopman and Longini, 1994). In an individual-level study that considers only the characteristics of the individual becoming infected, that information is never examined. Not only is the prevalence in a population important, but also the characteristics of the source of a pathogen are central to transmission dynamics. Similarly with HIV, higher viral load of the sexual partner or mother increases risk of transmission, sexually or vertically. The entire distribution of risk is greater in malnourished, parasite-laden populations because those characteristics increase viral load and viral shedding in HIV-infected individuals, and the risk is compounded when the prevalence of HIV is already high. As in the case of dengue, an individual-level study of HIV transmission and schistosomiasis in the HIV-negative population might not exhibit a significant correlation because it would abstract from schistosomiasis in the infecting population and from other cofactor conditions of the HIV-negative population. By examining a number of poor populations—and understanding the mechanisms by which malnutrition and parasites increase infectiousness and vulnerability—we learn that there is more to HIV transmission besides the immediate sexual or vertical contact.

As we saw in the appendix to chapter 1, sexual behavior varies more within populations than between populations. Sexual behavior, therefore, is one important factor in interindividual differences in infection, along with other host factors. But population factors, which are sometimes ubiquitous in a population, not interindividual variations, are important for explaining overall prevalence, differences in prevalence between populations, or changes in prevalence over time.

Because the individual behavioral paradigm so dominates thinking about HIV transmission, considering other examples of public health problems can help move the analysis beyond fixation on the sex act. Schwartz and Carpenter (1999) explored multilevel causation of obesity in the United States. Genetic makeup, family environment, or individual behavior might explain interindividual differences in body mass within a society at a given point in time. But they do not explain the overall prevalence of obesity in the United States compared with other countries or the rapid increase in obesity over the past few decades. Ubiquitous or environmental factors, which are overlooked in individual-level study, play an important role. Food advertising, food quality, portion size, sedentary lifestyle, and the shift of focus in schools away from physical activity and play to academic competition are ecologic variables that influence obesity prevalence and its change over time. They frame the context in which individual behavior, family, and genetics operate. If they are overlooked, then the vulnerability to obesity of increasing numbers of individuals is not recognized (Schwartz and Carpenter, 1999).

An obesity model that fails to take into account such environmental factors cannot explain differences between populations or changes over time. If a model does not explain differences in prevalence between populations, it also does not explain why many individuals in one population but few people in another population are affected. In the case of HIV, a valid transmission model must incorporate the fact that population average viral load is higher in sub-Saharan Africa, not only because more people are HIV-infected but also because viral load in each HIV-infected person is higher. That alters the whole distribution of risk.

Individual bias and HIV-transmission models used by policy organizations

The exclusive focus on individual-level effects and behavioral variables is evident in the HIV-transmission models developed by the major policy organizations. This focus is also evident in their prevention strategies, which incorporate an implicit transmission model. The variables they include indicate the organizations' underlying theory of HIV transmission. None of the transmission models used by the major organizations in the AIDS field takes into account ecologic factors or in any way reflects the population health of the regions under study. They assume very few factors in HIV transmission, all related to individual sexual behavior, and consequently incorporate only behavioral-intervention variables. The models generally include a variable for HIV prevalence in the population, which translates into the probability of contact with a person who is HIV-infected, and STD prevalence, which increases the probability that any contact will result in transmission but which is assumed to have only behavioral determinants. The models do not take into account other medically significant differences between populations. Ubiquitous or widespread factors, such as prevalence of malaria, TB, schistosomiasis, helminthic infection, or malnutrition, which affect the risk of transmission or infection, are not included. Three such models are discussed below.

The AVERT model, developed by Family Health International (FHI) for USAID, is intended to estimate intervention effects on the reduction of HIV transmission. The only descriptive variables (which the model calls *constant variables*) are population labels: occupation, type of partner (regular or casual), gender, partner gender, and HIV prevalence. Intervention variables are the average number of sex partners, average number of sex acts, prevalence of STDs, and condom use. The results generated by the program are the probable infections with and without the chosen interventions (Bouey et al., 1998). There is nothing in the model that pertains to the health profile of the population. Like all the other tools being promoted by USAID's consulting groups, AVERT can only generate answers to its own very narrow question about behavior.

The Futures Group International (TFGI), another USAID partner, developed the GOALS model "to support strategic planning at the national level" by linking goals and funding (www.tfgi.com). The model uses unit costs for interventions that are generally based on pilot studies from other locations; those estimates were exhaustively researched and, while imperfect, are the best available. More problematic is the fact that the only variables considered as affecting transmission of STDs and HIV are condom use, STD treatment, number of partners, and age at first sex, in a model that is promoted for use in heterogeneous populations around the world. The only interventions considered for prevention (except for blood safety) relate narrowly to individual behavior change through mass media, voluntary counseling and testing (VCT), peer counseling for commercial sex workers, workplace education programs, condom social marketing, and so on. The GOALS model could presumably be adapted to include treatment for malaria, schistosomiasis, helminth infection, and micronutrient deficiency. At present, however, this transmission model promoted by the Futures Group and USAID only includes behavior-change variables. It does not even include needle safety in medical and quasi-medical settings. The way that the GOALS model and the AVERT model are used can actually be pernicious because they presume to give answers to the questions: What are the determinants of HIV transmission and epidemic spread? And how can we best prevent HIV transmission? But those questions cannot be answered with only the variables they have chosen. The exclusive focus on behavioral variables leads to very narrow, stop-gap attemps at solutions by organizations that control a large proportion of HIV program funds.

In a background paper for *Confronting AIDS*, the World Bank's most widely disseminated book on HIV/AIDS of the 1990s, van Vliet et al. (1997) evaluate the effectiveness of HIV prevention strategies with the STDSIM model. It is a useful exercise to estimate the epidemics that result from different scenarios. STDSIM can accommodate different behavioral assumptions and presumably could be adapted to incorporate other variables in the health profile of the population. That is not done and, as the model on which World Bank interventions are based, it has serious limitations. It models only heterosexual transmission and omits transmission from blood transfusions or unsterile needles. It does not include a variable for population average infection rate with TB, malaria, helminths, and schistosomiasis or for levels of malnutrition. Abstracting from all the health factors that differentiate populations, it uses one value for male-to-female transmission risk for all populations and one value for female-to-male transmission risk for all populations. Interaction with other STDs is included in the model, but variations in viral load over the duration of infection or due to coinfection with various parasitic and infectious diseases are not. While the authors specifically mention that they are only dealing with heterosexual and vertical transmission in the model, they have provided the scenario on which the conclusions of *Confronting AIDS* are based. By leaving out other sources of transmission, and the greater vulnerability of people with compromised immune systems, they have constructed an account of the epidemic in which a high prevalence of HIV (a population characteristic) must result from a high rate of heterosexual partner change (an individual characteristic). Their conclusion, therefore, is that the most cost-effective intervention is a highly targeted intervention for condom promotion among commercial sex workers.[3] In various international fora, such as the international AIDS conferences, the World Bank line is that such targeted interventions are the proven cost-effective approach for preventing HIV spread. Behind that claim is the STDSIM model, which can give only that answer because its assumptions are so limiting.

The common theme in all of these models is that individual sexual behavior and prevalence of HIV and other STDs (themselves the aggregated result of individual behaviors) are the only significant variables in HIV transmission. The same models with the same variables are assumed to be valid for North America, Europe, sub-Saharan Africa, Latin America, or Asia, with the same two values used for heterosexual transmission probabilities (one for male-to-female and one for female-to-male). The one-risk-fits-all assumption ignores the wealth of evidence that host factors change the risk of transmission and of infection. Such models are also used to confirm the behavioral assumptions, for which data have not been collected, on which the models are based.

As we saw in chapter 2, malnutrition, parasite load, and endemic dis-

3. They also assumed that higher levels of behavior change can be achieved with commercial sex workers than among what they call the "general population," although one could certainly reason the opposite. Women whose livelihood depends on the inherently dangerous activity of engaging strangers on the street and interacting with pimps and the police could be less able than rural mothers living in at least somewhat supportive communities, with their mothers and sisters and cousins, to adapt their behavior to protect themselves and their children. Another bias is the assumption that the number of condoms distributed equals the number of condoms used—there is no waste—a patently incorrect assumption.

eases interact to reduce immune response and make people more vulnerable to disease acquisition, whether transmission occurs through food, water, air, sexual activity, or contact with contaminated instruments. Chapter 3 explained some of the nutritional, parasitic, and disease interactions that specifically increase the transmission and acquisition of HIV. The vulnerability profile of each HIV-negative person, like the virulence profile of each HIV-infected person, is unique. Nevertheless, it is clear that the aggregate risk in a malnourished, microbe-burdened population is much greater than in a well-nourished, healthy population.

A transmission model for HIV or any disease should take into account the substantial differences among populations in order to correctly predict prevalence and incidence. The standard transmission models for HIV—AVERT, GOALS, and STDSIM among them—do not incorporate what is known about the complexity of HIV transmission. Those standard models essentially assume a universal dose-response, given in a per-contact transmission risk that is a constant or one-risk-fits-all. As we have seen, the transmission of HIV is considerably more complex, because characteristics of both the person transmitting and the person contracting the infection affect the risk of transmission. The core of the standard model is as follows:

$$I = N \times P \times T$$

where I is probability of sexual infection, N is the number of partners, P is the prevalence rate in the population, and T is the per-contact transmission risk, which is assumed to be the same for every population. Since we have estimates for prevalence (P) and incidence (I), and T is constant, then the use of such an equation generates an imputed value for the number of sexual partners (N). Because the model does not include other relevant population characteristics, the only way it can explain incidence of infection is through the behavioral variables. If incidence is found to be 40 or 400 times higher in Botswana than in Sweden, then assumed values of the behavioral variable must be adjusted upward. The dependent variable, incidence (I), is known or estimated, so the model, in effect, determines the independent variable, N, or the number of partners.

Amplified HIV-transmission model

In order to model HIV transmission adequately and hence determine the appropriate prevention strategies, we need a transmission model that reflects the complexity of disease transmission. The outlines of an amplified HIV-transmission model are sketched here. For sexual transmission of HIV, it is clear that a universal per-contact transmission-risk term, as is used in the standard model, is incorrect. Instead, transmission risk should reflect two sets of variables: one that estimates the per-contact risk of the transmitting person, and the other the per-contact risk of infection on the part of the HIV-negative person. Whether those variables should be included in a multiplicative model or an additive model is not essential to the present argument. Interaction terms for synergies between conditions should also be included. It may not be possible or mathematically meaningful to aggregate all conditions across all individuals. What is most important is that the numerous factors that demonstrably contribute to HIV transmission be recognized in any model of HIV spread that is used to formulate intervention policy.

The last term in the equation above, T, should represent

$$T = V^{-} + C^{+} \text{ (or perhaps } T = V^{-} \times C^{+}\text{)}$$

and include both of the following equations:

$$V^{-} = f\{\text{standard risk}, H^{-}, M^{-}, F^{-}, TB^{-}, STD^{-}, SCH^{-}\}$$

where V^{-} is the per-contact infection risk (vulnerability) of an HIV-negative person. For the independent variables, H^{-} is the helminth factor, M^{-} is the malaria factor, F^{-} is the nutrition factor, TB^{-} is the tuberculosis factor, STD^{-} is the STD factor, and SCH^{-} is the schistosomiasis factor, where each of the factors represents the acquisition-enhancing risk of the corresponding condition. Additional factors that diminish the immune response through the barrier defenses or cell-mediated immunity may need to be added as well.

$$C^{+} = g\{\text{standard risk}, H^{+}, M^{+}, F^{+}, TB^{+}, STD^{+}, SCH^{+}\}$$

where C^{+} is the per-contact risk of transmitting HIV (virulence or contagiousness) of an HIV-infected person and the other symbols are the same as above, except that they pertain to the HIV-infected person. Any other factors found to increase viral load and/or viral shedding in the HIV-infected person can be added to the formula.

Similarly, a new transmission model for vertical transmission is necessary, that would follow the lines of the equation below:

> Probability of vertical transmission = standard risk × (mother is vitamin-A deficient + mother is anemic + mother has an STD + mother has genital schistosomiasis + mother has high viral load + mother has no access to C-section + baby is malnourished + baby's immune system is disrupted by exposure to helminths in utero or after birth in food or unclean water)

If we include these other factors that affect transmission of HIV, we can better understand the global distribution of HIV and AIDS. Clearly, there are myriad opportunities to intervene. In fact, it is apparent that it is necessary to treat coinfection while also facing HIV directly.

In all of this, the issue is not that behavior is unimportant. It is that behavior explains so little about why poor people get sick. The models of all the major policy organizations and their consultants have made no attempt to capture the reality of life for poor people. They are extremely unsophisticated models. There are significant relative risks in poor environments, but they are not the ones that the models include. Why do 40 percent of the adult population in one country and only 1 percent in another country contract HIV? A conventional, but complex, epidemiological model to explain HIV prevalence that recognizes characteristics of pathogen, host, and environment, is long overdue.

Methods of health economics

The increasingly individual focus of epidemiology is aggravated by donors' growing demands for accountability in projects. It is reasonable and necessary to evaluate interventions with a notion of cost-effectiveness, or getting the most health improvement for a given expenditure. The aim of such an exercise is not merely to improve efficiency as an abstract goal. It is also compassionate since it tries to improve the most lives to the greatest degree with a given amount of money. That is not a substitute for the political decision to allocate more money, but economical use of resources is the responsible way to proceed, whatever the amount available.

While an evaluative process is necessary, the cost-effectiveness methods currently in use are inadequate. They are most easily applied to short-term, single-input, single-output interventions and do not lend themselves to multi-input, multi-output, or long-term programs. They are also not appropriate for comparing different interventions for different goals, or deciding on allocative efficiency. Nevertheless, bilateral and multilateral agencies rely on these limited tools to determine the allocation of resources for health-sector interventions, with the result that only narrow, short-sighted programs pass the test: "*How* allocative decisions are made has a major effect on the allocation itself, with different priority-setting mechanisms leading to very different results" (Green and Barker, 1988, 919). The use of limited tools appears to validate the superiority of single-input interventions because those tools cannot measure the benefits of programs with heterogeneous or diffuse benefits, unanticipated spillover benefits, or benefits that take some time to appear.

Cost-effectiveness analysis is best used when there are identical outcomes to alternative treatments or when it is easy to measure a single objective (outcome) of the intervention (Henderson, 1999). In practice, however, cost-effectiveness analysis is used to compare different objectives in different areas with an arbitrary cutoff in monetary terms for which investments are considered good deals.[4]

4. For the debate on cost-effectiveness analysis and disability-adjusted life years in evaluating health interventions, see Green and Barker, 1988; Jamison et al., 1993; World Bank, 1993a; Briggs et al., 1994; Murray, 1994; Morrow and Bryant, 1995; Barker and

A good example of the limitations of using cost-effectiveness analysis to compare and choose interventions when the outcomes are different, when there are diffuse outcomes for one intervention, and when the results accrue only in the long run is a controversy that erupted in 1979. On the eve of the "water decade" of the 1980s, in which safe water and sanitary facilities were to be expanded worldwide, a cost-effectiveness study evaluated the use of oral rehydration therapy (ORT) for reducing infant mortality from a specific form of diarrhea (Walsh and Warren, 1979). ORT is one of the greatest medical advances of the twentieth century. The lives saved by that single intervention, in conjunction with other elements of GOBI (growth monitoring, breast feeding promotion, and inoculations), should not be understated. But the results of the Walsh and Warren study are cited to make inappropriate comparisons of the value of a single-input, single-output curative intervention (ORT) with investment in water and sanitation for the elimination of numerous water-borne diseases, as well as the reduction in household effort expended for water, and other collateral benefits.

While ORT has been a profoundly important innovation and has saved millions of children's lives, it is not the only intervention that is required for alleviating the burden of water- and waste-borne diseases. Although child mortality from diarrhea decreased as a result of ORT, global incidence of diarrhea did not decrease over the 1980s and 1990s (WHO, 1997; Warner, 2001). The long-term effects of frequent episodes of diarrhea have not been remedied.

If cost-effectiveness studies attempted to calculate the full benefits of a village water pump, they would have to include: the direct reduction in morbidity and mortality for adults as well as children from water-borne pathogens; the reduction in calorie expenditure from hauling water; the increase in time spent on family gardens from time not spent hauling water; the increase in child school enrollment from being released from the drudgery of water hauling; the increase in child enrollment because of greater school success from fewer diarrhea-related absences; and numerous other benefits. The benefits from latrines and other waste-disposal infrastructure are even greater (Esrey, 2001; Warner, 2001). Since these are chronic and widespread concerns in poor countries, the cumulative costs of doing without clean water and sanitation are enormous—and probably incalculable, at least with tools currently available, and that is just the problem.

In 1979 one could not anticipate that an investment in water infrastructure for household use might also reduce the toll of HIV in Africa, but that was established in the 1990s in studies that linked genital schistosomiasis and helminths to HIV (see chapter 3). Nevertheless, interventions to reduce parasite cofactors are still not incorporated into any cost-

Green, 1996; Anand and Hanson, 1997; Walker and Fox-Rushby, 2000; Walker, 2001; and Walker, 2003.

effectiveness studies of HIV prevention carried out by UNAIDS, USAID, or the World Bank. Impossible to measure, of course, is the benefit to morale of not living in the midst of human and animal waste, or the change in attitudes toward oneself that can begin when one is liberated from that prison of filth.

Another problem with exclusive reliance on a curative intervention, such as ORT, is that without a change in the water supply, and even more important, in the disposal of human wastes, children will continue to become sick and will have to be brought back from the brink of death over and over again. What cost-effectiveness studies of ORT do not capture are the deaths that result from repeated diarrheal infections that weaken the child (although rescued for the moment by ORT). The child becomes stunted from repeated infections; her growth, mental development, and immune health are all undermined by the repeated bouts of disease and consequent malnutrition. She may succumb the following year to an acute respiratory infection. The cost-effectiveness study for ORT records her life saved, as indeed it should, but the child is no better protected the following year.

Investments in good health are complementary because the causes of diseases interact. A cost-effectiveness study of a program to put a roof on the child's house could appear to show that good housing does not save lives if she dies of pneumonia after the roof is on. She needed a roof, but a latrine would have helped by preventing repeated diarrheal diseases and thus strengthening her immune system. A latrine *and* a roof would almost surely have saved the child and should not have to compete with ORT for funds. A cost-effectiveness study for ORT or any single intervention does not show the competing threats to the child or the synergistic benefits of multiple preventive interventions. ORT programs must be continued, but their cost-effectiveness should not be used as the model to make programs for the prevention of water-borne diseases ineligible for funding. Similarly, narrow interventions for HIV prevention should not rule out more comprehensive programs that address fundamental causes of the epidemic simply because the tools to measure cost-effectiveness are inadequate for problems with real-world complexity.

There is another perversity to cost-effectiveness studies that can be seen at the individual or family level and at the population level. Much of the cost of a successful ORT program is in the initial phase of educating the community, mothers in particular, of the life-saving therapy. For a mother of seven children, the more squalid their living conditions, the more diarrheal attacks they suffer—and therefore the more cost-effective is ORT. Having had the life of one child saved (through contact made with nurses), she will surely bring in her other children as they fall ill, without additional expenditure for outreach. If she has 14 children, and still no latrine, the cost-effectiveness of ORT improves even further. Does that suggest that, at the family or population level, the worse the water supply and waste-disposal facilities, the less cost-effective is their improvement because ORT is more cost effective? There is something wrong with an evaluative tool that can only confer a positive rating on bringing a child to the jaws of death and snatching her back.

Cost-effectiveness and HIV interventions

HIV/AIDS policy is constrained by a simplistic cost-effectiveness approach that would do nothing to keep a 14-year-old off the streets, but would validate an internationally funded program to provide peer educators to warn her of HIV when she engages in survival sex with a tourist. Everyone understands that health and development are complex webs, but the interventions that are implemented are only those that pass the simplest test of single-input, single-output cost-effectiveness analysis, and such interventions are last-minute, curative, individual, and dead-end.

There are specific problems with the way that cost-effectiveness studies are applied to HIV interventions and similar programs. First, for most of the interventions for HIV prevention, it is not possible to measure outcomes. The studies substitute intermediate inputs for output measures, generally without attaching a probability to the estimate. It cannot be known (under normal circumstances) if a person who has been peer-counseled changes his or her behavior. It cannot be known if a person properly and consistently uses the condoms that are distributed. Nevertheless, these studies equate condoms distributed with condoms used and simply presume a certain number of infections prevented, concluding that the intervention is therefore effective.

Another problem with cost-effectiveness studies of HIV interventions is that they make comparisons between interventions for which full cost data are provided and others for which they are not. Damien Walker conducted a review of numerous cost-effectiveness studies of HIV interventions (such as voluntary counseling and testing, condom social marketing, etc.) and pointed out that none of the studies had complete cost data. Some studies have no data at all and simply model the expected value of costs and benefits (Walker, 2003). Those hypothetical models are then accepted as demonstrating the greater cost-effectiveness of targeted interventions. The use of modeled projects biases the selection of interventions against those for which the full costs are known in favor of those that are modeled on the basis of overly optimistic assumptions about costs and outcomes.

A third problem with cost-effectiveness studies of HIV interventions is that they cannot measure multiple outputs. Some types of interventions appear to be very expensive because the multiple uses of an intervention have not, or maybe cannot, be included in the benefits. Walker points out that programs targeted at children are very expensive. They are considered expensive, however, because the shared costs of general education and HIV-prevention cannot be considered together in a simple model. If children are already in school, then the marginal cost of HIV-prevention education is not very high. Training a science teacher to teach HIV-prevention as well is much cheaper than stand-alone programs for children and is a spillover benefit of general education.

A fourth problem with cost-effectiveness studies of HIV prevention is that they do not include interaction variables. None of the cost-effectiveness studies of HIV prevention published by the policy groups ever evaluated an intervention to eradicate schistosomiasis or malaria. Even if a study were to evaluate the cost-effectiveness of treating schistosomiasis for HIV prevention or other population-health problems that affect HIV transmission in a multiburdened population, the beneficial effects might not be demonstrated at the individual level if only one intervention were included. In combination with other interventions, however, the results would certainly be cost-effective (although perhaps unmeasurable with current tools), especially in light of the treatment costs of HIV infection now being projected.

Externalities: applying an economic concept to epidemiology

The weaknesses inherent in single-input, single-output cost-effectiveness studies can be further illuminated with a concept long recognized in economics but not used in health economics: the notion of externalities. To economists, externalities (or "spillovers," in common parlance) are costs or benefits that fall on someone who is not a party to a transaction. If my neighbor buys a sound system and plays it at high volume, I do not have to pay the merchant or my neighbor (the two parties involved in the purchase of the sound system) for the pleasure I get from listening to the music. If I do not want to hear it, neither the merchant nor my neighbor has to compensate me for my irritation (a cost). If the social cost of unwanted music (a negative externality) were included in the purchase price, sound systems would be more expensive and fewer would be bought. When a positive externality exists, too little of a good is produced because the market only reflects the interests of the two parties to the sale, not others who could benefit from the production of the good.

The recognition of environmental spillovers as a market failure stimulated the elaboration of the economic analysis of externalities. If a factory can dump waste products into a stream without penalty, then downstream users bear the cost of pollution, rather than the firm and its customers (the parties to the transaction). The notion of externalities is linked to pricing in a market system. If no price is assigned to a good—if no value is assigned to clean water—then firms can pollute without absorbing the costs. Environmental protection, therefore, has proceeded on two fronts: prohibitions, such as noise ordinances, and taxation systems that essentially assign prices or values to environmental goods.

The failure to price goods accurately due to externalities leads to another type of problem, called *missing markets*. Because women's work time is assigned too little value, for example, communities have failed to invest adequately in easily accessed supplies of water for domestic use (Griffin and McKinley, 1994). Similarly in the health field, failing to recognize the personal and national cost of widespread parasite infection, governments have not invested adequately in safe water supplies. The market for deworming is missing because a market can only value the benefits of better health to the individual who has money and who buys the medicine. The market does not capture what the improved health of that individual could mean to community members and to employers whose hiring would be more efficient and whose investment in human capital enhancement would have a higher return. If we recognize the synergies between parasitic diseases, considered low priority in the past, and HIV, the problem of the missing market for basic health care becomes even more obvious.

Another concept linked to the notion of externalities is that of complementary markets. If coffee and sugar are always consumed together, then the absence of supply of either good eliminates the incentive for producers of the other good to enter the market. If either good is supplied, the other becomes worthwhile (Stiglitz, 2000, 83). Applied to investments in development, it is difficult to see the benefit of school construction when children are worm-burdened, of low birth weight, and stunted since children with those conditions do not learn much in school. In a parallel manner, it is hard to measure the effect of deworming on school attendance if there are no schools to attend or if household tasks, such as gathering water and firewood, prevent children from attending school regularly. Providing piped water to houses might be judged too expensive or not cost-effective for a single measured outcome, but that does not take into account the increase in the effectiveness of a clinic nearby that would then be relieved of very numerous, time-consuming visits to treat water-borne diseases.[5]

The trials in Malawi that administered vitamin A to pregnant women in order to prevent mother-to-child transmission of HIV were considered inconclusive (see chapter 3). With endemic malaria and all the other health problems of poor Malawians that could not be addressed in that trial, it is

5. I visited a newly built clinic on the outskirts of Mendoza, Argentina. The construction of the clinic necessitated the laying of a water line to the site. The neighborhoods along the way were provided with piped water, and doctors noted an immediate and dramatic drop in parasite infection in the population. That not only contributed to the greater efficiency of the investment in the clinic, since doctors, nurses, and medicines could be applied to other urgent needs, but it also made investment in schools more beneficial, since children without parasites attend more days and are more attentive when present.

impossible to say that vitamin-A supplementation is not efficacious for HIV-infected mothers. Using conventional cost-effectiveness analysis, however, vitamin-A supplementation would be abandoned because the results were inconclusive. Other trials might determine that malaria eradication or treatment should be abandoned because each, by itself, is insufficient to stop the AIDS epidemic. Either intervention might require a complementary intervention in order to be effective in reducing HIV transmission. There are complementary markets, or interventions, for HIV prevention that go unfunded because the methods used to measure cost-effectiveness cannot detect the benefits of those single interventions.

Biomedical analysis can comprehend disease synergies, although much of medical and biological research remains narrow and disconnected. Economics can comprehend externalities, missing markets, and complementary markets, although the notions of complementarities and synergies need to be incorporated into health economics and specifically into cost-effectiveness analysis. Externalities or spillovers are ubiquitous in any economy or health environment, but they play an especially crucial role in the prescriptions proposed in chapter 11 for remedies to the AIDS epidemics. That gives us reason for optimism. Just as opportunistic infections take advantage of reduced immune defense, opportunistic investments with multiple inputs and outputs increase their own cost-effectiveness and that of other projects.

Conclusion

Understanding the population dynamics of HIV transmission is trammeled by methods that examine only individual, and generally behavioral, variables. Evaluation of interventions for cost-effectiveness is similarly constrained by inadequate economic tools that measure only single inputs and single outputs. Each year 5 million more people are becoming infected with HIV, 95 percent of them in low- and middle-income countries. Yet epidemiology and health economics attempt to analyze and confront the epidemic in countries with 25 to 40 percent of the adult population HIV-infected with the same models and programs they would use in countries with less than 1 percent infected. The next chapter demonstrates the kinds of policies that result from the flawed methodology discussed here.

IV

Consequences

9

HIV/AIDS Policies

Too Little, Too Late

International AIDS policy continues to be ad hoc in approach, unscientific in conception, and narrow in focus. Current strategies for HIV prevention do not address the causes of susceptibility or the causes of behaviors and have been largely unsuccessful. Fixation on the proximate cause of HIV transmission reinforces tunnel vision among policy makers and analysts who continue to push for more money for the same kinds of end-game interventions, rather than tackling the broad array of cofactors that fuel the spread of HIV.

Poverty is recognized as one of the key factors promoting the epidemic, and yet some economists are urging developing countries to abandon poverty-eradication programs and dedicate all their resources to HIV alone. Plans of the international community to spend billions of dollars to prevent HIV transmission fail to get beyond the sex act to address the larger context of disease in poor communities. Similarly, the strategies that policy makers offer rarely encompass changes in gender relations or the status of women, although it is widely understood that gender relations play an important role in the epidemic. Condoms can be effective in minimizing transmission of HIV, but they are only of use to women who already have some degree of power in their sexual relationships.

The policy responses were initially conceived in an atmosphere of crisis. The problem we now face is the widespread transmission of an infectious disease in poor populations around the globe. That context is almost entirely absent from the emergency, last-minute measures that still comprise virtually all of global AIDS policy. If 1, 5, 10, or 20 years into the epidemic we are doing little more than handing out condoms, when will we deal with fundamental causes? This chapter examines the narrow range of policies offered by the major funders in the global AIDS arena.

Policy and path dependence

AIDS policy is greatly influenced by the perspective of the major funding and administering agencies. As in any field, people who become experts in a particular technique often find it difficult to consider other options. Experts not only carry with them a limited set of tools, but they also take on a preset view of how things work. AIDS policy options are limited in part because policy makers tend to see the problem as an extension of the work they have already done. They might repeat the refrain that AIDS is a development issue, but they tend to see it as a behavioral problem if their life's work is behavior-change communication. Organizations that have received hundreds of millions of dollars over the past three decades from USAID and other donor-country aid organizations for behavior-change communication or for condom social marketing have strong institutional momentum for continuing to receive funding for the same kinds of programs.

Because of the limitations of the methodology and the experience of major players that trammel the discourse, advocates call for more of the same narrow range of interventions.[1] Although this chapter criticizes the current HIV-prevention policies, it does not in any way call for completely abandoning the strategies now in place. It is necessary to fight HIV at all stages of susceptibility, even at the last possible moment. Nevertheless, the policies offered thus far are woefully inadequate and short-sighted, and, because of their narrowness, often useless or counterproductive.

The central theme of this chapter is that the HIV epidemic arises from social, economic, and biological conditions and cannot be solved with narrow behavior-modification programs. End-game interventions do not exploit biological synergies of host factors that would have a direct impact on reducing HIV transmission, and they do not change the environment in which people make decisions about their behavior. In policy documents, recognition of the context of HIV in poor countries is restricted to intro-

1. More of the same is not necessarily inappropriate if the programs are subject to increasing returns—for example, if people's behavior will start to change because of the campaigns' often repeated message. On the other hand, we have perhaps gotten all the mileage possible from this attempt at social engineering if people have become inured to the perpetual din of safe-sex messages.

ductory materials, slogans, and cover photos. The menu of policy options is quite uniform across organizations, regardless of the issue or group ostensibly targeted, and has no connection with the context in which HIV is spreading in the developing world and transition countries.

Postwar development agenda and impact on HIV/AIDS policy

The national and international strategies needed to advance human development and address the AIDS epidemics are already known. To select them from the larger set of possible strategies, tried and untried, will require us to ask what are our goals, to what extent have past or current policies helped to achieve those goals, and what is the best way to proceed, given that history and the current health crisis.

Our goal is a world of healthy people who have the freedom and resources to live in dignity. Rich and poor countries have expended billions of dollars, and uncounted thousands of skilled people have dedicated their lives to achieve that goal. The result of that effort has been generally disappointing because of several fundamental problems, including the nature of foreign aid, the type of investment favored, the misguided reforms of the 1980s and 1990s, and the legacy of racial policy in the development agenda.

First, the beginning of the era of development programs coincided fatally with the Cold War. The United States and the Soviet Union and their respective allies directed their aid to and distorted the operations of governments they wished to support for their geopolitical ends. The rivalry engendered numerous wars, brutal dictatorships, millions of refugees, and ongoing misery and the neglect of food security, health, education, and the construction of viable democracies.

Second, economists and donors alike overestimated the importance of large capital investments and underestimated the importance of a healthy, free workforce for human development and economic growth. That bias reinforced and was reinforced by the interests of corrupt government officials who could skim more from physical capital projects than from investment in human capital. Again, the billions spent in aid did not protect those populations from poverty and disease.

Third, when it became clear that bad policy and corrupt governments (rich and poor) had produced development failures, the opportunity for economic and institutional reform was squandered. The structural adjustment programs promoted and approved by the International Monetary Fund and lender governments did not embody thoughtful strategies to transform stagnant economics and suffocating and repressive states. They exhibited a quick-fix mentality and were built on ideologically driven, simple-minded concepts of how market economies actually function. Harsh austerity programs were supposed to immediately transform sick economies and dependent sectors into beacons of economic growth. Of course, some of the people involved—in borrowing countries, in banks, and in firms shopping for bargains—were only interested in stripping the countries of capital assets with no regard for the well-being of the economy or of the population. (For my analysis of the Argentine case, see Stillwaggon, 1998.)

There was a serious need for economic and political reform in the developing and transition economies in the 1980s. Instead, poor and working people were considered expendable; social spending was cut, jobs were eliminated, and state enterprises were looted. The international organizations insisted on opening the markets of poor countries to the exports of rich countries. That is a good thing if done properly because it encourages quality improvements and price reductions. But it cannot be done rapidly, especially in the poorest countries, without ruining domestic producers and vendors. What would have been less harmful would have been guidance and encouragement to modernize government institutions to make them more transparent and more efficient for the delivery of needed services. Technical and financial assistance to restructure local and regional trade, to create regional free trade zones, and to provide the road and rail links to support that trade would have been constructive structural adjustment.

If the rich countries wanted to help restructure the poor countries, the tools were there to do it constructively. Instead, they stood by or actively encouraged the stripping of state assets and the destruction of social service systems. Structural adjustment programs in many countries exacerbated the vulnerability of individuals and populations to epidemics of infectious disease, including HIV. Rural livelihoods suffered, and cities swelled with the unemployed. The economic collapse led to both more risky behaviors and a more risky health environment.

There is a fourth fundamental problem with past efforts to promote economic development, and one that is especially relevant to a critique of current AIDS policy. Development planning was, from the beginning, wedded to Western fears of the Third World "population bomb." Politicians of the late nineteenth century very explicitly enunciated geopolitical phobias that whites would be overpowered by people of color and poor people of their own countries (Furedi, 1997). Support for those fears was provided by the pseudoscience of eugenics, whose proponents favored procreation by "fit" members of society and the prevention of births among the "unfit." Eugenic thinking was explicitly embodied in the social hygiene and contraceptive movements of the early twentieth century. Numerous members and officers of the American Eugenics Society were also members and officers of International Planned Parenthood Federation and Planned Parenthood Federation of America. Frederick Osborn, long-time official and president from 1946 to 1952 of the American Eugenics Society, was a cofounder of the Population Council, along with John D. Rockefeller III. (John D. Rockefeller was also a member of the American Eugenics Society, and his son, John D. Rockefeller Jr., was a patron of the organization.) Alan Guttmacher was vice president of the American Eugenics Society from 1956 to 1963 and was president of Planned Parenthood Federation of America from

1962 until his death in 1974 (http://www.africa2000.com/ENDX/aedata.htm). (People who today work for the Population Council, Planned Parenthood, and similar organizations may even be unaware of their organization's roots in the eugenics movement.)[2]

Economic and social planning for development emerged in the 1950s, and population control quickly became a dominant theme of the development agenda. In a perverse twist of logic for what were supposed to be programs for human development, births became the problem, not poverty, sickness, and early death. That shifted the blame to poor people and away from the gross inequality, national and international, that makes so many people poor and sick. Development strategies in general and HIV/AIDS policies specifically are indelibly marked with that history.

It is certainly true that millions of women have had pregnancies that were unintended, and even coerced, and that a need exists for information about family planning. But many millions of women or couples have chosen to have numerous births because they wanted large families. For decades the population-control organizations saw their job as twofold: satisfying the actual unmet demand for contraceptive services, and convincing women in developing countries that they did not really want as many children as the women thought they wanted. They did not accept that poor women were making rational choices in having numerous pregnancies in their attempts to assure the survival of some children to maturity. A human development program built around the interests of parents would have been centered on child survival. Programs devised in New York (or in developing countries) that failed to see infant deaths as the problem spent decades and billions of dollars trying unsuccessfully to convince people to have fewer births. Bad philosophy makes for impractical policy. If the organization's goal had been helping women and children live healthy lives, instead of just preventing births, they could even have achieved their family-planning goals more efficiently. A reduction in infant mortality would have increased the demand for their family-planning services.[3]

2. It is very important to recognize the extent of influence of eugenic ideas, even in modern times. The reader is encouraged to browse through the lists of members, directors, and officers of the American Eugenics Society (AES) and its successor, the Society for the Study of Social Biology (SSSB). SSSB was the new name chosen for the organization in March 1973 because the term *eugenics* had strong associations with the Holocaust. Many AES and SSSB members and officers held or hold professorships at the most influential universities and were or are advisors to UN organizations or private foundations (http://www.africa2000.com/ENDX/aedata.htm).

3. Finally in 1994, developing-country representatives were successful in raising the issues of women's health and child survival at the UN International Conference on Population and Development in Cairo. Population Services International then applied its experience in social marketing of condoms to the sale of insecticide-treated bed nets, since malaria kills over 1 million infants a year in Africa alone, necessitating repeated

That history of development programs dominated by population control is very relevant for HIV/AIDS for two reasons. First, global HIV/AIDS policy is dominated by organizations whose institutional mission for nearly a half-century was population control in developing countries through behavior change. Second, HIV/AIDS programs, even in other organizations, have taken the same narrow behavioral approach and end-game tactics that population-control programs use. Population-control groups tried to change behavior to prevent births without offering people alternative ways of achieving desired family size or the security in widowhood and old age that children provide. Now behavior-change organizations try to prevent AIDS at the last minute, without changing any of the circumstances that lead to vulnerability to HIV, social or biological. A practical approach would be to ask what are the problems people face, and what can be changed in their environment that would reduce HIV transmission. Instead, HIV/AIDS programs are based on assumptions about how poor people behave and the paternalistic task of the West to change that behavior. Those often-unexamined assumptions are reinforced by an unscientific, narrow approach to preventing disease that ignores the biological context of susceptibility.

In part, the narrow approach of attempting to prevent HIV in isolation from other social and economic problems derives from the fears of the international organizations and rich countries, just as the fear of a "population bomb" motivates much of foreign aid. They are afraid of AIDS because it could affect them ultimately. They are not afraid of the ongoing misery of hunger, worms, and endemic diseases; of women who live in fear of their husbands and their communities; of boys and girls who live on the street or as prisoners in brothels. Preventing HIV transmission in brothels in Eastern Europe or the developing world, for example, protects high-cost health-care systems in Western Europe from the burden of citizens who return from sex tourism with HIV. Self-interest is not the only reason that European, Scandinavian, and U.S. aid agencies have contributed to AIDS programs. But it does, in part, explain the greater interest generated by AIDS than all the other miseries of poverty and lack of freedom that plague the developing and transition countries.

Major funders in global AIDS policy are UNAIDS, the World Bank, European aid agencies, and USAID and its major consultancy and supply partners, in particular, Population Services International (PSI), Family Health International (FHI), and the Futures Group International (TFGI), which includes the Policy Project. Although the organizations involved were established with different purposes, they have all converged on the same narrow track. PSI, FHI, and TFGI, for example, were established as

pregnancies for women to achieve their desired family size. In spite of that important change of focus, much bilateral and multilateral aid continues to reflect the old view that poor people are the problem.

population-control groups, so it is not so surprising that their strategies are chiefly restricted to condom distribution and behavior-change communication. (See their Web sites for organizational histories.) The other organizations were established as recovery and development agencies. The World Bank's mandate is poverty eradication and development. USAID is the development-assistance agency of the U. S. government. UNAIDS is the United Nations' umbrella organization for HIV/AIDS and, as such, represents the UN Children's Fund (UNICEF), the International Labour Organization (ILO), the UN Development Programme (UNDP), the World Health Organization (WHO), the UN Food and Agriculture Organization (FAO), the UN Population Fund (UNFPA), and a few other agencies. Each of those organizations, except UNFPA, is charged with a broad human development agenda that is to a greater or lesser extent affected by AIDS. Unfortunately, the human development agenda is lost in the very narrow programs that comprise global AIDS policy.[4]

There are a few new players on the scene, including the Bill and Melinda Gates Foundation and the Global Fund for AIDS, TB, and Malaria. Both have a broader health focus, although, so far, the programs they have funded for HIV/AIDS prevention have been essentially the same as those of the other organizations. Nevertheless, they are structured in a way that allows for much more creativity in devising programs that take advantage of biological and investment synergies, and they already direct much of their funding to broader health investments.

USAID

The U.S. Agency for International Development (USAID) is the U.S. government's foreign aid agency. It has projects in about 100 countries, providing assistance in agriculture, government operations, economic growth, environment, education, health, and humanitarian needs. USAID funds for AIDS programs since 1986 have amounted to over US$2.3 billion, which the agency reports is more than any other public or private organization in the world (www.usaid.gov). USAID reorganized its AIDS strategies in 1997 in an attempt to improve coordination among programs for prevention, treatment, and support. Prevention of new infections is considered USAID's top priority and absorbs about 70 percent of the agency's HIV/AIDS budget. USAID's listing of prevention activities is limited to the following:

4. There is one notable exception. The UNDP South-East Asia HIV and Development Project, under the direction of Lee-Nah Hsu, produced a significant number of studies and financed projects that addressed the development context of HIV spread in southeast Asia. For their varied, useful programs, see http://www.hiv-development.org.

- Developing interventions to change or prevent high-risk sexual behavior
- Treating other sexually transmitted infections, which increase the efficiency of HIV transmission
- Increasing demand for and access to condoms and other essential commodities
- Preventing mother-to-child transmission of HIV
- Promoting voluntary HIV counseling and testing, which is an effective way to achieve sustainable behavior change (www.usaid.gov).

The first and third items in the list are behavioral and last minute, and the other three are ex post. Additional components of USAID's program are care and treatment for those already infected, support for children affected by HIV/AIDS, increasing surveillance capacity to monitor the epidemic, increasing the capacity of developing-country health systems, and funding some biological and behavioral research. A final element of USAID's program is called "creating a supportive environment," which, as the Web site explains, means combating the social and political environment of stigma. They do not mean the biological environment of malnutrition and parasitic and infectious disease. All of USAID's components are essential, but they fall far short of an adequate response to AIDS from a development agency. The prevention component, in particular, is completely myopic. USAID has over 40 years' experience in agricultural development, environmental projects, education, and governance, which it could use and enhance to reduce upstream causes of the HIV epidemic.

In 2001 USAID published a lengthy summary detailing its activities throughout the world related to HIV/AIDS. At that time USAID had spent more than US$1.6 billion, and the United States was providing about half of the global resources spent on AIDS, according to USAID (USAID, 2001). The only mention of food security in the entire report refers to the impact of HIV/AIDS on agricultural output, and the only nutrition-related programs provide food to AIDS orphans. Incorporating the agriculture sector into HIV prevention consisted exclusively of printing HIV/AIDS messages on 800,000 fertilizer sacks in Zambia, hopefully not pasted on top of instructions on the safe handling of farm chemicals.

The 2001 report lists USAID programs in country after country that consist of condom distribution through Population Services International and usually include programs for voluntary counseling and testing as well. There are also projects to increase access to health services for treatment of sexually transmitted infections and for prevention of mother-to-child transmission. USAID also publishes country profiles on its web site (www.usaid.gov), in which it details the programs financed. In 21 countries in Africa with HIV/AIDS programs, 16 included condom social marketing and 13 financed behavior-change communication (BCC). Only two funded blood safety programs, and only three provided funds for preventing mother-to-child transmission. Only two country profiles, for Zambia and Kenya, listed intersectoral or multisectoral programs that integrate development programs with HIV prevention or care and support, and those are primarily postinfection or BCC in focus. Those are all useful programs, but the narrowness of USAID's approach reflects its heavy reliance on a few private-sector firms whose long-term interest has been in family planning. Hence, the solutions they offer rely almost exclusively on condom distribution and behavior-change communication. USAID has failed to integrate HIV into a broader development agenda, although the 2001 report contains a two-word reference to the "larger context." As for gender issues, the report says that "USAID programs . . . acknowledge and, where possible, address the economic and political conditions that put women at a disadvantage" (USAID, 2001, 41), a very weak statement indeed. And the list of actual programs shows that gender relations do not constitute a main component of USAID policies for HIV/AIDS.

The profiles provide some social and economic information as background for HIV programs in each country. The disconnect between the context of profound poverty and civil strife and the solutions they offer approaches high farce. For Rwanda, the country profile reports that rape played a very important role in spreading HIV. It has also been reported that rape continued to be a problem in refugee camps. The Rwandan national response financed by USAID, however, lists no element that addresses security for women, only the usual interventions: behavior-change communication, voluntary counseling and testing, promoting condom use. The military played a role in the rapes during the crisis period, but USAID interventions with the military do not deal with violence against women.

The full text of what the country profile says about USAID's involvement with the military is that "[i]n 2001, USAID supported three activities targeted at Rwanda's military: an 'HIV and the Military Town Meeting,' with call-in questions from six brigades nationwide; a behavior change communication campaign entitled 'A Hero Is Always Prepared' to promote condom use; and establishment of a voluntary counseling and testing center at a military hospital" (USAID, 2003, 4).

USAID recognizes the importance of engaging the Rwandan military, but it squanders the opportunity to make any real improvement. What could be more fundamental than criminalizing rape and inculcating civic responsibility among Rwandan military men? The most obvious behavior change that needs to take place is to stop rape, and yet it is not a part of USAID's program, not even for a part of Rwandan society over which USAID has some financial control. Nor is there any program for women's self-defense or funding to arm and train a women's militia. In the billions of dollars spent on HIV/AIDS programs, there are too many missed opportunities: instead of lecturing male soldiers that they ought to have used a condom to protect themselves in their last rape, USAID could work aggressively with that same captive audience on issues of gender oppression.

Other USAID activities in Rwanda include collecting data on sexual behavior in order to target the more vulnerable segments of the population. In a country where 40 percent of the population lives on less than US$1 a day, 26 percent of the population has malaria, and HIV prevalence is already 9 percent—who would not be vulnerable?

USAID partners

USAID has outsourced much of its research and program activities to a small number of key consulting firms, in particular PSI, FHI, and TFGI. Each of those large organizations has subsidiaries for specific USAID projects, and all three organizations had population control as their primary initial purpose. Their expertise is in behavior change communication and condom provision, and so it is not surprising that they would see those tasks as key to preventing AIDS and would promote them at every opportunity to USAID. When USAID scaled back its activities and outsourced much of its work to a small number of firms, it shackled its ability to confront an epidemic of infectious disease in the developing world because its priority was no longer social and economic development, but population control. Nevertheless, it must be said that because of their familiarity and comfort with issues of sexuality, the population-control organizations were willing to tackle AIDS when other groups ignored it. To the extent that any start was made in battling AIDS, those groups deserve the credit. Nevertheless, the end-game approach of population-control strategy—paternalistic behavior-change communication programs without change in the context of choices about family size—illustrates the narrow thinking that those groups bring into the AIDS battle.

Family Health International

Like the other USAID partners, FHI has smart and dedicated people who have enough time in the field to know that the context is an important determinant of the success or failure of their programs. Their publications have begun to acknowledge the environment of behavior, but their solutions still do not grapple with that environment. FHI publications promise a contextual approach, but they do not deliver on that promise in their policy recommendations. One such report argues that "[o]riginal models of HIV behavior change put far too much emphasis on individualistic approaches and failed to consider the social, cultural and economic environment and context in which the behaviors occurred" (Brown et al., 2001, 18). It goes on to assert that the recognition of factors beyond the control of the individual "led to the realization that individually targeted prevention efforts alone are insufficient to produce sustained behavior change" (Brown et al., 2001, 19). The chapter on recommended prevention strategy in that report, however, is entirely about behavior change communication, which it says is the cornerstone of policy, although there is one mention of seeking alternative employment for women engaged in sex work.

Another FHI book promises "Strategies for an Expanded and Comprehensive Response (ECR) to a National HIV/AIDS Epidemic" (Lamptey et al., 2001). The report admits that the rate of transmission has not been diminished by the interventions in place but proposes extending coverage of those same interventions. By "expanded response" FHI does not mean expanding the range of interventions. It means what others call scaling up, or "increasing coverage to different population types" (Lamptey et al., 2001, 3). When it refers to "synergies," it means providing condoms plus treating STDs, which are important but still represent a narrow range of interventions. By "comprehensive" they mean the same HIV-prevention strategies and HIV care and involving all organizations, governmental and nongovernmental. In their "situation assessment," there is nothing about the health profile of the population. Essentially, populations are portrayed as differing with regard to their sexual behavior (or in the case of Eastern Europe and former Soviet Union, drug-using behaviors), but not with respect to their health status. They do point out that "women at high risk" in a mining community "indicated that they were tired of receiving condom messages while other health issues were ignored" (Lamptey et al., 2001, 26). Even after reporting the women's expressed needs, this comprehensive response cannot comprehend the women's demand for good health rather than just the absence of HIV.

The report raises a number of important issues, but it fails to answer them with appropriate interventions. It points out that many countries do not have a safe blood supply and that contaminated blood accounts for perhaps 10 percent of primary HIV transmission in poor countries (p. 31), but ensuring the safety of the blood supply is not listed among "essential activities" (p. 79). It mentions that the lack of maternal-care infrastructure impedes the prevention of vertical transmission, but it fails to recognize that situation as an opportunity for an investment in primary health care that has positive spillovers for HIV prevention. It points out that a major barrier to voluntary counseling and testing is fear of stigma but does not recognize that stand-alone programs for STDs and HIV increase stigma and discourage use because everyone in town knows why you are going there.

Resources for HIV prevention are scarce relative to the need, but they are lavishly expended in narrow and repetitive studies, reports, analyses, and conferences that represent a serious diversion of funds that could be spent improving the lives of poor and sick people. Family Health International produced a book entitled *HIV/AIDS Prevention and Care in Resource-Constrained Settings* (Lamptey and Gayle, 2001). In its more than 700 pages, it never manages to convey what the implications of resource constraints are for poor people in poor countries. (There are resource constraints everywhere, but malnutrition in Zambia differs from water scarcity for golf courses in Phoenix.) The book is burdened with consultancy jargon and lacks any concrete evaluation of what are the biological and economic factors in the HIV/AIDS epidemics in poor ("resource-constrained") countries. Out of 28 chapters, there is only one that addresses "development constraints," and that one is brief, general, and essentially limited to the proposition that structural adjustment programs, trade liberalization, and development schemes led to more high-risk behavior. Even the case study in that chapter is not about a program to alleviate a development constraint but discusses instead a behavior-change program in a hospital in Zambia.

There are seven chapters about telling people to behave differently. There are no chapters about the health and nutrition profiles of the "resource-constrained" populations to whom all this preaching is to be directed. This 700-page work, subtitled *Handbook for the Design and Management of Programs,* never mentions the hundreds of articles in scientific journals that demonstrate the myriad ways in which malnutrition, malaria, schistosomiasis, helminths, and other endemic problems of poor people interact with viral load, immune response, and mucosal and epithelial integrity to promote HIV transmission. Even one chapter on the health profiles of poor people would have lent an air of reality to this otherwise surreal treatment of resource-constrained settings. Mainstreaming (to use a term popular in the AIDS literature) the reality of poverty into every chapter would have made it a much more useful document. The final chapter, on future challenges for prevention and care, covers only vaccines, antiretroviral therapy, barrier methods, male circumcision, orphans, and stigma.

Development opportunities foregone

An example of the shortsighted and narrow approach that results from the choice of USAID's "partners," its contract program consultants, is the project called Corridors of Hope, which is aimed at reducing HIV transmission along trucking routes and at border crossings. USAID has four partners for that project: PSI, FHI, TFGI, and the University of North Carolina (for statistical work). Delays at border crossings have been an important source of HIV spread because truckers find that no hotels are available or that staying with a commercial sex worker is cheaper than staying in a hotel. Border delays for customs clearance can take as much as 10 days in Zimbabwe, and up to 7 days in other sub-Saharan African countries (FHI, 2003). There is an immediate, policy-sensitive, and obvious solution to that problem, if it is looked at as a development issue. Border delays are costly to trucking companies, shippers, and the consumer. Cumbersome trade regulations raise costs, discourage trade and investment, and are both a symptom of a country's economic weakness and a cause. For a solution to this structural economic and political problem, USAID contracted the Corridors of Hope project to three organizations whose primary activity is behavior-change communication and condom distribution. Their solution is, not surprisingly, behavior-change communication and condom distribution. The primary cause of the border delays is a problem of economic development—costly trade regulation and corruption—that falls outside their expertise and is not addressed at all in this massive undertaking. USAID is trapped in a market-failure problem familiar to microeconomists. This is a case of supplier-induced demand.[5] USAID, a development agency with a talented staff of economists and political scientists, many of whom are experts on governance and trade issues, outsourced the analysis of what should be done about border delays (transport logistics and customs procedures) to organizations experienced in other fields (population control and behavior-change communication). It did not use the resources of the World Bank, which has already developed strategies for trade facilitation, nor did it enlist the help of the International Chamber of Commerce (ICC), which has a division for trade facilitation.

Obviously behavior-change communication is part of the answer, but it does not attack the problem in a sustaining way geared at maximum impact. In fact, one can imagine that truckers trained as peer educators for behavior-change communication would spend extra days at the border (putting up posters, educating their peers, and taking care of administrative details), imposing greater costs on their employers and possibly spending additional nights with sex workers. Another strategy offered is convincing sex workers to use condoms, but that might not be a sustainable solution, since even the same reports on the border problem acknowledge that sex with a condom brings the women a lower price.

Programs such as reforming border procedures are within the direct control of policy makers because they only require enforcement of administrative changes within the government. Behavior change, in contrast, can only be the target of programs, but it is not subject to the direct control of governments. Governments can educate and exhort; they cannot enforce behavior change. They can, however, enforce border procedures. The priority in strategies should always be those over which the agency can reasonably expect to exert control and those that have the broadest, most sustainable impact because they get to the fundamental cause.

USAID chose partners with the wrong incentive structure for solving the border problem. The 10-day delays at a border mean 10 days worth of condoms that PSI needs to provide. The longer the wait, the more it seems an emergency for which no other solutions can be offered. FHI's website makes that posture clear, as do many others, when they say they offer an expanded response through "proven interventions." Leaving aside for the

5. The case of supplier-induced demand is very clear in the market for medical services, for example. Patients are reluctant to reject the urging of doctors for additional tests or invasive procedures because they feel they do not have the knowledge to evaluate a doctor's suggestion, especially when third parties pay for the additional services that doctors supply.

moment that BCC interventions have not been proven to be successful in most places, the intimation is that there is no room for more complex ideas like structural change in the economic, social, or bureaucratic setting.

If USAID had sought the advice of different organizations, the problem would have been framed differently. For trucking companies, importing and exporting firms, and consumers, 10-day delays at a border mean:

- 10 days of idle capital (the trucks)
- 10 days of wages for idle skilled and semi-skilled truckers and their assistants
- 10 days of truckers' expenses
- bribes to petty officials to clear the paperwork
- higher health costs for trucking firms for HIV-infected employees
- higher training costs to replace workers who have died from AIDS
- impediments to shipping high-value goods because of increased risk of theft
- impediments to shipping perishable goods
- impediments to shipping low-value goods because the high fixed costs of border delays cannot be recovered in a competitive market
- cost to consumers from pressure by firms on government to reduce market competitiveness because of high fixed costs

That is just the beginning of a list of the impacts of border delays and the ways in which the resources of USAID, the World Bank, the International Chamber of Commerce, the UN Development Program, the World Trade Organization, and other organizations could be enlisted for HIV prevention. It is the basis for collaboration with the business community in ways that give them incentives to cooperate.

The Synergy Project also published a report on HIV transmission along trucking routes. The authors emphasize the "broader structural context" of HIV risk and comment that "typical intervention points for HIV/AIDS programs continue to focus on targeted groups of individuals, their behavior, and/or their health problems" (Synergy Project, 2002, 3). They cite reports that border delays in Zimbabwe can take up to 10 days, that in Uganda border officials do not work on Saturday or Sunday, and that in some places crossings close at four in the afternoon. The health toll on drivers who stay with sex workers at border posts is high. One estimate predicted that among truckers in South Africa, by 2005, there would be 403 AIDS-related deaths for every death from other causes. A Zambian trucking company lost 39 of its 144 drivers to AIDS in 3 years (Synergy Project, 2002, 23).

The Synergy report then evaluated 12 intervention programs. Although none of the programs addressed the legal/regulatory or corrupt practices that created border delays, the Synergy Project gave them high marks. Even programs that consisted of nothing more than peer education and condom distribution were said to have addressed the broader structural context. As in many other reports for USAID, FHI, TFGI, and UNAIDS, the status quo in condom promotion and distribution, generally with the same organizations, is said to be a success, even when the same reports state that there has been no apparent change in behavior and the environment of risk has not changed. The Synergy report concludes with 53 specific recommendations, of which 42 deal with condom distribution and peer education and eight address detailed aspects of treating STDs (including a separate recommendation for not naming a clinic "STD Clinic"). The specific recommendations are strongly worded when proposing the usual interventions, such as "[c]onvince trucking companies . . . to carry high quality condoms" (Synergy Project, 2002, 71). But they are weak and nonspecific in the few that refer to the structural context: "Advocate for government regulation and policy changes to support the overall program. For example, speeding the process of passing through checkpoints" (Synergy Project, 2002, 69). Even more vague is the recommendation to "[a]ddress, or at least take into account, the relevant socioeconomic and power issues—particularly in terms of women" (Synergy Project, 2002, 69). Finally, in the very last section of table IV-3 on the last page of text, out of 47 possible interventions, there is the two-word inclusion of "political pressure" (Synergy Project, 2002, 78) on ministries of immigration and commerce, without elaborating on strategies or providing models of streamlined regulatory framework.

The discourse on AIDS includes much discussion of behavior change and empowerment. The behavior change, however, is only expected from people in inferior social status to those seeking the change. And policy makers seem to lose their own sense of empowerment when it comes to talking to government or business, even about strategies that would increase government or business revenue or lower costs.

World Bank

The World Bank also failed to forge an integrated solution to a development problem and the spread of HIV/AIDS. Instead, their response to HIV transmission caused by the logistical stalemate at national borders relies on the standard package of behavior-change communication and condom distribution, even though the World Bank already has a well-argued, well-planned program for trade and transport facilitation. The guidelines for modernizing logistics in the region are clearly laid out in working papers published by the Sub-Saharan Africa Transport Policy Program (SSATP), under the auspices of the World Bank and the U.N.'s Economic Commission for Africa (de Castro, 1993; de Castro, 1996). If funded sufficiently, the plans would contribute substantially to development in the region and would both directly and indirectly stem the AIDS epidemic. The work of the transport division is of critical direct importance for the prevention of HIV spread. That fact is overlooked in the Strategic Review of SSATP conducted by the Netherlands Economic Institute. Their report put HIV/

AIDS in the category of issues that should be left to experts in "dedicated organisations" (NEI, 2001, 13). The people in the best position to do the most about HIV prevention at the borders were told to defer to behavior-change specialists who know little to nothing about trade facilitation.

At the same time, the World Bank also has a division of HIV prevention that is almost entirely focused on the standard package of behavior-change communication and related activities. The report, *AIDS and Transport in Africa* (World Bank, 2003a), illustrates the lack of integration of the bank's thinking. In an ironically apt disconnect, the forword, written by a World Bank highway engineer, presents various data on the epidemic in Africa, all of which were taken from a newspaper article rather than from the bank's own ample data on HIV. In the 78-page report, only a few sentences mention the importance of reducing border delays. The "core prevention interventions" listed are behavior-change communication (BCC), condom use, STD care, voluntary counseling and testing, and creating an enabling environment (being able to talk about sex) (World Bank, 2003a, 9). They do not include measures to facilitate the passage of trucks, goods, and drivers across borders, which would be beneficial in numerous ways. When the report discusses integrating HIV programs into the transport sector, it means actions such as painting AIDS ribbons on rail cars and including BCC in job training (p. 10). Surveillance means surveys of sexual behavior, not truck-release times in customs. The obsession with sexual behavior obscures the most obvious of solutions.

The World Bank is an organization one should expect to be concerned with how things work. The transport division should be interested in making trucking work. With that clear objective, it should be easier to do their job.

Global Business Coalition on HIV/AIDS

One of the most promising and yet perplexing developments in HIV prevention is the formation of the Global Business Coalition on HIV/AIDS. A consortium of over 150 businesses uses a Web site and face-to-face meetings and publications to promote HIV prevention in the workplace. For a group that one would expect to be pragmatic and interested in the bottom line, their suggested interventions are surprisingly superficial. What is completely lacking from the Global Business Coalition perspective is any suggestion that 150 large firms could have any influence in changing the conditions that everyone agrees promote HIV transmission. Large firms can and do exert influence on governments in the pursuit of conditions that will help them maximize their profits. For virtually no cost, in addition to their usual contacts with government, they could direct their lobbying to the reform of border regulations for international trade and other structural problems that provide the environment for HIV transmission.

What makes the most sense is for Global Business Coalition to concentrate on measures that improve the functioning of businesses in developing countries, by lowering costs and raising revenues in ways that are sustainable and that also support human development. Both businesses and their critics too often think that maximizing profits can only be achieved by worsening conditions for workers or the society as a whole. That reflects the very short-term mentality of profit maximization that has already caused untold damage to workers' health and to the environment. But companies in poor countries cannot flourish indefinitely by those means. The only companies that will actually benefit from an impoverished and diseased Third World will be pharmaceutical companies, and then only if aid is provided to pay for their products. Firms that sell products to well people, from beverages to furniture to tools and appliances, benefit from a healthy and affluent population.

It has taken a long time for it to dawn on businesses that grinding poverty is bad for profits ultimately. Now that it has, it should be clear that reacting to only one epidemic with only last-minute measures, the effects of which cannot be guaranteed or even adequately measured, is not a very business-like way to proceed.

Specific problems of HIV programs

In addition to the criticisms above that relate to narrow, behavioral policy in general, there are shortcomings to many of the elements of those programs. That is not a topic I will develop at great length because the larger problem is more important: that all of the money is taken up in such a limited range of programs, which cannot bring about a solution. Nevertheless, a few points need to be made.

Condom use has the potential of saving many lives and needs to be part of a program supporting safe sex. But condoms are useless if a person does not have the power in a relationship to insist on their use. Much more emphasis has to be devoted to changing sexual power relationships, and this does not apply only to populations in the developing world. Equality in sexual relationships is far from a reality all over the world, perhaps especially for young people.

Peer-education interventions require a serious reexamination. Money invested, for example, in training commercial sex workers to be peer educators is money that is not spent in enabling them to get another job. It is hard to see how the contradictions of sex-worker peer-education programs are not obvious to their proponents. Sex workers could well perceive each other as competitors, whereas in a factory, fellow workers would not generally see each other that way. Consequently, exhortations from competitors are likely to be viewed with suspicion, unless all the sex workers can organize collectively. In addition, sex workers face market pressure that militates against policy ends because not using a condom generally gets a higher price. Finally, some of the peer-education programs attempt to reduce transmission by convincing sex workers to have fewer clients. It takes very little business sense to understand that prostitutes work on a piece rate, and having fewer clients means lower income.

Another widely acknowledged problem with behavioral interventions is that there is a serious gap between what people know and what they put into practice (Guttman and Salmon, 1998). Consequently, policies that put all resources into attempting to influence behavior will get a relatively low return on investment compared with policies that affect controllable variables, such as government procedures.

Another weakness pertains to the overall design of most of the interventions that currently operate. HIV/AIDS is not an issue that can be addressed in isolation. There are serious conceptual and practical problems with the use of interventions that are narrowly focused on HIV and other STDs. Among the reasons HIV and AIDS, along with other STDs, should not be addressed in issue-specific and, even more so, stand-alone, programs are the following:

1. Stand-alone programs encourage the divorce of sex and sexuality from other aspects of a healthy lifestyle. Rather than integrating sexuality and STD prevention into health awareness, they ultimately add to the stigmatization of STDs, singling them out as requiring isolation and separate treatment.
2. They force people to use clinics and programs that are known to deal with the specific issues of sexuality and STDs, denying them the privacy that would enhance use of the service. Workers using STD-only clinics can reasonably expect howling derision or silent shunning from coworkers in almost all cultures. Community STD clinics would have the same effect among neighbors.
3. STD- or HIV-specific programs attempt to win people over to a healthy lifestyle by exclusively addressing the issue that for many people might be the most difficult place to begin. There are many other areas that could be incorporated into a health education plan that would ease people into a preventive approach.
4. Workplace and community programs narrowly addressing sexual behavior do nothing to change the environment that produces the unhealthy behaviors.

HIV interventions will only be effective if they are situated in a health program that is comprehensive, addressing a broad array of health problems that undermine immune response and act as cofactors for infectious transmission, along with a social and economic program that changes the context in which people make decisions about protecting their own health.

It is important to clarify what are and what are not problems in international HIV policy. Very often the literature in both development economics and public health is combative, impugning the motives and sensibilities of the players (on the other side). The problem in international HIV policy is not, for the most part, the players. They are smart, dedicated people who are sincerely interested in finding solutions to HIV. Few have a personal vested interest in a particular program or intervention, but most only have experience in one field. They have been trained in a narrow behavioral approach, and, in their experience at school and in international organizations, only such narrow studies are approved and funded. The professionals in this field often produce very good models that address the specific topic they want to address. The overall effect, however, is to restrict the options that are considered possible because of the weight of methodological bias and path dependence. The most important problem is that the same strategies are recycled over and over again, and there is very little thinking outside that box.

HIV/AIDS is a complex biological issue, with complex social and economic contributing causes. It can only be tackled in a multidisciplinary manner. At present, most scientific efforts are in very specialized subfields. The vast majority of HIV research does not address interactions between HIV and other biological conditions. Prevention is considered the province of behavioral scientists and health economists. The approach of health economics, at least as it is seen in the literature of AIDS economics, is really more cost accounting, which should be just one important step in a much wider project.

The way that services are structured is also a waste of resources. There are enormous economies of scale and scope in situating HIV prevention and care in primary care clinics, in workplaces, and in the community. The same facilities and occasions that are used for voluntary counseling and testing, condoms, and STD treatment, can be used to promote good nutrition, counsel against substance abuse, raise awareness about spousal abuse, or distribute antiparasitals.

Primary-care clinics save money not just because of economies of scale and scope but also because of the substantial externalities and positive spillover effects in health programs. Children treated for worms learn better and stay in school longer. In school they can learn how to protect themselves from unsafe sex, and protected from worms, they suffer less malnutrition and its consequent immunosuppression. Adults treated for worms or tuberculosis work better and longer. Healthy, more prosperous people have more chance to use the information of prevention campaigns.

Chapter 10 examines workplace HIV/AIDS programs as an example of the limitations of global AIDS policy.

10

Workplace Interventions for STD and HIV/AIDS Prevention

HIV policy, while very uniform in the types of programs it comprises, goes through phases in the locations or groups that are the focus of those programs. One such phase is seen in the substantial new literature regarding, and many new policy initiatives for, workplace interventions. USAID, FHI, UNAIDS, ILO, the U.S. Department of Labor, and other organizations all issued major reports on workplace interventions between 2000 and 2003. The workplace is one very promising venue for health-promotion activities, but the proposals for workplace HIV interventions thus far are mired in paternalistic and narrow behavior modification, as are most other HIV-prevention programs. They are limited by their own single-issue, end-game approach. This chapter examines the proposals for workplace intervention and proposes a model for health programs that are appropriate to the workplace and address the needs of workers and employers. The chapter first considers the advantages of the workplace for HIV interventions, then the problems with a workplace focus for AIDS prevention, and finally a plan for workplace health promotion that incorporates the broader economic and social context of health.

The biggest advantage of siting HIV-prevention interventions, and by extension broader-purpose clinics, in the workplace is a pragmatic one. The workforce is a captive clientele, and the workplace is a convenient location to dispense and receive services. In the case of HIV/AIDS prevention and treatment, the workplace is especially opportune because most HIV prevalence occurs in the working-age population.

The workplace is a good location, for example, for treating tuberculosis, with or without HIV coinfection. A formal-sector workplace has the operational structure to manage directly observed therapy (DOTS), the best method for maintaining drug treatment over the long period necessary for curing tuberculosis. Since people show up every day for work, and their attendance is recorded, they need not go anywhere else for the treatment and a system of recording doses already exists in the attendance monitoring. Treatment of opportunist infections can make improvements in quality of life that increase productivity and compensate firms for the expense of managing the system (Morris, 2003).

Workplace intervention, however, is only feasible in large, formal-sector workplaces that have the infrastructure and budget to launch the program and a workforce large enough to guarantee a certain degree of anonymity for the workers. There are serious practical, political, philosophical, and economic problems that the bilateral and multilateral organizations fail to acknowledge when they promote the workplace for HIV intervention.

Practical problems

The first problem is that focusing HIV-prevention efforts on the workplace omits about 60 percent of the workforce and an even larger percentage of the adult population and total population. That model could work to some extent (for those who are employed) in Germany, France, Japan, or the United States. In the developing world, however, the majority of people are employed in small workshops of just a few people; in single-table markets alongside the highway; or at bus stops, in train stations, on sidewalks in cities; in gas stations; in large markets, as sweepers, mechanics, and shop helpers; and as agricultural and construction day laborers. Those workplaces and employment arrangements are unlikely situations for an employer-financed HIV-prevention and treatment clinic.

Informal or small-firm employment represents the majority of workers in the developing world. In Argentina, which was once among the more industrialized of developing countries and had an extensive employment-based health-care system, only 60 percent of the workforce is now in the formal sector. Of those, nearly 20 percent work in firms with five or fewer workers. In Bolivia, there are more than twice as many people who are *cuentapropistas* (on their own account) and family workers as there are wage and salary workers. In Colombia, 40 percent of the workforce is in the informal sector. In Indonesia, two-thirds of the workforce is reported to be self-employed, casually employed, or unpaid labor. In Malawi, 38 percent of the workforce is employed by micro- and small enterprises, and even in

Mexico, a much richer and more industrialized economy, 42 percent of the workforce is thus employed. In the Philippines, there are more own-account and unpaid laborers than wage and salary workers. In Thailand, of 34 million total employed, almost two-thirds are own-account or unpaid family workers. (ILO provides links to many national statistical offices at www.ilo.org/dyn/lfsurvey.)[1]

Nevertheless, the formal-sector workplace is a very convenient venue. The choice is sensibly opportunist because it provides a captive audience. Workplace interventions would make it possible to reach as much as 40 percent of the workforce. The workplace clinic can also serve as a model for neighborhood clinics to meet the needs of informal-sector workers, unemployed persons, at-home workers, children, and the elderly.

Political problems

Health-care provision that is workplace-sited is a step backward from the principle of health as a human right or health care as a civil right. Situating prevention as part of a health-care program in the workplace makes health a part of the wage contract. In a developing country, the aristocracy of labor already enjoys an aristocracy of health care. Furthermore, when health care is tied to the wage, it limits workers' mobility and bargaining power on other issues. Neither of those flaws is an impediment if health care for a worker and a worker's family is also available outside the workplace and is therefore not contingent upon securing or continuing in employment.

This is a very important distinction and needs to be kept in mind when a developing country is expanding the scale of health services. The nation should begin with a clear conception of the political decision that is being made. An example of the difference between an employment-tied system and a citizenry-tied or residency-tied system can be seen in Argentina, which had a very good national health system until the 1950s and then introduced a European-style social security system for its formal-sector workers. When the formal sector failed to expand and encompass most of the workforce, a health crisis of grave proportions overtook the country. The corporatist solution was not even feasible, even if it had been desirable (Stillwaggon, 1998). Countries that are less industrialized than Argentina, including most

1. Data were obtained from national statistical offices. The national sites are: Argentina, INDEC at www.indec.mecon.ar; Bolivia, INE at www.ine.gov.bo; Colombia, DANE at www.dane.gov.co/inf_est/cont_empleo.index.html; Indonesia, NLFS at www.bps.go.id/employ/index.html; Malawi, ILO Subregional Office for Southern Africa at http://www.ilo.org/public/english/region/afpro/mdtharare/scripts/indicator.php; Mexico, STPS at www.stps.gob.mx; Philippines, CENSUS at www.census.gov.ph; and Thailand, NSO at www.nso.th/eng/stat/lfs/lfse.htm.

African and Caribbean and some Asian countries, are no more capable of maintaining a comprehensive employment-based social security system that covers the entire population than was Argentina.

Neither the pragmatic nor the political difficulty need be a barrier to workplace interventions and health-care provision, as long as the workplace is recognized as just a convenient venue for delivering services for one segment of the population, with the service replicated for unemployed or informal-sector workers in community clinics. Poor countries initiating or expanding primary health-care services should not use a model that promises, at best, an aristocracy of health and limits workers' freedom by tying health benefits to their jobs.

Philosophical problems

If the workplace is to be used for health programs, we must then ask what kind of program is appropriate. It can only be the enormity of the AIDS epidemic that has propelled so many people and organizations to promote HIV prevention and education in the workplace without examining some of the implications of such an approach. All of the literature on workplace HIV interventions confidently exhorts employers to take an activist role in persuading employees to change their sexual behavior. They make the case that such employer activism will protect firms from the costs of an AIDS-burdened workforce and that it will help national prevention efforts.[2] Except in unusual—and often illegal—situations, however, employers are not party to workers' sexual relationships. In fact, under other circumstances, employers' attempts to insinuate themselves into workers' sex lives would have been opposed by civil libertarians and workers' representatives. Such an intrusion needs to be acknowledged as a change in the nature of the employer-employee relationship.[3]

To what extent are we willing to alter employer-employee relations? Maybe we do have a health emergency in the HIV/AIDS crisis such that a suspension of the normal rules of the game is warranted. If that emergency exists in sub-Saharan Africa, does it also exist in Latin America and the Caribbean, in Asia, and in Eastern Europe? A number of recent publications on workplace interventions include directions or suggestions to firms of

2. Whether an activist policy protects an individual firm and whether a firm can be expected to provide, without compensation, a prevention program that is a public good are discussed below.

3. The Ford Motor Company took such a paternalistic approach with its workforce in the early part of the twentieth century. It formed a Department of Social Work that employed social workers who visited the homes of Ford employees and checked on their hygiene and family life.

initiatives to take on HIV/AIDS, such as to include in new employee orientation the HIV/AIDS prevention behavior that is expected of all employees. Do we really want to insist that employers tell workers how to conduct their personal lives?

And if such an emergency exists that governments, international organizations, and nongovernmental organizations (NGOs) are willing to tell private firms how to run their businesses, why are the measures so limited? In the workplace literature, the list of things that managers are told to do is extraordinarily narrow when one considers the myriad ways in which workers' lives could be affected, even just for HIV, let alone broader health concerns. Why such a paternalistic interest in sex, which also happens to be an area most vulnerable to exploitation of confidentiality?

The workplace-intervention guides exhort managers to tell their workers to use condoms. ILO, FHI, USAID, and the Global Business Coalition see it as within their province to tell private firms what managers should say to workers about condoms, but nowhere in the literature do they exhort employers to make those managers stop the ongoing, daily, hourly degradation of women that often occurs in the workplace, that contributes to an abusive attitude toward women in personal relationships, and that prevents people from thinking clearly about safe sex. If the Global Business Coalition and USAID and ILO and FHI and the Policy Project can all tell employers that they should hand out condoms, why can they not tell employers to hire more women and let the women decide what kind of sexual relationships they would have in a world in which they have independent incomes?

The programs now promoted aim to change the relationship of government and business, of employers and employees. If the health crisis justifies overhauling the rules of the game, then that change needs to be more creative. If the workplace is to be used in this way, less myopic goals would yield more provident results, including a reduction in HIV transmission. Why should firms get involved in workers' sex lives and not in their economic lives, which are more directly related to work and wage issues?

The workplace-intervention guides urge firms to include HIV prevention in the orientation of new managers. To adequately manage a workforce, especially given the skewed income distribution of most developing countries, managers should receive orientation on workers' housing, water supply, income relative to a standard consumer basket, status of their civil liberties vis-à-vis the police, and so on. That is not only the logical concomitant of changing the rules of the game, it is also necessary to comprehend the context in which people make choices regarding their sexual behavior. There is little reason to assume that people will change their behavior significantly if the environment that produces that behavior does not change. If workers have miserable, alienating lives, then orienting managers about workers' sex lives without information about workers' lives in a broader context will not yield any solution.

Economic problems

The momentum for workplace interventions for HIV prevention comes from bilateral aid agencies and international organizations. It seems that they see firms as potentially deep pockets of untapped funds for HIV prevention and treatment. A two-pronged appeal to social conscience and the firms' self-interest is the approach taken. The argument for using the workplace is framed either as a human rights issue or as a way for firms to protect themselves from the costs of HIV. The arguments for workplace intervention go together with a policy of nondiscrimination against workers who are, or who are suspected to be, HIV-infected because stigma and fear of job loss are serious obstacles to effective national prevention programs. Neither argument, however, is likely to be convincing to the businesses that are expected to absorb the costs of nondiscrimination, prevention, education, and even treatment.

The normative argument—that firms *should* provide HIV-prevention programs—asserts a human rights position (see AIDS Law Project, 1997) without recognition of the fact that key players (the firms) are not constituted to make decisions on the basis of rights. There is a fundamental disjunction between the language of human rights lawyers and advocates and that of business. It is unlikely in any economy based on profit-maximization that firms will invest when they cannot be sure to reap the benefits. For the most part, the substantial literature in the field of law and human rights addressing HIV/AIDS does not acknowledge the very different perspective of the business community. The demands of stockholders and the exigencies of the market compel the firm to see this year's or this quarter's bottom line as the key variable in decision making. The objective of the firm is to maximize profits.

The clash of ideologies is muddled further when strategies that are merely pragmatic are asserted as "workers' rights." A United Nations document on workplace interventions for HIV prevention listed, among the rights of workers, the "right" to supplies of free condoms readily at hand at work. ("Laws, regulations and collective agreements should be enacted or reached so as to guarantee the following workplace rights: . . . Adequate supplies of condoms available free to workers at the workplace" [United Nations, 1998, 20–21]). Unless the workers are brothel-based commercial sex workers, condoms are not really a workplace issue. The "right" to condoms has not played a role in the long struggle for workers' rights, alongside the 8-hour-day and collective bargaining. Having condoms readily available at work is a good idea and an opportune use of location. Mixing up pragmatic strategies with "workers' rights," however, makes a dialogue with business more difficult.

Business-oriented literature on HIV/AIDS addresses the concerns of firms better, but it still provides little hard evidence to convince firms that compassion should override profits. It tends to express wishful thinking and generalizations rather than convincing evidence of the benefits to firms of joining in a national campaign against HIV. Whether produced by the ILO, USAID, any of the consulting firms that write for USAID, or the Global Business Coalition, they cover the same menu of options and do not distinguish between positive and normative statements. Often they do a good job of positive analysis (costs of a workplace plan) but then slide into saying what firms should do, without acknowledging the difference. Often that elision is disguised with, "Firms are finding that . . ." or "Firms are increasingly recognizing that . . . ," but without providing evidence.

In reality, most firms will do everything they can to shift the burden of a HIV-infected workforce from themselves to the individual or the government. Whether or not firms provide health benefits, firms become responsible for a stream of costs when workers become infected (Simon et al., 2000; Rosen et al., 2002b). Those costs are considerably greater for firms that do provide health benefits. Firms have several options when faced with high costs from HIV. They can: (1) reduce benefits, including sick leave, health care, and pensions; (2) avoid hiring "risky" workers; (3) outsource production that involves workers in risk groups (drivers); and (4) shift from labor-intensive to capital-intensive techniques. By reducing their costs, firms move the burden to households and government. (For discussion of shifting the burden of HIV/AIDS, see Simon et al., 2000; Rosen et al., 2002b.) In high-prevalence settings, firms have already taken those steps. Governments can constrain those actions, but then companies might fail or relocate. In sub-Saharan Africa, the economies of Botswana, Namibia, and South Africa are protected because firms cannot relocate their diamond and other mining operations. South Africa dominates the sub-Saharan economies, and its superior infrastructure makes it less likely that nonmining firms will move north to less HIV-affected countries. The possibility of firms relocating is much greater for small countries with few unique resources, including those in the Caribbean, Central America, Southeast Asia, and the transition economies.

When considering a prevention program, firms have no guarantee that they will be among the beneficiaries of any investment they make in better health for the workforce. Calculating benefits that firms cannot capture from prevention programs that they are expected to finance does not help make the case with business leaders about the constructive role they can play in a national HIV-prevention strategy. In an economy of free wage labor, firms cannot force HIV-negative workers to stay in their employ on the basis of the firms' prior investment in the workers' health.

In order to make a dialogue between human rights advocates and businesses feasible, governments must recognize the public-goods nature of HIV prevention and the necessity to enlist firms in ways that enhance, rather than reduce, productivity. HIV prevention is a public good because everyone benefits from a healthier workforce, but no individual firm has an interest in bearing all the costs of nondiscrimination or running an HIV-prevention program because it cannot claim a return on its investment.[4] Having a healthy workforce is good for all firms in the economy, but it is too expensive for any one firm to launch a comprehensive HIV-prevention scheme, and even if a firm was successful in preventing HIV among its workers, it could not prevent those workers from changing jobs or, for that matter, from being killed in a bus accident.

There are economic benefits from a national prevention program based on nondiscrimination and workplace intervention, but those benefits are diffuse. The costs of continuing to employ workers who are, or who will be, sick are specific to the firm. Conventional economic analysis recognizes the difference between private costs and benefits and social costs and benefits and allows for the existence of public goods where private and public interests diverge.

The workplace and health promotion

Once firms have been enlisted in a national HIV-prevention program, there are important economies-of-scale and economies-of-scope arguments for siting those programs in comprehensive workplace primary-care clinics. HIV/AIDS has raised awareness of issues that should have been resolved long ago. Malaria, tuberculosis, cholera, worms, STDs, and violence have always been costly to workers, employers, and developing economies. A workforce free of disabling disease is beneficial for the economy, but no firm is willing to incur the full costs of protecting workers' health. A human rights approach to good health, including HIV prevention, is compatible with economic health, as long as the private and social costs and private and social benefits are calculated in a transparent manner. The developing world is in a health emergency. The dismal performance of their economies even before HIV/AIDS was evidence enough. Now governments, business councils, and nongovernmental organizations seem ready to confront the crisis. Using the workplace productively requires first that it not be the only place that health education and health care is available, although it can serve as a model for other locations. There are three additional requirements for a successful program. Health promotion has to be recognized as a public good. The medical approach has to be acknowledged as only part of the solution. And the programs have to offer comprehensive health promotion, not just HIV prevention.

4. A public good is one that confers a benefit on everyone; the enjoyment of the benefit is nonexcludable and nonrival. The classic example is national defense. Protection from invasion is good for all individuals and firms in the economy, but it is too expensive for any one firm or individual to provide, and no firm can capture all of the benefits of such an investment.

Governments have to recognize that health promotion is a public good. In an economy based on profit maximization, it is pointless to argue or plan for what firms *should* do by any other standard. Sometimes firms will do things that are not in the interests of short-term profit maximization, but that is very unusual. Some firms are providing antiretroviral medications to their employees (often just to their managers) although they have found that it is not cost-saving (Rau, 2002). In general, firms will try to avoid costs and shift the burden of sick employees to their families or the government (Simon et al., 2000; Rosen et al., 2002a).

The second requirement is that HIV prevention and treatment must be part of a larger program to address the causes of vulnerability and unsafe behaviors. Firms have to hire more women and take an active role in stopping the degradation of women in the workplace. The workplace guides tell firms to make HIV avoidance part of the requirements of a job (although it is unenforceable). It can certainly make degradation of women in the workplace a dismissible offense.

Considering that so many organizations have recently launched programs on "workplace interventions" for HIV prevention (ILO, USAID, FHI, and the Global Business Coalition), it is odd that there is so little suggested that would actually change aspects of the workplace or work time. There are cursory suggestions to provide migrant workers with housing for their families, but that generally comes as one line after 45 pages of minutiae on condom-distribution strategies. Mine and factory workers, such as those in southern Africa who live 11 months of the year away from their families, have a whole grab-bag of health problems that result from that separation. That is a workplace issue. Nutrition suffers in single-sex hostels. Stress and violence are endemic; loneliness and depression and substance abuse are more likely in such a setting. Along with numerous synergistic health problems, single-sex hostels and family disruption also produce STDs and HIV transmission. How does it even occur to the organizations to offer those men only condoms and a lecture?

As noted earlier, a few publications have made brief mention of changing customs procedures to reduce waiting time at borders. Organizations with significant political power, such as the Global Business Coalition, could have a very important impact if they were to band together to insist that governments take apart the system of corruption that keeps the truckers at the border. That would be a workplace and business intervention that would save workers' lives and corporations' money. Uniting to tackle corruption should be a major theme of business-oriented HIV literature, not an occasional footnote.

Finally, workplace health interventions should be comprehensive. Since the various organizations are attempting to incorporate firms in the provision of public goods, then the interventions should exhibit more vision and wider impact. None of the guidelines for workplace interventions explains why firms should intervene only in the case of STDs and not other diseases.

A key WHO training manual for workplace clinics (not specifically aimed at HIV) asks the important question, "What are the main objectives of your programme?" (Creese and Parker, 1994, 45). This is an important issue in workplace interventions. Is the objective a healthy workforce or just a workforce without HIV? None of the articles or documents on workplace interventions for HIV prevention explains how a firm is better off if it saves a skilled worker from HIV, only to lose her to spousal abuse, tuberculosis, or malaria.

There are myriad health concerns that affect poor and working populations in developing countries, from worms and other parasites to on-the-job hazards, intoxication from unsafe food and water, toxic wastes in their neighborhoods, poor nutrition, and chronic diseases (see Stillwaggon, 1998). Workers are very familiar with these health concerns. They provide a good starting point for health education and prevention programs. In its HIV-education program NAMDEB Diamond Corporation in Namibia found that a problem with HIV/AIDS communication programs was that "information is repeated to a point where audiences 'tune out' " (Rau, 2002, 87). This important information was noted in one of eight case studies in appendix D to a 100-page report. They also found that workers needed a wide range of health information, and that HIV-prevention information was better absorbed when it was one issue in a series of 10 monthly topics on a broader range of adult and family health concerns, including malaria, alcohol, child abuse, and stress. People are eager to have information that will help them protect the health of their families. After building trust and experience with health promotion, interventions related to the socially and emotionally charged issues of sexuality and STDs will have much greater effect.

Decades of experience have shown that broad access to primary health care is the most cost-effective way to improve health. Many of the firms whose HIV-prevention successes are listed on the Web site of the Global Business Coalition for HIV/AIDS already had primary-care clinics in the workplace for their employees. They were able to launch HIV-prevention campaigns because the workers were already integrated into a health-promotion program. The lesson to be learned is that HIV-prevention advocates have failed to look to successful examples of health care in the developing world and have narrowed their approach to a model of paternalistic behavior modification.

Chapter 11 offers a few strategies to change the environment of risk and the ecology of disease for poor people in poor countries.

V

Solutions

11

Opportunistic Investments for Health and Human Development

This book has made the argument that the AIDS epidemics in the developing world and the transition countries are neither random nor inexplicable events. They are the predictable outcome of an environment of poverty. Just as the health of the natural environment depends on a complex network of ecosystems, so, too, does the health of human populations depend on the interaction of numerous biological factors and their interplay with social, economic, and environmental circumstances that comprise the ecology of poverty.

In the face of myriad health problems in developing and transition countries and billions of dollars spent on HIV/AIDS prevention with little effect, the prospects for combating the AIDS epidemic might seem bleak. The message of this chapter, however, is optimistic. As daunting as is the list of necessary interventions to improve health in developing and transition countries, we already know what to do and how to do it. Furthermore, correcting the wide array of health and related human development problems is far more affordable, even profitable, than is generally recognized.

As we saw in chapters 4, 5, and 6, the conditions that increase the vulnerability of a population to HIV/AIDS are widespread in developing and transition countries. In spite of the unprecedented wealth in the world as a whole, the precarious existence of billions of people made the emergence of pandemic HIV/AIDS possible, through biological, social, and economic routes. The solutions proposed in most AIDS discourse for this biological and economic disaster address neither the biological nor the economic causes of widespread transmission. The interventions that are now funded remain almost exclusively behavioral. Proponents of those policies argue that their methods are more economical because they are aimed directly at the act that leads to transmission of HIV from one person to another. But in few places are the epidemics slowing down. Why should we expect simplistic methods to solve complex problems? Furthermore, since poor people and poor economies have so many health problems that threaten their viability, why should we put all of our funds into preventing just one disease, one act at a time?

Synergies, bad news and good

Few diseases are monocausal or so virulent that they can spread rapidly without supporting conditions. Most epidemics require a supportive context of economic, social, and environmental factors. Even fewer diseases have purely behavioral causes. There are, of course, behavioral elements to virtually every disease transmission. Drinking contaminated water is a behavior, but one can hardly say that people get sick with cholera because they have a drinking problem. Becoming sick with cholera should not be viewed as the result of drinking behavior but of the infectious dose in the water consumed and the immune strength of the person consuming the contaminated water. Poor people have worse water, and they are less resistant. They probably do not drink more water.

Tuberculosis infection depends on the virulence of the cases around the person exposed to the disease and on that person's immune status. The problem is not the behavior of breathing, but where and with whom one does the breathing and the personal vulnerability of the person engaged in the breathing behavior.

As we have seen, the same can be said for HIV and other diseases that are transmitted sexually or vertically. Sexual contact or maternal infection is a necessary, but not a sufficient, condition for transmission. (The risk of infection through needle-sharing or blood transfusions is much greater, and the importance of cofactor vulnerability is consequently less significant.) Transmission depends on who transmits the virus (because identical behaviors produce different amounts of transmitted virus) and who receives it (how vulnerable a person is to infection). The viral load of the HIV-infected person is generally higher if that person is malnourished; has untreated bacterial STDs; has malaria, TB, or other diseases; harbors helminths and other parasites; is burdened with schistosome worms and eggs; or has other cofactor conditions. Having sex with a person who has one or more of those conditions is far more dangerous than having sex with an otherwise healthy HIV-infected person. An infant is more likely to become infected with HIV from the mother if the child is malnourished in utero, if the mother has malaria, or if the child's immune system is activated by the mother's exposure to helminths and other parasites. Furthermore, all of those conditions weaken the immune status of HIV-negative persons. Exposure to the same amount of HIV virus, therefore, leads to sharply different likelihoods of contracting the infection between persons who are otherwise healthy and those who are burdened with malnutrition or parasites.

Not only are there numerous health conditions that contribute to vulnerability to disease, but also those conditions behave synergistically. Synergies make the impact of one condition more potent because of its interaction with others. For example, undernutrition is a serious problem on its own. Combined with contaminated drinking water, it can lead to more serious gastrointestinal results than in a well-nourished person, since the undernourished person lacks specific nutrients to resist disease-causing microbes in the water. Undernutrition combined with lack of vaccination can lead to catastrophic results from immunopreventable diseases such as measles. Measles depletes vitamin A, which is necessary for healthy eyes and resistance to infection. In vitamin-A-deficient children, measles can cause blindness and death. Malnutrition and parasite infection also have synergistic relationships (see chapters 2 and 3). As we have seen earlier, malnutrition and parasite infection also have a synergistic effect on HIV transmission. In the language of current discourse on HIV/AIDS, malnutrition and parasitosis are cofactors for infectious disease, including HIV/AIDS.

But synergies are not just bad news. They are opportunities for intervention. Adding vitamins or other nutritional supplements to a program for control of infectious or parasitic disease increases the effectiveness of the latter investment. In a parallel manner, providing antiparasitals or mosquito nets means that expenditures on nutrition programs are not wasted due to excretion of vitamins through diarrhea or burning calories through malarial fever. Investments in health, education, water and sanitation, transportation, and other sectors have significant positive spillovers in other areas.

Spillovers can be good or bad, or, as is the case with the health conditions discussed here, they have the potential of being both. The conditions have negative effects, but interventions to remediate them can have positive spillovers that are substantial. As discussed in chapter 8, the methods generally used in epidemiology and health economics to measure the effectiveness of health interventions are too limited to detect such spillovers. Cost-effectiveness studies rarely attempt to model more than a single input and a single output. Decontextualized analysis, such as randomized controlled trials or single-input/single-output cost-effectiveness analysis, is useful for some purposes, but it cannot be the only approach we use to examine complex ecologic questions. In order to prevent HIV/AIDS, we have to recognize and exploit the synergies that undermine health and well-being in general.

We know that good diet, clean water, worm elimination, and protection from schistosomes and malaria are good for people, and we know that the effects of each individual intervention would be enhanced by any of the others. And we know that each of those makes people less likely to transmit HIV to others and better able to resist HIV infection if they are exposed. Healthy people also can evaluate information better and choose safer behaviors (within the constraints of their economic and social situation). Complementing these health strategies, economic interventions to eradicate poverty and provide economic alternatives expand those choices for people even more.

This book has shown that HIV/AIDS is indeed a development issue. The origins of epidemic AIDS in developing and transition countries can be found in the same weaknesses of those economies and social structures that produce so many other kinds of suffering. It has long been recognized that myriad aspects of underdevelopment interact in a vicious circle that thwarts efforts to raise living standards. In the macroeconomic and macrosocial environment there are synergies of underdevelopment. At the community level, too, social and economic factors interact with climate, history, and even chance to advance or retard human development. At the individual level, there is synergy as well, since nutrition, parasite load, exposure to pathogens, and access to health care interact in negative or positive cycles toward illness or toward health.

In the face of this global health emergency some have suggested that resources be ever more concentrated and targeted on interventions aimed solely at the immediate threat, HIV/AIDS. That has always been a mistake and continues to be a mistake even as the pandemic worsens. Every year more young people confront an environment with the same biological, social, and economic risks. At the same time, other analysts are claiming that poor countries will reach the limits of their absorptive capacity if too much help comes their way. Together those two arguments—spend only on HIV/AIDS, but only up to the limited absorptive capacity—save donors from spending much of the money that has been promised but abandon poor people to the same unhealthy environment.

In fact, there is no problem of absorptive capacity if the right investments are chosen. The solutions that this book would offer are perhaps by now obvious. The most cost-effective solutions are those that exploit the synergies that exist: biological, social, and economic. The most important investments for health might not be in the health sector, just as the most important investments for productivity in agriculture and industry are probably in the health of the labor force in poor countries.

Health and non-health interactions

Chapters 2 and 3 explored a number of health synergies, including those among nutrition, parasites, STDs, and tuberculosis. An important health and behavior interaction that cannot be included in cost-effectiveness studies of single interventions is the effect that one health intervention has on other health behaviors. Survival from one disease provides incentive to invest personally in other preventive measures (Dow et al., 1997). In addition to synergies between different health conditions and between successful health outcomes and behavior, there are externalities between and among investments in health and other aspects of economic and human development (see chapter 8 on externalities). These interventions are needed to address HIV as a development issue, although they may be also, or even primarily, intended for other purposes. Because the HIV epidemic is neither random nor inexplicable, interventions to prevent or reverse it must be aimed upstream, as well as at the immediate causes of transmission. Education, agriculture, commerce, government, transport, and other sectors all shape the environment of health. The following section explores just a few of the ways that investments in human development have positive spillovers or externalities that have immediate benefit for individual and group health and development and long run benefits as well.

Nutrition and learning

A substantial literature supports the importance of good nutrition for learning. Certainly, the school breakfast and school lunch programs in the United States and other industrialized countries are in part based on the recognition of nutritional needs of children. They also attempt to increase school attendance by offering meals, since regular attendance is assumed to contribute to the learning process as well. Nutrition alone, however, is not as effective as combined interventions that exploit the interactions of better nutrition and a better learning environment (Sigman and Whaley, 1998). Another aspect of good nutrition that receives inadequate attention is the physiological impact on psychological well-being. Malnutrition promotes a sense of fatalism as a direct physiological effect. That fatalism undermines confidence in learning or other actions that would help to lift someone out of poverty. Confidence speeds learning, which then has a self-fulfilling momentum.

In particular for addressing HIV and AIDS, some upstream investments have value that has been little appreciated. Education of girls is important to develop productive workers; cultivate aesthetic, intellectual, and other capacities that are important in their own right; and reduce infant mortality. Children in school are a captive audience for HIV and other health-education programs. Girls in school are less likely to become pregnant, which might mean they are postponing sex. (For a review of the literature on the externalities of girls' education, see Schultz, 2002.)

Girls' education, however, is linked to community infrastructure. In order to keep girls in school, it is important to have easy access to water for the family, since the girls may spend several hours per day fetching water. Health has an important feedback on education because healthy children are absent less often and are better able to learn when they are in school. Consequently, clean water supplies increase the state's return on its educational expenditure, the children's return on their time expenditure, and the parents' return on the opportunity cost of giving up the children's labor at home.

Another complementarity that must be considered so that keeping girls in school will have the desired effect of preventing HIV is that it is probably necessary to rescind school fees. The cost to parents of girls' schooling might be prohibitively high or just not valued sufficiently by them. Numerous works assert that schoolgirls have sugar daddies who pay their school fees in return for sex. If that is true, then canceling school fees is an easy solution to that part of the problem. The amount that parents are willing to pay for schooling for girls does not represent the full value to society of educating girls and protecting them and their children from HIV and other risks. This is an example of market failure, as discussed in chapter 8.

There are also intergenerational spillovers that are widely recognized. A mother's education has a significant effect on child survival and also on child development. The effect of mother's education on child height (an indicator of healthy development) is explained by improved access to information rather than through income. There is also a significant interaction between the impact of mother's education and the extent of infrastructure in her community (Thomas et al., 1991). Her capacity to use information is not of much use if the health-care facilities are not available. Complementarities abound for investment in human development.

Parasites and learning

An important adjunct to the literature on nutrition and learning is the research on parasite load and learning. Numerous kinds of parasites afflict a large proportion of the population of developing countries, as was discussed in chapter 2. Lack of clean water, sanitary facilities, clean storage areas for food, and adequate hygiene practices are among the reasons for endemic parasitosis. Many parasites produce significant morbidity in children and adults, but because they are rarely fatal, they tend to be underappreciated as a source of misery, as well as a cause of significant loss of productivity (Gallup and Sachs, 2000; Fischhoff et al., 2002). Numerous studies document the effect of parasite load on cognitive function, highlighting again the spillover effect of health on education, achievement, and community participation (Kvalsig et al., 1991; Nokes et al., 1992; Adams et al., 1994; Levav et al., 1995; Gallup and Sachs, 1999; Hastaning et al., 1999).

Miguel and Kremer expand the analysis of deworming programs and learning through the concept of externalities. They found that children who were treated for worms increased their school attendance. Furthermore, untreated children in the same school and even untreated children in nearby schools without treatment benefitted and increased school attendance because their play areas were less contaminated with excreted worms. The single-dose therapy can cost as little as 49 cents per person per year. The treatment was the most cost-effective way of increasing school attendance, and the authors conclude that the externalities in community-wide health improvement justify fully subsidizing treatment (Miguel and Kremer, 2001).

Anderson and May reported similar externalities in treatment of schistosomiasis. They found that treating "a random ten percent of the local population would lead to a 37 percent reduction in the total local worm burden, with over three quarters of this reduction due to the externality, while mass treating a random 30 percent of the local population against worms would lead to a reduction of 89 percent of the total local worm burden" (cited in Miguel and Kremer, 2001, 21–22). Miguel and Kremer argue that naive estimates that ignore externalities severely underestimate cost-effectiveness: "To the extent that the treatment of other tropical infectious diseases also generates spillover benefits similar to deworming, the externality findings of the current study may also provide an additional rationale for a substantial public role in subsidizing medical treatment for infectious diseases in less developed countries" (Miguel and Kremer, 2001, 44).

Treating children for worm infestation makes them healthier, eliminating a constant challenge to their immune system and the constant drain on their nutrition. Treating a single child, however, affects many others. Reducing the diarrhea that worms produce reduces the number of other children who will become infected with worms since they are spread through fecal contamination of play areas and drinking water. The mother's and siblings' time spent in caring for the sick child is now freed up to produce food or contribute to the family in other ways. The child is able to attend school, and the community as a whole benefits from having one more educated member. Given the new information on worm infection and vulnerability to HIV transmission (see chapter 3), the urgency to relieve over 1.5 billion people of this serious obstacle to health and well-being becomes even greater. Treating worm infection is an effective and inexpensive measure that could slow the HIV/AIDS epidemic, with important collateral benefits in the health, comfort, and productivity of a large segment of the world's population.

Other benefits of parasite eradication

There are other examples of positive spillovers from health investment into other sectors. Programs for the eradication of river blindness and the control of tsetse flies opened up millions of acres of farmland and pasture, expanded agricultural potential, with a feedback for food security. Eradication of dracunculiasis (guinea worm infection) has the collateral benefit of providing clean drinking water, which prevents other parasitic and infectious diseases, and the training of community health workers who can deliver other health services (Aylward et al., 2000).

Malaria-related illnesses kill 5 percent of children under age 5 in sub-Saharan Africa, which means that mothers must replace 5 percent of births to achieve the desired number of children. The mortality rate among adults is lower, but malaria saps productivity through frequent episodes of fever (McCarthy et al., 2000). Malaria has a significant effect on economic growth through various routes, which likely include "the effect of repeated worker absences on production patterns and specialization, malaria-prevention motivated reductions in internal and external labor mobility, and potential loss of investment projects" (McCarthy et al., 2000, 6). Other growth effects of malaria include work absenteeism, coping required of co-workers and family members, school absenteeism, losses in long-term learning capacity, and losses in accumulation of capital. Because of frequent absenteeism, firms have to overstaff and workers have to be less specialized. In agriculture, frequent illness of family members forces farmers to change planting patterns (McCarthy et al., 2000).[1]

In the case of endemic diseases, the effect on economic growth is largely invisible because of the factors that are never measured. Diseases that are always there are built into investment plans or the decision not to invest. Only the scale of the AIDS epidemic and the high profile it had achieved in the United States and Europe brought adequate worldwide attention to the effect of health on economic growth in developing and transition countries. There are scores of studies of the economic burden of guinea worm, river blindness, hookworm, and malaria. The puzzle is why the weight of such evidence has not been enough to mobilize resources for eradication of all those diseases, or why there is still any question about how to help countries develop. The solution, or at least a large part of the solution, to HIV is to solve the myriad other problems that afflict poor people in the developing world and hinder human development. HIV did not develop in a vacuum, and it will not be stopped in isolation.

The obligation of optimism

Development programs were molded by the perspective and interests of affluent countries. That had a direct impact on HIV/AIDS because it kept

1. When I taught at the University of Dar es Salaam in Tanzania, the department always kept two professors in reserve, without course assignments. They knew that during the year every member of the department would come down with malaria at some point and would need to be replaced for a period of time. The prediction did prove true for all except the two expatriate professors who were taking malaria prophylaxis.

policy makers from seeing the obvious: that we still have not secured a dignified safe standard of living for half the world's people. This time it is AIDS, but before it was cholera and next it may be flu, or something else. The route from poverty to death can be direct, or it can be mediated through behaviors that people are compelled to adopt or that they choose to adopt, but in either case, they are behaviors that are conditioned by their environment.

The environment of poverty is complex, but the solutions are rather simple to the extent that we know what investments directly improve people's health and freedom and that also help to prevent the spread of HIV. There are countless ways to intervene, in every sector. Many of them are costless, at least in financial terms. The good news is that so many of the required interventions have synergistic effects that the package of programs will actually cost less, and have greater impact, than is currently projected. All of them bring about improvements in the quality of people's lives that we should not have left until now.

We can't throw up our hands and say it can't be done. The truth is that we have the means. And the scandal is that all this suffering results from the failure to allocate resources to human needs and the failure to challenge oppressive systems.

There is no problem of poor countries being able to absorb the right investments. There is no problem of gender relations that cannot be attacked immediately. There is no culture in Africa, Asia, or Latin America that makes poverty there any more acceptable than it is in the rich countries. The fundamental differences are not between people but between the environments in which we live—and that we can change.

This chapter concludes with a dozen plans that contribute to HIV prevention. The goals sound ambitious, but we already have the knowledge and the tools required. In most cases the organizations already exist to execute the needed investments. The first plan is for eradication of helminth and *Schistosoma* infection. It aims to achieve a health goal with a health-sector investment. The rationale for eradication is abundantly clear from the foregoing discussion. The outlines of the plan are given in Objective #1. The second plan aims to achieve a health goal with a nonhealth investment. The rationale and approach for Objective #2 are provided, then the outlines of the plan. Ten more outlines follow.

Objective # 1

Objective: Eradicate helminth and *Schistosoma* infection

Methods: Cheap, effective deworming medications and hygiene education

Intestinal worms (hookworm, roundworm, and whipworm) can be eliminated with a single once-a-year pill. Either albendazole or mebendazole can be used, and the cost is US$0.02 per capsule. Mass treatment is advised, requiring no diagnostic resources, because the treatment is easily tolerated (Montresor et al., 2001; World Bank, 2003b).

Cost per child per year of deworming (hookworm) is US$0.08 (Stoltzfus et al., 1998).

Schistosomiasis can be treated for US$0.20, once per year, using a single dose of praziquantel. Dosage can be determined on the basis of a child's height through a simple dose-pole. Teachers can be trained easily, making administration in school feasible and cheap. Teachers already have the means for keeping records on children. Deworming pills have a long shelf-life and are heat stable, allowing easy delivery in the tropics (World Bank, 2003b).

Recommended complementary investment: Water systems, latrines
Problems alleviated:

- Malnutrition due to worm infections
- Cost-effective in reducing moderate and severe anemia (Stoltzfus et al., 1998).
- High work and school absenteeism
- Poor school performance and early dropout
- Externality infections, even in untreated population
- HIV/AIDS cofactor eliminated

Sources of technical advice and aid:

- TDR (Special Programme for Research and Training in Tropical Diseases), an organization sponsored by UNICEF, UNDP, World Bank, and WHO, at http://www.who.int/tdr
- World Bank, at http://www.worldbank.org/hnp
- PPC (Partners for Parasite Control) founded by the World Health Assembly in 2001
- Bill and Melinda Gates Foundation
- Carter Center
- Partnership for Child Development

Note: The significant externalities between education and hygiene and of labor productivity on both education and hygiene make this a particularly good investment.

Solving a development problem with economic and health impact: trade and trucking

Sometimes the best investment to solve a health problem will be outside the health sector. There are countless ways to promote development and reduce the risk of HIV transmission. In every sector—agriculture, industry, commerce, government, education, and others—there are opportunities to make the changes that should have been made long ago, and that could have helped to prevent the health crisis in the developing and transition countries. This section proposes the modernization of trucking and trade, as just one example of obvious ways to help prevent HIV transmission while achieving other worthwhile goals.

Lengthy delays at border crossings are repeatedly mentioned in the policy literature as contributing to HIV transmission, particularly in sub-Saharan Africa. It is clear that border delays are costly in themselves, even if HIV did not exist. Well-developed trade corridors are essential for the flow of goods and also for the diffusion of new technology, both of which contribute to job creation and opportunities for higher incomes in the hinterland. Border delays raise the cost of shipping and discourage investment. Some goods, including agricultural products, are not worth shipping because of the unpredictability and high cost of delivery. (A longer list of the cost of border delays appears in chapter 9.)

The knowledge of how to facilitate trade is already well established. One need only travel from Eastern Europe, where as many as 50 trucks are lined up at border crossings at any given time,[2] to the European Union to see that borders need not be an obstacle to the free flow of truck traffic. Of course, there are numerous historical and political obstacles to the free flow of goods and factors of production across international borders. Most developing countries have elaborate and suffocating trade barriers that are intended to protect domestic industry. An ideological hostility to free trade on the part of many people concerned with human development has hindered the promotion of trade facilitation for poverty eradication. The vested interests of those who collect bribes and fees also support the system. Rarely in the last 40 years, however, have those restrictive systems promoted domestic growth and development.

This is not the place to evaluate all the arguments for and against protectionist trade policy, generalized or specific. It is safe to say, however, that little is to be gained from competitive restrictions between similarly impoverished countries. That is true for poor landlocked states, such as Zambia, Zimbabwe, Botswana, Lesotho, and Swaziland, and for countries with good ports but few products or just one product to export, such as Mozambique and Angola (Lakshmanan et al., n.d.). Cooperation, rather than competition, between countries such as Zambia and Zimbabwe, would have beneficial results. Even between countries unevenly developed, such as Zimbabwe and South Africa, integration offers numerous advantages. South

2. In spring 2003, I crossed borders many times among all the countries between Estonia and Croatia. Each time I would count the trucks waiting to clear customs. Often their number exceeded 50, whether at major crossings or on small roads off the main routes. When I visited the truck lots at Messina, South Africa, in 2005, I counted well over 200 trucks waiting to be cleared to enter Zimbabwe.

Africa already relies on labor migrants from throughout southern Africa, and the other countries depend on remittances from workers who migrate south for work.

The Maputo Corridor provides an example of the benefits of connecting the interior to the coast. The Southern African Development Community has been trying to revive the Maputo Corridor to provide a shorter route to the ocean for goods from Johannesburg and to help Mozambique. The route would lower prices for imports inland and lower the cost of shipping exports. Intermediate goods could move more rapidly among regions, and along the corridor new sources of employment would provide opportunities at home to discourage migration to the largest cities. Transport development would also lead to the improvement of water and sanitation in communities along the way. The physical infrastructure of a road system will be wasted, however, if it is not accompanied by smooth border operations and good logistics (Lakshmanan et al., n.d.).

The European Union is built on the principle that market integration is beneficial. The larger market offers opportunities predicted by all the theories of international trade. Even if the integration of poor countries represents only the pooling of poverty, however, and none of the growth promise of the EU, it is still worthwhile to reduce the costs of trade barriers. These countries receive no growth stimulus from the border regulations. The costs of those regulations are numerous, including the costs to the government of maintaining the system, the private costs listed in chapter 9, and the pervasive corruption and its insidious effect on good governance, efficiency, and personal incentives. To all that we must now add the mushrooming costs of the AIDS epidemic, which is partly fueled by border delays.

Border regulations could be dismantled in a very short time. The system does not need to be invented. The EU has 40 years' experience with progressive trade facilitation. Removing trade barriers between developing countries need not take anywhere near that long because the process is already well known.

North America already has computerized systems for paperless truck logs and truck surveillance systems that allow trucks to maintain highway speeds while passing weighing stations, ports of entry, and agricultural inspection stations (see PrePass at www.prepass.com). The International Chamber of Commerce (ICC) also has a well developed program for trade facilitation, including paperless customs procedures and other border surveillance, such as agricultural and security checks (www.iccwbo.org).

There is a very valuable opportunity here for the Bill and Melinda Gates Foundation or other funding groups to modernize trucking and trade by financing the computerization of customs for the trade corridors in Africa, Asia, and Latin America. Low national income is not an obstacle to trade facilitation. India is computerizing truck checks at state borders. The intention was probably to reduce corruption, a worthwhile goal. But the new procedures also improve oversight and increase profits in other ways, including reduced travel time, lowering capital and labor costs for shippers (Nachiket Doshi, personal communication). Compared with the economic and health costs of border delays, a laptop computer and a transponder for every truck are a small investment.

Objective # 2

Objective: Alleviate border delays
Methods:

- Paperless customs procedures
- Barrier-free trade among developing countries

Problems alleviated:

- Long stays away from home for truckers
- Costly delays for trucking and shipping firms

Sources of technical advice and aid:

- International Chamber of Commerce
- World Bank
- European Union
- Bill and Melinda Gates Foundation
- PrePass

Ten more plans for health and development

This section gives ten more examples of obvious, important interventions that should be undertaken in order to enable people to live healthier, freer lives and to prevent HIV transmission. The selection is not meant to be limiting but, rather, suggestive. People in every sector will think of similar interventions they can undertake. The ways to promote human development and lessen vulnerability to HIV epidemics are already known; they just have to be funded and carried out.

Objective # 3

Objective: Bolster immune systems
Methods: Cheap, effective nutrient supplements

- Vitamin-A fortified sugar: US$0.29 per person per year (this adds only 1.6% to the price of sugar) (Sommer et al., 1996)
- Vitamin-A capsules, US$0.02 per capsule (Sommer et al., 1996)
- Iron supplementation costs US$0.02 per child per year if given weekly, or US$0.08, if given daily (Stoltzfus et al., 1998).

- Iron supplementation increases the efficacy of iodine supplementation (Hess et al., 2002).

Sources of technical advice and aid:

- Sommer, Alfred, and Keith West, with J. A. Olson and A.C. Ross. 1996. *Vitamin A Deficiency: Health, Survival, and Vision.* New York: Oxford University Press.
- UNICEF
- United Nations Food and Agriculture Organization
- International Food Policy Research Institute (IFPRI)

Note: A healthy population is a public good since it is beneficial to everyone but is not within the means of any one firm to finance. Government attempts to compel the food industry to absorb the full cost of vitamin-fortification programs have failed (Sommer et al., 1996, 419).

Objective # 4

Objective: Keep girls in school
Methods: Eliminate family burden for school fees
Problem eliminated: Sugar daddies for school fees
Sources of aid: Faith-based organizations in wealthier countries
Note: This is an excellent activity for faith-based organizations since some are reluctant to finance HIV-prevention programs that entail controversial issues of sexuality. Faith-based organizations should readily finance school fees. Individual mosques, synagogues, or parishes could adopt one or a number of schools, or a large organization, such as Lutheran World Relief or Catholic Charities, could adopt an entire national school system. Concerns about the participatory aspect of user fees can be resolved through students' contribution of time, such as tutoring younger children, caring for school gardens, and so on.

Objective # 5

Objective: End oppression of women
Methods: Behavior-change communication through government, school, religious, and community campaigns
Problems alleviated:

- Violations of human rights
- Child and maternal mortality due to women's lack of control over income, food, health decisions
- Inability to negotiate safer sex

Sources of aid:

- Religious organizations
- Government

Note: In this matter it is essential to involve religious organizations. They all claim to be in favor of the equality and dignity of women, at least in the home. All of the things they detest—pornography, sex work, casual sex—are supported by the low status of women. If they want to protect the sanctity of the family, they must support the equality of women in the household. To ignore the practice of husbands using sex workers or having mistresses is to collaborate in gender inequality. In Latin America, for example, it is common for men to stand outside on the steps of the church while women and girls attend Mass. The priests need to stand outside with the other men and take their message out there. If the men leave, the priests should follow them and talk to them in the bars. The religious groups—churches, mosques, or temples—have to lead the campaign for gender equality so that it is more than a theoretical part of their faiths and so that they can have a positive influence on change. At present, some people use religion as an excuse to prevent gender equality.

This seems like a very large agenda. Nevertheless, how will it be accomplished if it is not begun? Furthermore, it is not as formidable as it seems. It does make a difference to change the legal status of women and to have faith-based organizations support women's equality. Completely changing men's views and women's status will, of course, take time. But a combination of BCC and regulatory enforcement has been used successfully against problems as varied as tobacco use, drunk driving, and littering. To accept that we are powerless against sexist oppression is to grant it a special status that is unwarranted and incorrect.

Objective # 6

Objective: Extend health care services
Methods:

- Use Global Fund money to expand primary-care networks
- Provide mobile clinics in buses, trains, boats
- Use religious and community buildings for part-time and visiting clinics

Problem alleviated:

- Lack of primary care
- Lack of health-promotion consciousness
- Lack of venue for HIV education and administration of antiretroviral medication

Sources of technical advice:
There are numerous models for community-based comprehensive pri-

mary health care. In Maharashtra State in India, Doctors Mabelle and Raj Arole built a system of health care through training community health workers. They accomplished social and medical goals simultaneously by training Dalit (so-called untouchable) women to be health workers. The caste barriers were overcome because people wanted the health services that only the Dalit women could provide (Arole and Arole, 1994).

Mobile clinics have been found to allow very efficient use of health staff time. Calculating all costs, including travel costs of patients, mobile clinics definitely reduce cost per contact. Travel costs are especially high for mothers who are part-time wage workers because they have to give up work to go to a clinic. Mobile clinics also increase coverage of the population (Vos et al., 1990).

Objective # 7

Objective: Mass communication for health information

Methods: Radio, television, street theater

Problem alleviated: Lack of information about healthy living and about personal rights

Sources of technical advice and aid: Communication Initiative. The Web site and mailings of the Communication Initiative have extensive information on and models for using communication for health and other social objectives (http://www.comminit.com).

Some models: As with community health care, there are many good models of health education using the media. One example of effective communication of health information in a readily available format on a variety of topics is the radio show, nationally syndicated in the United States, "Cuidando su Salud." The program is relatively inexpensive to produce, is well planned for the target population, and covers a range of health topics. There are several features of the programming that make it successful: repetition of key themes, long enough format to be really informative, no use of jargon, a constant feature of the daily news, and sensitivity to community views (Huerta and Weed, 1998).

In Tanzania, radio soap opera was used to educate and change attitudes and behaviors for HIV prevention. In the absence of a conscious preventive message, in television and radio there is already a message about appropriate behavior (Vaughan et al., 2000).

Objective # 8

Objective: Change in hiring practices and status of women at work

Methods: Behavior-change communication

Target: Corporate and government managers

Problems alleviated:

- Waste of workforce
- Abusive attitudes toward women in the workplace and community
- Higher incomes for women improve their options vis-à-vis partners

Sources of technical advice and aid:

- Global Business Coalition
- USAID

Note: The Global Business Coalition has already developed the network for assisting businesses to train managers for BCC programs for workers. What is needed is BCC for managers to make fundamental changes in hiring practices and in respect for women in the workplace. Employers can enforce behavior in the workplace. Both the Global Business Coalition and USAID already promote behavior-change communication. They just have not applied it to fundamental change in the way managers approach their jobs. Behavior change should not be limited to people whose economic status is subordinate.

Objective # 9

Objective: Eliminate trafficking of women and children
Methods:

- Criminalize soliciting but not prostitution
- Close brothel towns

Targets:

- Organized crime groups
- Police who abet gangs
- Clients

Problems alleviated:

- Source of HIV and STDs
- Other effects of slavery
- Social dysfunction in consuming countries. Industrialized counties are ignoring social problems at home (distorted gender relations and pedophilia) by tolerating trafficking, sex tourism, and Internet shopping for sex tourism.

Sources of technical advice and aid:

- Interpol
- International Office for Migration
- Human rights groups

Objective # 10

Objective: Sustainable agricultural systems in developing countries

Methods: This is obviously a complicated issue, but one thing that can be done, regardless of climate, labor resources, technology, and so on, is for the United States, Japan, and the European Union to drop their tariff barriers that make it more difficult, if not impossible, for poor countries to compete in developed-country markets.

Problems reduced:

- Rural and urban employment
- Famine
- Excessive urbanization

Source of technical advice: World Trade Organization: the system is there; it has to be used against the tariff walls that do the most harm—tariffs of industrialized countries against developing-country imports. Industrialized countries are exporting their agricultural-sector problems to the Third World, as they export their social problems by not addressing distorted gender relations, and their labor shortages by recruiting nurses from developing countries.

Objective # 11

Objective: Blood screening, safe needles in medical and quasi-medical settings

Problem alleviated: Transmission of HIV as well as numerous other infections, including hepatitis B, Hepatitis C, and Chagas disease

Sources of technical aid and advice:

- Physicians for Human Rights (http://www.phrusa.org)
- World Health Organization
- U.S. Centers for Disease Control and Prevention (http://www.cdc.gov)

Objective # 12

Objective: Reuniting families

Methods: Bus service. It would, of course, be preferable if families could live together close to their work. Mine, factory, and plantation managers should make every effort to enable workers' families to migrate with the workers and organize services so that family members can also find work. If it is impossible for family members to accompany workers because they are tending family farms, then easy, cheap transportation should be available. There are extensive bus services throughout Africa, Asia, and Latin America. But as anyone knows who has traveled by bus, indirect routes can use up all the free time one has. Migrant labor is essential to the operation of those firms. The workers' value should be acknowledged in the services provided to them by the firms. Since many migrants come from the same regions, it is not that difficult to run bus services that are easy to use. Firms in the same area can cooperate in organizing the pools. Work time could also be reallocated so that workers have four 10-hour shifts and can spend 3 days of every week as part of their families and communities.

Problems alleviated:

- Divided families
- Shortages of rural labor at peak times
- Boredom and isolation at work sites

Sources of technical aid and advice:

- Commuter van services, such as those organized by Commuter Connections in the metropolitan Washington area or any other urban area, http://www.mwcog.org/commuter/ccindex.html
- College ride boards
- Any of the thousands of van services that operate, often in the informal sector, throughout the developing world

Create your own models. Use the Blank Plans at the end of this chapter to devise strategies for your own sector or to correct a problem that you have seen. Photocopy the template or vary it to suit your plan, since you can probably think of many more interventions.

There are plenty of other examples of problems with easy solutions. See below a partial list of fairly easy but extremely beneficial actions or resources:

Four relatively uncomplicated legal changes

- Abolish school fees
- Eliminate border restrictions
- Allow women to inherit land
- Change immigration laws to encourage families to migrate with workers

Four cheap health expenditures

- Deworming medications
- Vitamin and mineral supplements
- Treated bed nets for mosquito protection and malaria control
- Water filters made from buckets or other simple materials

Four unused, misused, or underused institutions

- Religious groups
- World Bank
- UNAIDS
- USAID, its partners, and other bilateral aid organizations

Objective #

___

___

Methods:

___

___

Problems alleviated:

___

___

Sources of technical aid and advice:

___

___

Objective #

___

___

Methods:

___

___

Problems alleviated:

___

___

Sources of technical aid and advice:

___

___

Works Cited

Abel, David. 1999. "Aids Linked to Infidelity in Dominican Republic." *Boston Globe,* December 28, pp. A2, A4.

Actor, J., M. Shirai, M. Kullberg, et al. 1993. "Helminth infection results in decreased virus-specific CD8+ cytotoxic T-cell and Th1 cytokine responses as well as delayed virus clearance," *Proceedings of the National Academy of Sciences* 90:948–952.

Adams, E., L. Stephenson, M. Latham, and S. Kinoti. 1994. "Physical Activity and Growth of Kenyan School Children with Hookworm, *Trichuris trichiura* and *Ascaris lumbricoides* Infections Are Improved after Treatment with Albendazole," *Journal of Nutrition* 124:1199–1206.

Adeyi, O., G. Chellaraj, E. Goldstein, et al. 1997, "Health status during the transition in Central and Eastern Europe: development in reverse?" *Health Policy and Planning* 12(2):132–145.

AIDS Law Project and Lawyers for Human Rights (South Africa). 1997. *HIV/AIDS and the Law: A Resource Manual.* Johannesburg: AIDS Law Project.

Altschuler, E. L. 2000. "Plague as HIV Vaccine Adjuvant," *Medical Hypotheses* 54(6): 1003–1004.

Anand, S., and K. Hanson. 1997. "Disability-Adjusted Life Years: A Critical Review," *Journal of Health Economics* 16:685–702.

Arole, Mabelle, and Raj Arole. 1994. *Jamkhed: A Comprehensive Rural Health Project.* London: Macmillan.

Ashforth, Adam. 2002. "An Epidemic of Witchcraft? The Implications of AIDS for the Post-Apartheid State," *African Studies* 61(1):121–143.

Attili, V. R., S. Hira, and M. K. Dube. 1983. "Schistosomal Genital Granulomas: A Report of 10 Cases," *British Journal of Venereal Disease* 59:269–72.

Aylward, B., K. A. Hennessey, N. Zagaria, et al. 2000. "When Is a Disease Eradicable? 100 Years of Lessons Learned," *American Journal of Public Health* 90(10): 1515–1520.

Bachrach, J. 2002. "Tricks for Treats: Shocking Confessions of Shameless Women: Free Clothes, Free Jewels, Free Lipo," *Allure* July:144–147, 152, 154.

Badhwar, Inderjit. 1994. "The Emperors of Garbage," *New York Times,* November 5, p. 23.

Barker, Carol, and Andrew Green. 1996. "Opening the Debate on DALYs," *Health Policy and Planning* 11(2):179–183.

Barnett, Tony, and Alan Whiteside. 2002. *AIDS in the Twenty-First Century: Disease and Globalization.* Hampshire and New York: Palgrave Macmillan.

Barraclough, Solon. 1997. "Food and Poverty in the Americas: Institutional and Policy Obstacles to Efficiency in Food Aid." *Development in Practice* 7(2):117–129.

Barreto, M. L., L. Rodrigues, R. Silva, et al. 2000. "Lower Hookworm Incidence, Prevalence, and Intensity of Infection in Children with a Bacillus Calmette-Guérin Vaccination Scar," *Journal of Infectious Diseases* 182:1800–1803.

Barry, Michele, M. Cullen, J. Thomas, and R. Loewenson. 1990. "Health Care Changes after Independence and Transition to Majority Rule," *Journal of the American Medical Association* 263(5):638–640.

Baruch, Y., and P. Clancy. 2000. "Managing AIDS in Africa: HRM Challenges in Tanzania," *International Journal of Human Resource Management* 11(4):789–806.

Baum, Marianna, and Gail Shor-Posner. 1998. "Micronutrient Status in Relationship to Mortality in HIV-1 Disease," *Nutrition Reviews* 56(1, Part 2):S135–139.

Baum, M. K., G. Shor-Posner, S. Lai, et al. 1997. "High Risk of HIV-Related Mortality Is Associated with Selenium Deficiency," *Journal of Acquired Immune Deficiency Syndrome and Human Retrovirology* 15(5):370–374.

Bean, R. B. 1906. "Some Racial Peculiarities of the Negro Brain," *American Journal of Anatomy* 5:324–342.

Beck, Melinda. 1997. "Increased Virulence of Coxsackievirus B3 in Mice Due to Vitamin E or Selenium Deficiency," *Journal of Nutrition* 127:966S–970S.

Beck, Melinda. 1998, "The Influence of Antioxidant Nutrients on Viral Infection," *Nutrition Reviews* 56(1, Part 2);S140–146.

Beck, Melinda. 2000. "Nutritionally Induced Oxidative Stress: Effect on Viral Disease," *American Journal of Clinical Nutrition* 71(suppl):1676S–1679S.

Beisel, William. 1996. "Nutrition and Immune Function: Overview," *Journal of Nutrition* 126:2611S–2615S.

Bentwich, Z., A. Kalinkovicj, and Z. Weisman. 1995. "Immune Activation Is a Dominant Factor in the Pathogenesis of African AIDS," *Immunology Today* 16:187–191.

Bentwich, Zvi, A. Kalinkovich, Z. Weisman, et al. 1999. "Can Eradication of Helminthic Infections Change the Face of AIDS and Tuberculosis?" *Immunology Today* 20(11):485–487.

Bernier, R., B. Barbeau, M. Tremblay, and M. Olivier. 1998. "The Lipophosphoglycan of *Leishmania donovani* up-regulates HIV-1 transcription in T cells through nuclear factor-kappa B elements," *Journal of Immunology* 160:2881–2888.

Billy, John O. G., Koray Tanfer, William R. Grady, and Daniel H. Klepinger. 1993. "The Sexual Behavior of Men in the United States," *Family Planning Perspectives* 25(2):52–60.

Black, M. 1979. "More about Metaphor," in A. Ortony (ed.), *Metaphor and Thought,* pp. 19–43. Cambridge: Cambridge University Press.

Blanc, Ann K., and Ann A. Way. 1998. "Sexual Behavior and Contraceptive Knowledge and Use among Adolescents in Developing Countries," *Studies in Family Planning* 29(2):106–116.

Bloland, Peter, J. Wirima, R. Steketee, et al. 1995. "Maternal HIV Infection and Infant Mortality in Malawi: Evidence for Increased Mortality Due to Placental Malaria Infection," *AIDS* 9(7):721–726.

Bongaarts, J., P. Reining, P. Way, and F. Conant. 1989. "The Relationship between Male Circumcision and HIV Infection in African Populations," *AIDS* 3(6):373–377.

Bonnell, V., and L. Hunt. 1999. "Introduction," in V. Bonnell and L. Hunt (eds.), *Beyond the Cultural Turn: New Directions in the Study of Society and Culture,* pp. 1–32. Berkeley: University of California Press.

Borkow, Gadi, and Zvi Bentwich. 2002. "Host Background Immunity and Human Immunodeficiency Virus Protective Vaccines: A Major Consideration for Vaccine Efficacy in Africa and in Developing Countries," *Clinical and Diagnostic Laboratory Immunology* May:505–507.

Borkow, G., Q. Leng, Z. Weisman, et al. 2000. "Chronic Immune Activation Associated with Intestinal Helminth Infections Results in Impaired Signal Transduction and Anergy," *Journal of Clinical Investigation* 106(8):1053–1060.

Borkow, G., Z. Weisman, Q. Leng, et al. 2001. "Helminths, Human Immunodeficiency Virus and Tuberculosis," *Scandinavian Journal of Infectious Disease* 33: 568–571.

Bouey, Paul, T. Seidel, and T. Rehle. 1998. *AVERT, Version 1.0: A Tool for Estimating Intervention Effects on the Reduction of HIV Transmission.* Washington, D.C.: Family Health International. Available at: http://www.fhi.org.

Boulton, Ian, and Scott Gray-Owen. 2002. "Neisserial Binding to CEACAM1 Arrests the Activation and Proliferation of $CD4^+$ T Lymphocytes," *Nature Immunology* 3:229–236.

Breman, J., A. Egan, and G. Keusch. 2001. "The Intolerable Burden of Malaria: A New Look at the Numbers," *American Journal of Tropical Medicine and Hygiene* 64(1–2 Suppl):iv–vii.

Breslin, M. 1998. "Abortion Rate among Young Romanians Declines: Those Not in Union Report Rise in Contraceptive Use," *International Family Planning Perspectives* 24(3):150–152.

Brewer, D., S. Brody, E. Drucker, et al. 2003. "Mounting Anomalies in the Epidemiology of HIV in Africa: Cry the Beloved Paradigm," *International Journal of STD and AIDS* 14:144–147.

Briggs, A., M. Sculpher, and M. Buxton. 1994. "Uncertainty in the Economic Evaluation of Health Care Technologies: The Role of Sensitivity Analysis," *Health Economics* 3:95–104.

Brooker, S., E. A. Miguel, S. Moulin, et al. 2000. "Epidemiology of Single and Multiple Species of Helminth Infections among School Children in Busia District, Kenya," *East African Medical Journal* 77(3):157–161.

Brown, T., B. Franklin, J. MacNeil, and S. Mills. 2001. *Effective Prevention Strategies in Low HIV Prevalence Settings.* Washington, D.C.: Family Health International.

Brundtland, Gro Harlem. 2000. "Nutrition and Infection: Malnutrition and Mortality in Public Health," *Nutrition Reviews* 58(2, Part 2):S1–S4.

Bullough, C. 1976. "Infertility and Bilharziasis of the Female Genital Tract," *British Journal of Obstetrics and Gynaecology* 83:819–822.

Burkhalter, Holly. 2003. "Unsafe Health Care and the HIV/AIDS Pandemic: Testimony of Holly Burkhalter," 31 July. Available at: http://www.phrusa.org/campaigns/aids/release080103.html.

Caldwell, J. 2000. "Rethinking the African AIDS Epidemic," *Population and Development Review* 26(1):117–135.

Caldwell, J., and P. Caldwell. 1985. *Cultural Forces Tending to Sustain High Fertility in Tropical Africa.* PHN Technical Note 85–16. Washington, D.C.: World Bank.

Caldwell, J., and P. Caldwell. 1987. "The Cultural Context of High Fertility in Sub-Saharan Africa," *Population and Development Review* 13(3):409–437.

Caldwell, J., and P. Caldwell. 1993. "The Nature and Limits of the sub-Saharan African AIDS Epidemic: Evidence from Geographic and Other Patterns," *Population and Development Review* 19(4):817–48.

Caldwell, J., and P. Caldwell. 2002. "Africa: The New Family Planning Frontier," *Studies in Family Planning* 33(1):76–86.

Caldwell, J., P. Caldwell, and P. Quiggin. 1989. "The Social Context of AIDS in Sub-Saharan Africa," *Population and Development Review* 15(2):185–234.

Caldwell, J., P. Caldwell, and P. Quiggin. 1991. "The African Sexual System: Reply to Le Blanc et al.," *Population and Development Review* 17(3):506–515.

Caldwell, J., I. Orubuloye, and P. Caldwell. 1992. "Underreaction to AIDS in Sub-Saharan Africa," *Social Science and Medicine* 34(11):1169–1182.

Campa, A., G. Shor-Posner, F. Indacochea, et al. 1999. "Mortality Risk in Selenium-Deficient HIV-Positive Children," *Journal of Acquired Immune Deficiency Syndromes and Human Retrovirology* 20(5):508–513.

Caraël, Michel. 1995. "Sexual Behaviour," in J. Cleland and B. Ferry (eds.), *Sexual Behaviour and AIDS in the Developing World,* pp. 75–123. London: Taylor and Francis for the World Health Organization.

Cassel, J. 1976. "The Contribution of the Social Environment to Host Resistance," *American Journal of Epidemiology* 104:107–123.

Castro-Leal, Florencia, J. Dayton, L. Demery, and K. Mehra. 1999. "Public Social Spending in Africa: Do the Poor Benefit?" *World Bank Research Observer* 14(1): 49–72.

CDC (Centers for Disease Control and Prevention). 1992. "Famine-Affected, Refugee, and Displaced Populations: Recommendations for Public Health Issues," *Morbidity and Mortality Weekly* 41(RR-13).

CDC (Centers for Disease Control and Prevention). 1997. "*Chlamydia trachomatis* Genital Infections—United States. 1995," *Morbidity and Mortality Weekly* 46(9):193–198.

CDC (Centers for Disease Control and Prevention). 1998. "Prevention and Treatment of Sexually Transmitted Diseases as an HIV Prevention Strategy." Atlanta: CDC. Available at: http://www.cdc.gov/nchstp/hiv_aids/pubs/facts/hivstd.htm.

CDC (Centers for Disease Control and Prevention). 1999. "STD Morbidity Count." Atlanta: CDC. Available at: http://wonder.cdc.gov/DataSets.shtml.

CDC (Centers for Disease Control and Prevention). 2003. "Plague." Atlanta: CDC. Available at: http://www.cdc.gov/ncidod/dvbid/plague/qa.htm.

CEE-HRN (Central and Eastern European Harm Reduction Network). 2002. *Injecting Drug Users, HIV/AIDS Treatment and Primary Care.* Vilnius, Lithuania: CEE-HRN.

Centro Cultural "La Pájara Pinta." 1996. *El amor en el maíz: migración, sexualidad y VIH-SIDA en comunidades rurales de Azuay y Cañar.* Cuenca, Ecuador: La Pájara Pinta.

Cetron, M., L. Chitsulo, J. Sullivan, et al. 1996. "Schistosomiasis in Lake Malawi," *Lancet* 348:1274.

Chandiwana, Stephen, and Paul Taylor. 1990. "The Rational Use of Antischistosomal Drugs in Schistosomiasis Control," *Social Science and Medicine* 30(10):1131–1138.

Chandra, R. K. 1997. "Nutrition and the Immune System: An Introduction," *American Journal of Clinical Nutrition* 66:460S–463S.

Cleland, J., and B. Ferry (eds.). 1995. *Sexual Behaviour and AIDS in the Developing World.* London: Taylor and Francis for the World Health Organization.

Cleland, J, B. Ferry, and M. Caraël. 1995. "Summary and Conclusions," in J. Cleland and B. Ferry (eds.), *Sexual Behaviour and AIDS in the Developing World,* pp. 208–228. London: Taylor and Francis for the World Health Organization.

Cockerham, W. C. 1997. "The Social Determinants of the Decline of Life Expectancy in Russia and Eastern Europe: A Lifestyle Explanation," *Journal of Health and Social Behavior* 38:117–130.

Coetzee, J. M. 1988. *White Writing: On the Culture of Letters in South Africa.* New Haven: Yale University Press.

Cohen, Bernard. 1994. "Invited Commentary: In Defense of Ecologic Studies for Testing a Linear No-Threshold Theory," *American Journal of Epidemiology* 139(8):765–768.

Cohen, M., I. Hoffman, R. Royce, et al. 1997. "Reduction of Concentration of HIV-1 in Semen after Treatment of Urethritis: Implications for Prevention of Sexual Transmission of HIV-1," *Lancet* 349(9069):1868–1873.

Cookson, S., R. Waldman, B. Gushulak, et al. 1998. "Immigrant and Refugee Health," *Emerging Infectious Diseases* 4(3):427–428. Available at: http://www.cdc.gov/ncidod/eid/v014n03/cookson.htm.

Corbett, E., R. Steketee, F. ter Kuile, et al. 2002. "HIV-1/AIDS and the Control of Other Infectious Diseases in Africa," *Lancet* 359:2177–2187.

Corbett, E., C. Watt, N. Walker, et al. 2003. "The Growing Burden of Tuberculosis: Global Trends and Interactions with the HIV Epidemic," *Archives of Internal Medicine* 163:1009–1021.

Coutsoudis, A., R. Bobat, H. Coovadia, et al. 1995. "The Effects of Vitamin A Supplementation on the Morbidity of Children Born to HIV-Infected Women," *American Journal of Public Health* 85(8):1076–1081.

Creese, Andrew, and David Parker. 1994. *Cost Analysis in Primary Health Care: A Training Manual for Programme Managers.* Geneva: World Health Organization.

Cunningham-Rundles, Susanna. 1998. "Analytical Methods for Evaluation of Immune Response in Nutrient Intervention," *Nutrition Reviews* 56(1, Part 2):S27–37.

Davies, Rob, and David Sanders. 1988. "Adjustment Policies and the Welfare of

Children: Zimbabwe, 1980–1985," in Giovanni Andrea Cornia, Richard Jolly, and Frances Stewart (eds.), *Adjustment with a Human Face.* Volume 2: *Country Case Studies,* pp. 272–299. Oxford: Clarendon Press.

de Castro, Carlos. 1993. *Trade and Transport Logistics Facilitation Guidelines.* SSATP Working Paper No. 4. Washington, D.C.: World Bank.

de Castro, Carlos. 1996. *Trade and Transport Facilitation.* SSATP Working Paper No. 27. Washington, D.C.: World Bank.

Delius, P., and C. Glaser. 2002. "Sexual Socialisation in South Africa: A Historical Perspective," *African Studies* 61(1):27–54.

Demery, Lionel, and Lyn Squire. 1996. "Macroeconomic Adjustment and Poverty in Africa: An Emerging Picture," *World Bank Research Observer* 11(1):39–59.

Deng, Francis. 1999. "Don't Overlook Colombia's Humanitarian Crisis," *Christian Science Monitor,* October 6.

Domingo, Esteban. 1997. "Rapid Evolution of Viral RNA Genomes," *Journal of Nutrition* 127:958S–961S.

Dow, W., T. Philipson, X. Sala-i-Martin, and J. Holmes. 1997. *Health Investment Complementarities under Competing Risks.* Economics Working Papers 192. Department of Economics and Business, Universitat Pompeu Fabra, Barcelona.

Drucker, E., P. Alcabes, and P. Marx. 2001. "The Injection Century: Massive Unsterile Injections and the Emergence of Human Pathogens," *Lancet* 358:1989–1992.

Dubow, S. 1995. *Scientific Racism in Modern South Africa.* Cambridge: Cambridge University Press.

Dumont, L. 1966/1980. *Homo Hierarchichus: The Caste System and Its Implications.* Chicago: University of Chicago Press.

Eidukiene, Virginija, 2002. "Poverty and Welfare Trends over the 1990s in Lithuania." Background Paper for *Social Monitor (2002),* UNICEF.

Elliott, A., J. Nakiyingi, M. Quigley, et al. 1999. "Inverse Association between BCG Immunisation and Intestinal Nematode Infestation among HIV-1-Positive Individuals in Uganda," *Lancet* 354(9183):1000–1001.

El-Mahgoub, S. 1998. "Pelvic Schistosomiasis and Infertility," *International Journal of Gynecology and Obstetrics* 20:201–206.

Escudé, Carlos Andrés. 1989. "Health in Buenos Aires in the Second Half of the Nineteenth Century," in D.C.M. Platt (ed.), *Social Welfare, 1850–1950: Australia, Argentina and Canada Compared,* pp. 60–70. London: Macmillan.

Esrey, Steven. 2001. "Environmental Sanitation and Its Relation to Child Health," in Ernest Bartell and Alejandro O'Donnell (eds.), *The Child in Latin America: Health, Development, and Rights,* pp. 121–137. Notre Dame, IN: University of Notre Dame Press.

Faiola, Anthony. 1999. "Drug War on the Home Front: Latin America, Long an Exporter, Fights Growing Addiction," *Washington Post,* September 15, p. A18.

Fairchild, Amy, and G. Oppenheimer. 1998. "Public Health Nihilism vs. Pragmatism: History, Politics, and the Control of Tuberculosis," *American Journal of Public Health* 88(7):1105–1117.

FAO (Food and Agriculture Organization). 2003a. *FAO/GIEWS: Africa Report.* Washington, D.C.: FAO. Available at: ftp://ftp.fao.org/docrep/fao_J1119e/J1119e00.pdf.

FAO (Food and Agriculture Organization). 2003b. *Food Balance Sheets. FAOSTAT: Nutrition Data.* Washington, D.C.: FAO. Available at: http://apps.fao.org/page/collections?subset–utrition.

Fawzi, W. W., and D. J. Hunter. 1998. "Vitamins in HIV Disease Progression and Vertical Transmission," *Epidemiology* 9(4):457–466.

Fawzi, W. W., and G. I. Msamanga. 2000. "Randomized Trial of Vitamin Supplements in Relation to Vertical Transmission of HIV-1 in Tanzania," *Journal of Acquired Immune Deficiency Syndromes* 23(3):246–254.

Fawzi, W. W., M. G. Herrera, P. Nestel, et al. 1997, "Risk Factors of Low Dietary Vitamin A Intake among Children in the Sudan," *East African Medical Journal* 74(4):227–232.

Fawzi, W. W., G. I. Msamanga, D. Spiegelman, et al. 1998. "Randomised trial of effects of vitamin supplements on pregnancy outcomes and T cell counts in HIV-1-infected women in Tanzania," *Lancet* 351(9114):1477–1482.

Feldmeier, H., G. Poggensee, I. Krantz, and G. Helling-Giese. 1995. "Female Genital Schistosomiasis," *Tropical and Geographical Medicine* 47(2, Suppl.):2–15.

Feldmeier, H., P. Leutscher, G. Poggensee, and G. Harms. 1999. "Male Genital Schistosomiasis and Haemospermia," *Tropical Medicine and International Health* 4(12):791–793.

Feldmeier, H., G. Helling-Giese, and G. Poggensee. 2001. "Unreliability of PAP Smears to Diagnose Female Genital Schistosomiasis," *Tropical Medicine and International Health* 6(1):31–33.

FHI (Family Health International). 2003. *Findings: Chirundu, Zimbabwe.* Available at: http://www.FHI.org/en/HIV/AIDS/Publications/manualsguidebooks/corrhope/corrfin3.htm.

Fiore, J., B. Suligoi, L. Monno, et al. 2002. "HIV-1 Shedding in Genital Tract of Infected Women," *Lancet* 359:1525–1526.

Fischer, David. 1996. *The Great Wave: Price Revolutions and the Rhythm of History.* Oxford: Oxford University Press.

Fischhoff, B., I. Fischhoff, E. Casman, and H. Dowlatabadi. 2002. "Integrated Assessment of Malaria Risk," in Elizabeth Casman and Hadi Dowlatabadi (eds.), *The Contextual Determinants of Malaria,* pp. 331–348. Washington, D.C.:Resources for the Future.

Fish, S. 1983. "Working on the Chain Gang: Interpretation in the Law and Literary Criticism," in W.J.T. Mitchell (ed.), *The Politics of Interpretation,* pp. 271–286. Chicago: University of Chicago Press.

Fleming, D. T., G. M. McQuillan, R. E. Johnson, et al. 1997. "Herpes Simplex Virus Type 2 in the United States, 1976 to 1994," *New England Journal of Medicine* 337(16):1105–1111.

Fleming, Douglas, and Judith Wasserheit. 1999. "From Epidemiological Synergy to Public Health Policy and Practice: The Contribution of Other Sexually Transmitted Diseases to Sexual Transmission of HIV Infection," *Sexually Transmitted Infections* 75:3–17.

Ford, N. 1994. "Cultural and Developmental Factors Underlying the Global Pattern of the Transmission of HIV/AIDS," in D. Phillips and Y. Verhasselt (eds.), *Health and Development,* pp. 83–96. London: Routledge.

Forster, Peter. 2001. "AIDS in Malawi: Contemporary Discourse and Cultural Continuities," *African Studies* 60(2):245–261.

Fortes, M. 1959. *Oedipus and Job in West African Religion.* Cambridge: Cambridge University Press.

Fowler, Mary, and Martha Rogers. 1996. "Overview of Perinatal HIV Infection," *Journal of Nutrition* 126:2602S–2607S.

Fragoso, G., M. Lastra, A. Aguilar, et al. 2001. "Effect of Oral Zinc Supplementation upon *Taenia Crassiceps* Murine Cysticercosis," *Journal of Parasitology* 87(5): 1034–1039.

Franco Agudelo, Saúl. 1988. "Crisis y salud en América Latina," in *II jornadas de atención primaria de la salud,* pp. 177–192. Buenos Aires: n.p.

Friedman, J., J. Kurtis, R. Mtalib, et al. 2003. "Malaria Is Related to Decreased Nutritional Status among Male Adolescents and Adults in the Setting of Intense Perennial Transmission," *Journal of Infectious Diseases* 188:449–457.

Friis, H., and K. F. Michaelsen. 1998. "Micronutrients and HIV Infection: A Review," *European Journal of Clinical Nutrition* 52:157–163.

Furedi, F. 1997. *Population and Development: A Critical Introduction.* New York: St. Martin's Press.

Gallup, J. L., and J. Sachs. 1999. *Malaria, Climate, and Poverty.* Cambridge, Mass.: Harvard Institute for International Development. Available at: http://www.cid.harvard.edu/caer2/htm/content/papers/paper48/paper48.htm.

Gallup, J. L., and J. Sachs. 2000. *The Economic Burden of Malaria.* CID Working Paper No. 52. Cambridge, Mass.: Center for International Development, Harvard University.

Gasyuk, Galina. 2002. "Poverty and Welfare Trends in the Republic of Belarus (1990–2000)," Background Paper for *Social Monitor (2002),* UNICEF. Available at: http://www.unicef-icdc.org.

Giannini, A., R. Saravanan, and P. Chang. 2003. "Oceanic Forcing of Sahel Rainfall on Interannual to Interdecadal Time Scales," *Science* 302(5647):1027–1030.

Gilman, S. 1985. *Difference and Pathology: Stereotypes of Sexuality, Race, and Madness.* Ithaca, N.Y.: Cornell University Press.

Gilman, S. 1990. " 'I'm Down on Whores': Race and Gender in Victorian London," in D. Goldberg (ed.), *Anatomy of Racism,* pp. 146–170. Minneapolis: University of Minnesota Press.

Gilman, S. 1992. "Black Bodies, White Bodies: Toward an Iconography of Female Sexuality in Late Nineteenth-Century Art, Medicine and Literature," in J. Donald and A. Rattansi (eds.), *"Race," Culture and Difference,* pp. 171–197. London: Sage.

Gisselquist, D., J. Potterat, S. Brody, and F. Vachon. 2003. "Let It Be Sexual: How Health Care Transmission of AIDS in Africa Was Ignored," *International Journal of STD and AIDS* 14:148–161.

Good, Kenneth. 1999. "The State and Extreme Poverty in Botswana: The San and Destitutes," *Journal of Modern African Studies* 37(2):185–205.

Gopinath, R., M. Ostrowski, S. Justement, et al. 2000. "Filarial Infections Increase Susceptibility to Human Immunodeficiency Virus Infection in Peripheral Blood Mononuclear Cells In Vitro," *Journal of Infectious Diseases* 182(6):1804–1808.

Gould, S. J. 1981. *The Mismeasure of Man.* New York: W. W. Norton.

Green, Andrew, and Carol Barker. 1988. "Priority Setting and Economic Appraisal: Whose Priorities—The Community or the Economist?" *Social Science and Medicine* 26(9):919–929.

Greenland, Sander, and James Robins. 1994. "Invited Commentary: Ecologic Studies—Biases, Misconceptions, and Counterexamples," *American Journal of Epidemiology* 139(8):747–760.

Griffin, Keith, and Terry McKinley. 1994. *Implementing a Human Development Strategy.* New York: St. Martin's Press.

Grinstead, O., B. Faigeles, D. Binson, and R. Eversley. 1993. "Sexual Risk for Human Immunodeficiency Virus Infection among Women in High-Risk Cities," *Family Planning Perspectives* 25(6):252–256, 277.

Grosskurth, H., F. Mosha, J. Todd, et al. 1995. "Impact of Improved Treatment of Sexually Transmitted Diseases on HIV Infection in rural Tanzania: Randomised Controlled Trial," *Lancet* 346(8974):530–536.

Grosskurth, H., R. Gray, R. Hayes, et al. 2000. "Control of Sexually Transmitted Diseases for HIV-1 Prevention: Understanding the Implications of the Mwanza and Rakai Trials," *Lancet* 355:1981–1987.

Guttman, Nurit, and Charles Salmon. 1998. "Credibility of Information from Official Sources on HIV/AIDS Transmission," *Public Health Reports* 113:465–471.

Hahn, Beatrice, G. Shaw, K. De Cock, and P. Sharp. 2000. "AIDS as a Zoonosis: Scientific and Public Health Implications," *Science* 287(5453, January 28):607–614.

Harbige, Laurence. 1996. "Nutrition and Immunity with Emphasis on Infection and Autoimmune Disease," *Nutrition and Health* 10:285–312.

Harms, G., and H. Feldmeier. 2002. "Review: HIV Infection and Tropical Parasitic Diseases—Deleterious Interactions in Both Directions?" *Tropical Medicine and International Health* 7(6):479–488.

Hastaning, S., C. Nokes, W. S. Hertanto, et al. 1999. "Evidence for an Association between Hookworm Infection and Cognitive Function in Indonesian School Children," *Tropical Medicine and International Health* 4(5):322–334.

Hedberg, K., N. Shaffer, F. Davachi, et al. 1993. "Plasmodium Falciparum-Associated Anemia in Children at a Large Urban Hospital in Zaire," *American Journal of Tropical Medicine and Hygiene* 48(3):365–371.

Henderson, James. 1999. *Health Economics and Policy.* Cincinnati: South-Western College Publishing.

Herwaldt, Barbara. 1999. "Leishmaniasis," *Lancet* 354(9185):1191–1199.

Hess, S., M. B. Zimmermann, P. Adou, et al. 2002. "Treatment of Iron Deficiency in Goitrous Children Improves the Efficacy of Iodized Salt in Cote d'Ivoire," *American Journal of Clinical Nutrition* 75(4):743–748.

Hitchcock, Penny, and Lieve Fransen. 1998. *Preventing HIV Infection: What Are the Lessons from Mwanza and Rakai?* Available at: http://www.iaen.org/partmat/mwanza.htm.

Hlaing, T. 1993. "Ascariasis and Childhood Malnutrition," *Parasitology* 107(Suppl.): S125–136.

Hoffman, I., C. Jere, T. Taylor, et al. 1999. "The Effect of *Plasmodium falciparum* Malaria on HIV-1 RNA Blood Plasma Concentration," *AIDS* 13:487–494.

HRW (Human Rights Watch). 2003. "To Serve without Health? Inadequate Nutrition and Health Care in the Russian Armed Forces," *Human Rights Watch Report* 15(8D). Available at: http://www.hrw.org/reports/2003/russia1103.

Huerta, Elmer, and Douglas Weed. 1998. "Cuidando su salud," *Cancer* (Suppl.) 83(8): 1805–1808.

IAVI (International AIDS Vaccine Initiative). 1994. *Paris Report: Accelerating the Development of Preventive HIV Vaccines for the World. Summary Report and Recommendations of an International Ad Hoc Scientific Committee.* New York: IAVI. Available at: http://www.iavi.org/about/paris.asp.

IDB (Inter-American Development Bank). 1998. *Facing up to Inequality in Latin America: Economic and Social Progress in Latin America, 1998–1999 Report.* Washington, D.C.: Johns Hopkins Press.

"In Haiti, More Than Half of All Births Are Either Unwanted or Mistimed." 1996. *International Family Planning Perspectives* 22(4):181–182.

IOM (International Organization for Migration). 2002. *Public Perception and Awareness of Trafficking in Women in the Baltic States.* Vilnius, Romania: IOM.

Izazola-Licea, J. S. Gortmaker, K. Tolbert, et al. 2000. "Prevalence of Same-Gender Sexual Behavior and HIV in a Probability Household Survey in Mexican Men." *Journal of Sex Research* 37(1):37.

Izdebski, Zbigniew. 2002. *Selected Aspects of Evaluation of the National HIV/AIDS Prevention Program.* Warsaw: National AIDS Center, UNDP.

Jacobson, Maria. 2002. "Why Do Men Buy Sex? Interview with Professor Sven-Axel Mansson," *NIKK magasin* (Nordic Institute for Women's Studies and Gender Research; Oslo) 1:22–25.

Jamison, D. H., W. Mosley, A. Measham, and J.-L. Bobadilla, eds. 1993. *Disease Control Priorities for Developing Countries.* New York: Oxford University Press.

Jespersen, Eva. 1992. "External Shocks, Adjustment Policies and Economic and Social Performance," in Giovanni Andrea Cornia, R. Van der Hoeven, and T. Mkandawire (eds.), *Africa's Recovery in the 1990s: From Stagnation and Adjustment to Human Development,* pp. 9–50. New York: St. Martin's Press.

John, G., R. Nduati, D. Mbori-Ngacha, et al. 1997. "Genital Shedding of Human Immunodeficiency Virus Type 1 DNA during Pregnancy: Association with Immunosuppression, Abnormal Cervical or Vaginal Discharge, and Severe Vitamin A Deficiency," *Journal of Infectious Diseases* 175:57–62.

Kaisernetwork. 2003a. "HIV Infections among Libyan Children Due to Negligence, Not Intentional, Montagnier Says in Testimony," *Kaiser Daily HIV/AIDS Report,* Sept 5. Available at: http://www.kaisernetwork.org.

Kaisernetwork. 2003b. "WHO Leaders Say Billions More Condoms Needed to Fight HIV/AIDS in Asia," *Kaiser Daily HIV/AIDS Report,* Aug 18. Available at: http://www.kaisernetwork.org.

Kamarck, Andrew. 1988. "The Special Case of Africa," in David Bell and Michael Reich (eds.), *Health, Nutrition, and Economic Crises: Approaches to Policy in the Third World,* pp. 199–221. Dover Mass.: Auburn House.

Keeler, Laura, and Marjut Jyrkinen. 2002. "Racism in the Sex Trade in Finland," *NIKK magasin* (Nordic Institute for Women's Studies and Gender Research; Oslo) 1:33–36.

Khan, M., S. Hawkes, and D. Ali. 2002. "Economic Evaluation of MCH-FP Clinic-Based Syphilis Screening in Rural Bangladesh." Dhaka: International Center for Diarrhoeal Disease Research, Bangladesh. Available at: http://www.icddrb.org.

Khandait, D. W., N. D. Vasudeo, S. P. Zodpey, et al. 1998. "Subclinical Vitamin A deficiency in Undersix Children in Nagpur, India," *Southeast Asian Journal of Tropical Medicine and Public Health* 29(2):289–292.

Kidd, D. 1904. *The Essential Kafir.* London: Adam and Charles Black.

Kidd, D. 1906. *Savage Childhood: A Study of Kafir Children.* London: Adam and Charles Black.

Kidd, D. 1908. *Kafir Socialism and the Dawn of Individualism.* London: Adam and Charles Black.

Koopman, James, and Ira Longini. 1994. "The Ecological Effects of Individual Exposures and Nonlinear Disease Dynamics in Populations," *American Journal of Public Health* 84(5):836–842.

Kost, Kathryn, and Jacqueline Darroch Forrest. 1992. "American Women's Sexual Behavior and Exposure to Risk of Sexually Transmitted Diseases," *Family Planning Perspectives* 24(6):244–254.

Kovaleski, Serge. 2000. "Child Sex Trade Rises in Central America; Prostitution Is "Dark Side of Tourism," *Washington Post,* January 2, p. A17.

Krieger, Nancy. 1994. "Epidemiology and the Web of Causation: Has Anyone Seen the Spider?" *Social Science and Medicine* 39(7):887–903.

Kuhn, T. 1970. *The Structure of Scientific Revolutions,* 2nd ed. Chicago: University of Chicago Press.

Kvalsvig, J. D., R. M. Cooppan, and K. J. Connolly. 1991. "The Effects of Parasitic Infections on Cognitive Processes in Children," *Annals of Tropical Medicine and Parasitology* 85(5):551–568.

Lakshmanan, T. R., U. Subramanian, W. Anderson, and F. Léautier. N.d. "Integration of Transport and Trade Facilitation: Selected Regional Case Studies." Washington, D.C.: World Bank.

Lamptey, Peter, and Helene Gayle. 2001. *HIV/AIDS Prevention and Care in Resource-Constrained Settings: Handbook for the Design and Management of Programs*: Washington, D.C.: Family Health International.

Lamptey, Peter, Paul Zeitz, and Carol Larivee (eds.). 2001. *Strategies for an Expanded and Comprehensive Response (ECR) to a National HIV/AIDS Epidemic: A Handbook for Designing and Implementing HIV/AIDS Programs.* Arlington, Va.: FHI.

Landers, Daniel. 1996. "Nutrition and Immune Function II: Maternal Factors Influencing Transmission," *Journal of Nutrition,* 126:2637S–2640S.

Lang, B. 1997. "Metaphysical Racism (Or: Biological Warfare by Other Means)," in N. Zack (ed.), *Race/Sex: Their Sameness, Difference, and Interplay,* pp. 19–27. New York: Routledge.

Laughlin, C., and E. Laughlin. 1973. "The So of Karamoja District, Eastern Uganda," in A. Molnos (ed.), *Cultural Source Material for Population Planning in East Africa.* Vol. 3: *Beliefs and Practices,* pp. 352–364. Nairobi: East African Publishing House.

Le Blanc, M-N., D. Meintel, and V. Piche. 1991. "The African Sexual System: Comment on Caldwell et al.," *Population and Development Review* 17(3):497–505.

Leon, D., L. Chenet, V. Shkolnikov, et al. 1997. "Huge Variation in Russian Mortality Rates 1984–1994: Artefact, Alcohol, or What?" *Lancet* 350:383–388.

Leutscher, P., V. Ravaoalimalala, C. Raharisolo, et al. 1998. "Clinical Findings in Female Genital Schistosomiasis in Madagascar," *Tropical Medicine and International Health* 3(4):327–332.

Leutscher, P., C-E. Ramarokoto, C. Reimert, et al. 2000. "Community-Based Study of Genital Schistosomiasis in Men from Madagascar," *Lancet* 3555:117–118.

Levander, Orville. 1997. "Nutrition and Newly Emerging Viral Diseases: An Overview," *Journal of Nutrition* 127: 948S–950S.

Levav, M., A. F. Mirsky, P. M. Schantz, et al. 1995. "Parasitic Infection in Manourished School Children: Effects on Behaviour and EEG," *Parasitology* 110: 103–111.

Lévy-Bruhl, L. 1926. *How Natives Think.* London: George Allen Unwin.

Linné, C. von. 1758/1956. *Systema Naturae.* London: British Museum (Natural History).

Litsios, Socrates. 2002. "Malaria Control and the Future of International Public Health," in Elizabeth Casman and Hadi Dowlatabadi (eds.), *The Contextual Determinants of Malaria,* pp. 292–328. Washington, D.C.: Resources for the Future.

Little, K. L. 1973. *African Women in Towns: An Aspect of Africa's Social Revolution.* Cambridge: Cambridge University Press.

Loewenson, Rene, and Alan Whiteside. 2002. *HIV/AIDS: Implications for Poverty Reduction.* UNDP Policy Paper. New York: United Nations Development Programme.

Logie, Dorothy. 1993. "Zimbabwe: Health or Debt," *Lancet* 341: 950.

Lopez, Margarita. 2001. "Safe Sanctuary Found for Lucky Few," *Baltic Times,* July 12–18: 20.

Luby, Stephen. 2001. "Injection Safety," *Emerging Infectious Diseases* 7(3, Suppl.). Available at: http://www.cdc.gov/ncidod/eid/v017n03_supp/luby.htm.

Lush, Louisiana, Gill Walt, and Jessica Ogden. 2003. "Transferring Policies for Treating Sexually Transmitted Infections: What's Wrong with the Global Guidelines?" *Health Policy and Planning* 18(1): 18–30.

Lush, L., E. Darkoh, and S. Ramotlhwa. 2005. "HIV/AIDS and Health Systems: Botswana," in E. J. Beck, N. Mays, A. Whiteside, and J. M. Zuniga, (eds.), *The HIV Pandemic: Global Implications.* Oxford: Oxford University Press.

Lutz, C., and J. Collins. 1993. *Reading National Geographic.* Chicago: University of Chicago Press.

Lynggard, Trine. 2002. "Nordic-Baltic Campaign against Trafficking in Women," *NIKK magasin* (Nordic Institute for Women's Studies and Gender Research; Oslo), 1: 16–17.

MacDonald, N. E., G. A. Wells, W. A. Fisher, et al. 1990. "High-Risk STD/HIV Behavior among College Students," *Journal of the American Medical Association* 263: 3155–3159.

Madden, F. 1899. "A Case of Bilharzia of the Vagina," *Lancet* 1:1716.

Mahler, K. 1997. "Increased Risk of STD Infection among Peruvian Women Linked to Their Partners' Sexual Practices." *International Family Planning Perspectives* 23(1): 39–40.

Malhotra, I., P. Mungai, A. Wamachi, et al. 1999. "Helminth- and bacillus Calmette-Guérin-induced immunity in children sensitized in utero to filariasis and schistosomiasis," *Journal of Immunology* 162:6843–6848.

Marble, Michelle, and Keith Key. 1995. "Clinical Facets of a Disease Neglected Too Long," *AIDS Weekly Plus* August 7: 16–19.

Markus, M., and J. Fincham. 2000. "Worms and Pediatric Human Immunodeficiency Virus Infection and Tuberculosis (Correspondence)," *Journal of Infectious Diseases* 181:1873.

McCarthy, F. D., H. Wolf, and Y. Wu. 2000. *The Growth Costs of Malaria.* NBER Working Paper 7541. Cambridge, Mass.: National Bureau of Economic Research.

McDaniels, Andrea. 1998. "Brazil Turns to Women to Stop Dramatic Rise in AIDS Cases," *Christian Science Monitor,* January 9, p. 7.

McMurray, David. 1998. "Impact of Nutritional Deficiencies on Resistance to Experimental Pulmonary Tuberculosis," *Nutrition Reviews* 56(1, Part 2): S147–152).

McPherson, Malcolm, D. Hoover, and D. Snodgrass. 2000. "The Impact on Economic Growth in Africa of Rising Costs and Labor Productivity Losses Associated with HIV/AIDS." CAER II Discussion Paper No. 79. Cambridge, Mass. Available at: http://www.cid.harvard.edu/caer2/.

Meurs, Mieke, and Rasika Ranasinghe. 2003. "De-Development in Post-Socialism," *Politics and Society* 31(1): 31–53.

Meydani, Simin, and Alison Beharka. 1998. "Recent Developments in Vitamin E and Immune Response," *Nutrition Reviews* 56(1, Part 2): S49–58.

Michael, Robert, J. Gagnon, E. Laumann, and G. Kolata. 1994. *Sex in America: A Definitive Survey.* Boston: Little, Brown.

Miguel, E. A., and M. Kremer. 2001. *Worms: Education and Health Expenditures in Kenya.* NBER Working Paper 8481. Cambridge, Mass.: National Bureau of Economic Research.

Miner, H. 1956. "Body Ritual among the Nacirema," *American Anthropologist* 58: 503–507.

Ministerio de Salud Pública del Ecuador. 1999. "Estadística de las enfermedades de transmisión sexual." Photocopy of data from Dirección Nacional de Epidemiología, Quito.

Ministerio de Salud Pública del Ecuador. 2000. "Datos estadísticos sobre el SIDA. Ecuador, 1984–1999." Photocopy of data from the Programa Nacional de SIDA/ITS, Quito.

Montagu, M.F.A. 1952. *Man's Most Dangerous Myth: The Fallacy of Race.* New York: Harper and Brothers.

Montresor, Antonio, Mahdi Ramsan, Hababu M. Chwaya, et al. 2001. Extending Anthelminthic Coverage to Non-enrolled School-Age Children Using a Simple and Low-Cost Method. *Tropical Medicine and International Health* 6(7): 535–537.

Moore, A., G. Herrera, J. Nyamongo, et al. 2001. "Estimated Risk of HIV Transmission by Blood Transfusion in Kenya," *Lancet* 358: 657–660.

Morris, Chester. 2003. "Workplace HIV Programs in Malawi: A Case Study and Review of Evidence Based Interventions in HIV Care, Support and Prevention," in William Kosanovich (ed.), *Bureau of International Labor Affairs Research Symposium Papers.* Vol. 2: *HIV/AIDS and the Workplace in Developing Countries,* pp. 165–188. Washington, D.C.: U.S. Department of Labor.

Morris, J. Glenn Jr., and Morris Potter. 1997. "Emergence of New Pathogens as a Function of Changes in Host Susceptibility," *Emerging Infectious Diseases* 3(4). Available at: http://www.cdc.gov/ncidod/eid/v013n04/morris.htm.

Morrow, Richard, and John Bryant. 1995. "Health Policy Approaches to Measuring and Valuing Human Life: Conceptual and Ethical Issues," *American Journal of Public Health* 85(10): 1356–1360.

Morse, Stephen. 1997. "The Public Health Threat of Emerging Viral Disease," *Journal of Nutrition* 127: 951S–957S.

Moses, S., J. Bradley, N. Nagelkerke, et al. 1990. "Geographical Patterns of Male Circumcision Practices in Africa: Association with HIV Seroprevalence," *International Journal of Epidemiology* 19: 693–697.

Mosunjac, M., T. Tadros, R. Beach, and M. Majmudar. 2003. "Cervical Schistosomiasis, Human Papilloma Virus (HPV), and Human Immunodeficiency Virus (HIV): A Dangerous Coexistence or Coincidence?" *Gynecologic Oncolgy* 90(1): 211–214.

Moustgaard, Ulrikke. 2002. "Bodies across Borders," *NIKK magasin* (Nordic Institute for Women"s Studies and Gender Research; Oslo) 1: 4–9.

Murray, C.J.L. 1994. "Quantifying the Burden of Disease: The Technical Basis for Disability-Adjusted Life Years," *Bulletin of the World Health Organization* 72(3): 429–445.

Murray, C.J.L., and J. L. Bobadilla. 1995. *Epidemiological Transitions in the Formerly Socialist Economies: Divergent Patterns of Mortality and Causes of Death.* Boston: Center for Population and Development Studies, Harvard University.

Murray, N. J., L. S. Zabin, V. Toledo-Dreves, and X. Luengo-Charath. 1998. "Gender Differences in Factors Influencing First Intercourse among Urban Students in Chile," *International Family Planning Perspectives* 24(3): 139–144, 152.

Mwanga, J. R., P. Magnussen, C. L. Mugashe, et al. 2004. "Schistosomiasis-Related Perceptions, Attitudes and Treatment-Seeking Practices in Magu District, Tanazania: Public Health Implications," *Journal of Biosocial Science* 36: 63–81.

Myrdal, G. 1944. *An American Dilemma: The Negro Problem and Modern Democracy.* New York: Harper and Brothers.

Nacher, M. 2002. "Worms and Malaria: Noisy Nuisances and Silent Benefits," *Parasite Immunology* 24: 391–393.

Nacher, M., F. Gay, P. Singhasivanon, et al. 2000. "*Ascaris lumbricoides* Infection Is Associated with Protection from Cerebral Malaria," *Parasite Immunology* 22: 107–114.

Nacher, M., P. Singhasivanon, F. Gay, et al. 2001. "Contemporaneous and Successive Mixed *Plasmodium falciparum* and *Plasmodium vivax* Infections Are Associated with *Ascaris lumbricoides*: An Immunomodulating Effect?" *Journal of Parasitology* 87(4): 912–915.

Nacher, M., P. Singhasivanon, S. Yimsamran, et al. 2002. "Intestinal Helminth Infections Are Associated with Increased Incidence of *Plasmodium falciparum* Malaria in Thailand," *Journal of Parasitology* 88(1):55–58.

Nchinda, Thomas. 1998, "Malaria: A Reemerging Disease in Africa," *Emerging Infectious Diseases* 4(3). Available at: http://www.cdc.gov/ncidod/eid/v014n03/nchinda.htm.

Needham, C., H. Thi Him, N. Viet Hoa, et al. 1998. "Epidemiology of Soil-Transmitted Nematode Infections in Ha Nam Province, Vietnam," *Tropical Medicine and International Health* 3(11):904–912.

NEI (Netherlands Economic Institute). 2001. "Strategic Review, SSATP: Synthesis Report." Washington, D.C.: World Bank. Available at:www.worldbank.org.

Nimmagadda, A., W. O'Brien, and M. Goetz. 1998. "The Significance of Vitamin A and Carotenoid Status in Persons Infected by the Human Immunodeficiency Virus," *Clinical Infectious Diseases* 26:711–718.

Nokes, C., S. M. Grantham-McGregor, A. W. Sawyer, et al. 1992. "Parasitic Helminth Infection and Cognitive Function in School Children," *Proceedings of the Royal Society of London* B 247:77–81.

Oberhelman, R. A., E. S. Guerrero, M. L. Fernandez, et al. 1998, "Correlations between Intestinal Parasitosis, Physical Growth, and Psychomotor Development among Infants and Children from Rural Nicaragua," *American Journal of Tropical Medicine and Hygiene,* 58(4):470–475.

OSI (Open Society Institute). 2001. *Drugs, AIDS, and Harm Reduction.* New York: OSI.

Packard, Randall, and Paul Epstein. 1991. "Epidemiologists, Social Scientists, and the

Structure of Medical Research on AIDS in Africa," *Social Science and Medicine* 33(7):771–794.

PAHO (Pan American Health Organization). 1998. *Health in the Americas.* Vol. 1. Scientific Publication No. 569. Washington, D.C.: Pan American Health Organization.

PAHO (Pan American Health Organization). 2002. *Health in the Americas.* Vol. 1. Scientific Publication No. 569. Washington, D.C.: Pan American Health Organization.

PAHO (Pan American Health Organization). 2003. *Trafficking of Women and Children for Sexual Exploitation in the Americas.* Washington, D.C. Pan American Health Organization. Available at: http://www.paho.org/English/HDP/HDW/TraffickingPaper.pdf.

Pallangyo, Kisali. 2001. "Clinical Features of Tuberculosis among Adults in Sub-Saharan Africa in the 21st Century," *Scandinavian Journal of Infectious Disease* 33:488–493.

Pelletier, David. 1994a. "The Potentiating Effects of Malnutrition on Child Mortality: Epidemiologic Evidence and Policy Implications," *Nutrition Reviews* 52(12):409–415.

Pelletier, David. 1994b. "The Relationship between Child Anthropometry and Mortality in Developing Countries: Implications for Policy, Programs and Future Research," *Journal of Nutrition* 124:2047S–2081S.

Pelletier, D., E. Frongillo Jr., and J.-P. Habicht. 1993. "Epidemiologic Evidence for a Potentiating Effect of Malnutrition on Child Mortality," *American Journal of Public Health* 83(8):1130–1133.

Pelletier, D., E. Frongillo Jr., D. Schroeder, and J.-P. Habicht. 1994. "A Methodology for Estimating the Contribution of Malnutrition to Child Mortality in Developing Countries," *Journal of Nutrition* 124:2106S–2122S.

Pelletier, D. L., E. Frongillo, D. Schroeder, and J-P. Habicht. 1995. "The Effects of Malnutrition on Child Mortality in Developing Countries," *Bulletin of the World Health Organization* 73(4):443–448.

Philipson, T., and R. Posner. 1995. "The Microeconomics of the AIDS Epidemic in Africa," *Population and Development Review* 21(4):835–848.

Pio, Alessandro. 1994. "The Social Impact of Adjustment in Africa," in Giovanni Andrea Cornia and Gerald Helleiner (eds.), *From Adjustment to Development in Africa,* pp. 298–314. New York: St. Martin's Press.

Pitje, G. M. 1948. "Traditional and Modern Forms of Male Education among the Pedi and Cognate Tribes." Unpublished M.A. thesis, University of South Africa. [Cited in P. Delius and C. Glaser (2002) "Sexual Socialisation in South Africa: A Historical Perspective," *African Studies* 61(1):27–54.]

Poggensee, G., I. Kiwelu, V. Weger, et al. 2000. "Female Genital Schistosomiasis of the Lower Genital Tract: Prevalence and Disease-Associated Morbidity in Northern Tanzania," *Journal of Infectious Diseases* 181:1210–1213.

Pounds, N.J.G. 1994. *An Economic History of Medieval Europe.* 2nd ed. London: Longman.

Powell, Josh. 1996. *AIDS and HIV-Related Diseases.* New York: Insight Books, Plenum Press.

PPC (Partnership for Parasite Control). 2002. *Rome Meeting Notes, 2002.* Geneva: PPC. Available at: http:///www.who.int/wormcontrol/about_us/en/mtgnotes/april2002.pdf.

Quinn T., M. Wawer, N. Sewankambo, et al. 2000. "Viral Load and Heterosexual Transmission of Human Immunodeficiency Virus Type 1," *New England Journal of Medicine* 342(13):921–929.

Rau, Bill. 2002. *Workplace HIV/AIDS Programs: An Action Guide for Managers.* Washington, D.C.: Family Health International. Available at: http://www.fhi.org.

Ravigolione, M. C., H. L. Reider, K. Styblo, et. al. 1994. "Tuberculosis Trends in Eastern Europe and the Former USSR," *Tuberculosis and Lung Disease* 75:400–416.

Reinisch, June M., Stephanie A. Sanders, Craig A. Hill, and Mary Ziemba-Davis. 1992. "High-Risk Sexual Behavior among Heterosexual Undergraduates at a Midwestern University," *Family Planning Perspectives* 24(3):116–121, 145.

Remez, L. 1997. "Fertility Remains Elevated in Guatemala: One in Three Births Are Unplanned," *International Family Planning Perspectives* 23(1):40–42.

Renton, Adrian. 1993. "Epidemiology and Causation: A Realist View," *Journal of Epidemiology and Community Health* 48:79–85.

Rifkin, Susan, and Gill Walt. 1986. "Why Health Improves: Defining the Issues Concerning 'Comprehensive Primary Health Care' and 'Selective Primary Health Care,' " *Social Science and Medicine* 23(6):559–566.

Rose, G. 1985. "Sick Individuals and Sick Populations," *International Journal of Epidemiology* 14:32–38.

Rosen, S., and AIDS Economics Team of the Center for International Health. 2002a. *What Makes Nigerian Manufacturing Firms Take Action on HIV/AIDS?* World Bank Africa Region Findings No. 199. Washington, D.C.: World Bank. Available at: http://www.international-health.org/AIDS_economics/.

Rosen, S., J. L. Simon, W. MacLeod, et al. 2002b. *Investing in the Epidemic: Making the Business Case against AIDS in Africa.* Boston: Center for International Health, Boston University School of Public Health. Available at: http://www.international-health.org/AIDS_economics/.

Rowland-Jones, Sarah, and Barbara Lohman. 2002. "Interactions between Malaria and HIV Infection: An Emerging Public Health Problem?" *Microbes and Infection* 4: 1265–1270.

Ruel, M. T., J. A. Rivera, M. C. Santizo, et al. 1997. "Impact of Zinc Supplementation on Morbidity from Diarrhea and Respiratory Infections among Rural Guatemalan Children," *Pediatrics* 99(6):808–813.

Rushing, W. 1995. *The AIDS Epidemic: Social Dimensions of an Infectious Disease.* Boulder: Westview.

Ryu, J. S., H. K. Choi, D. Y. Min, et al. 2001. "Effect of Iron on the Virulence of *Trichomonas vaginalis*," *Journal of Parasitology* 87(2):457–460.

Sanders, David, and Abdulrahman Sambo. 1991. "AIDS in Africa: The Implications of Economic Recession and Structural Adjustment," *Health Policy and Planning* 6(2):157–165.

Sarin, A. R. 1995. "Severe Anemia of Pregnancy, Recent Experience," *International Journal of Gynecology and Obstetrics* 50(Suppl. 2):S45–S49.

Scanlon, Thomas, A. Tomkins, M. Lynch, and F. Scanlon. 1998. "Street Children in Latin America," *British Medical Journal* 316(7144):1596–1600.

Schön, D. 1979. "Generative Metaphor: A Perspective on Problem-Setting in Social Policy," in A. Ortony (ed.), *Metaphor and Thought,* pp. 254–283. Cambridge: Cambridge University Press.

Schultz, T. Paul. 1997. "Assessing the Productive Benefits of Nutrition and Health: An Integrated Human Capital Approach," *Journal of Econometrics* 77:141–158.

Schultz, T. Paul. 2002. "Why Governments Should Invest More to Educate Girls," *World Development* 30(2):207–225.

Schwartz, Sharon, and Kenneth Carpenter. 1999. "The Right Answer for the Wrong Question: Consequences of Type III Error for Public Health Research," *American Journal of Public Health* 89:1175–1180.

Scott, Marilyn, and Kristine Koski. 2000. "Zinc Deficiency Impairs Immune Responses against Parasitic Nematode Infections at Intestinal and Systemic Sites," *Journal of Nutrition* 130:1412S–1420S.

Scrimshaw, Nevin, and J. P. SanGiovanni. 1997. "Synergism of Nutrition, Infection, and Immunity: An Overview," *American Journal of Clinical Nutrition* 66:464S–477S.

Seitles, Marc D. 1997/1998. "Effect of the Convention on the Rights of the Child upon Street Children in Latin America: A Study of Brazil, Colombia, and Guatemala," *In the Public Interest* 16:159–193.

Sekula, W., K. Babinska, and S. Petrova. 1997. "Nutrition Policies in Central and Eastern Europe," *Nutrition Reviews* 55(11):S58–S73.

Semba, R. 1998. "The Role of Vitamin A and Related Retinoids in Immune Function," *Nutrition Reviews* 56(1, Part 2):S38–48.

Semba, R., N. Graham, W. Caiaffa, et al. 1993. "Increased Mortality Associated with Vitamin A Deficiency during Human Immunodeficiency Virus Type 1 Infection," *Archives of Internal Medicine* 153:2149–2154.

Semba, R., P. Miotti, J. Chiphangwi, et al. 1994. "Maternal Vitamin A Deficiency and Mother-to-Child Transmission of HIV-1," *Lancet* 343:1593–1597.

Shankar, A. H., B. Genton, R. D. Semba, et al. 1999. "Effect of Vitamin A Supplementation on Morbidity Due to *Plasmodium falciparum* in Young Children in Papua New Guinea: A Randomised Trial," *Lancet* 354(9174):203–209.

Sharp, David. 2003. "Dam Medicine," *Lancet* 362:184.

Shaw, Mary, Danny Dorling, and George Davey Smith. 1999. "Poverty, Social Exclusion, and Minorities," in Michael Marmot and R. G. Wilkinson (eds.), *Social Determinants of Health,* pp. 211–239. Oxford: Oxford University Press.

Shcherbak, Yuri. 1996. "Ten Years of the Chornobyl Era," *Scientific American* April 1996:44–49.

Shkolnikov, V., D. Leon, S. Adamets, et al. 1998. "Educational Level and Adult Mortality in Russia: An Analysis of Routine Data 1979 to 1994," *Social Science and Medicine* 47(3):357–369.

Sigman, Marian, and Shannon Whaley. 1998. "The Role of Nutrition in the Development of Intelligence," in Ulric Neisser (ed.), *The Rising Curve: Long-Term Gains in IQ and Related Measures,* pp. 155–182. Washington, D.C.: American Psychological Association.

Simon, J. L., S. Rosen, A. Whiteside, et al. 2000. "The Response of African Businesses to HIV/AIDS," in Commonwealth Secretariat (ed.), *HIV/AIDS in the Commonwealth 2000/01,* pp. 72–77. London: Kensington Publications. Available at: http://www.international-health.org/AIDS_economics/.

Simonsen, L. A. Kane, and J. Lloyd. 1999. "Unsafe Injections in the Developing World and Transmission of Blood Borne Pathogens: A Review," *Bulletin of the World Health Organization* 77:789–800.

Singh, Susheela, and Jacqueline E. Darroch. 1999. "Trends in Sexual Activity among Adolescent American Women: 1982–1995," *Family Planning Perspectives* 31(5): 212–219.

Singh, S., D. Wulf, R. Samara, and Y. Cuca. 2000. "Gender Differences in the Timing of First Intercourse: Data from 14 Countries," *International Family Planning Perspectives* 26(1):21–28, 43.

Sipaviciene, Audra. 2002. "You Will Be Sold Like a Doll," *NIKK magasin* (Nordic Institute for Women's Studies and Gender Research; Oslo) 1:10–15.

Skrabanek, P. 1992. "The Poverty of Epidemiology," *Perspectives in Biology and Medicine* 35:182–185.

Smith, Tom W. 1991. "Adult Sexual Behavior in 1989: Number of Partners, Frequency of Intercourse and Risk of AIDS," *Family Planning Perspectives* 23(3): 102–107.

Solomons, Noel. 1998, "Plant Sources of Vitamin A and Human Nutrition: Red Palm Oil Does the Job," *Nutrition Reviews* 56(10):309–311.

Sommer, Alfred, and Keith West, with J. A. Olson and A. C. Ross. 1996. *Vitamin A Deficiency: Health, Survival, and Vision.* New York: Oxford University Press.

"South Africa's President and the Plague." 2000. *Economist,* May 25. Available at: http://www.economist.com/editorial/freeforall/current/ir7632.html.

Spanger, Marlene. 2002. "Between Suppression and Independence: Transnational Prostitution of Black Women in Denmark," *NIKK magasin* (Nordic Institute for Women's Studies and Gender Research; Oslo) 1:18–21.

Stepan, N. L. 1982. *The Idea of Race in Science: Great Britain 1800–1960.* Hamden, Conn.: Archon Books.

Stepan, N. L. 1990. "Race and Gender: The Role of Analogy in Science," in D. Goldberg (ed.), *Anatomy of Racism,* pp. 38–57. Minneapolis: University of Minnesota Press.

Stephensen, C. B., J. O. Alvarez, J. Kohatsu, et al. 1994. "Vitamin A Is Excreted in the Urine during Acute Infection," *American Journal of Clinical Nutrition* 60(3): 388–392.

Stiglitz, Joseph E. 2000. *Economics of the Public Sector.* 3rd ed. New York: W. W. Norton.

Stephenson, L. 1993. "The Impact of Schistosomiasis on Human Nutrition," *Parasitology* 107(Suppl.):S107–123.

Stillwaggon, Eileen. 1998. *Stunted Lives, Stagnant Economies: Poverty, Disease, and Underdevelopment.* New Brunswick, N.J.: Rutgers University Press.

Stoltzfus, R., M. Albonico, H. Chwaya, et al. 1998. "Effects of the Zanzibar School-Based Deworming Program on Iron Status of Children," *American Journal of Clinical Nutrition* 68:179–186.

Storey, D. M. 1993. "Filariasis: Nutritional Interactions in Human and Animal Hosts," *Parasitology* 107(Suppl.):S147–158.

Sturm, A. W., D. Wilkinson, N. Ndovela, et al. 1998. "Pregnant Women as a Reservoir of Undetected Sexually Transmitted Diseases in Rural South Africa: Implications for Disease Control," *American Journal of Public Health* 88(8):1243–1245.

Suhrcke, Marc. 2000. *Are Reforms from a Centrally Planned to a Market System Bad for Health?* HWWZ Discussion Paper No. 105. Hamburg: Hamburg Institute of International Economics.

Susser, M. 1977. "Judgment and Causal Inference: Criteria in Epidemiologic Studies," *American Journal of Epidemiology* 105:1–5.

Susser, M. 1985. "Epidemiology in the United States after World War II: The Evolution of Technique," *Epidemiological Review* 7:147–177.

Synergy Project. 2002. "Putting on the Brakes, Preventing HIV Transmission along Truck Routes." Washington, D.C.: USAID. Available at: www.synergyaids.com.

Tagwireyi, Julia, and Ted Greiner. 1994. *Nutrition in Zimbabwe: An Update.* Washington, D.C.: World Bank.

Tarasevich, I., E. Rydkina, and D. Raoult. 1998. "Outbreak of Epidemic Typhus in Russia," *Lancet* 352:1151.

Terborgh, A., J. Rosen, R. Santiso Galvez, et al. 1995. "Family Planning among Indigenous Populations in Latin America," *International Family Planning Perspectives* 21(4):143–149, 166.

Thomas, D., J. Strauss, and M.-H. Henriques. 1991. "How Does Mother's Education Affect Child Height?" *Journal of Human Resources* 26(2):183–211.

Thompson, R., J. Reynoldson, S. Garrow, et al. 2001. "Towards the Eradication of Hookworm in an Isolated Australian Community, *Lancet* 357:770–771.

TransMONEE Data Base. 2003. Florence: UNICEF/IRC. Available at: http://www.unicef.org.

Turbayne, C. 1962. *The Myth of Metaphor.* New Haven: Yale University Press.

Turner, R. 1993. "Landmark French and British Studies Examine Sexual Behavior, Including Multiple Partners, Homosexuality," *Family Planning Perspectives* 25(2):91–92.

Umeta, M., C. West, J. Haidar, et al. 2000. "Zinc Supplementation and Stunted Infants in Ethiopia: A Randomised Controlled Trial," *Lancet* 355(9220):2021–2026.

UN (United Nations). 1998. *HIV/AIDS and Human Rights: International Guidelines.* HR/PUB/98/1. Geneva: United Nations.

UN (United Nations). 2000. http://unstats.un.org/unsd/demographic/ww2000/table1a.htm.

UN (United Nations). 2004. *Millennium Indicators Database.* Deparatment of Economic and Social Affairs, Statistics Division Available at: http://millennium indicators.un.org.

UNAIDS (Joint United Nations Programme on HIV/AIDS). 1998. *Report on the Global HIV/AIDS Epidemic.* Geneva: UNAIDS. Available at: http://www.unaids.org.

UNAIDS (Joint United Nations Programme on HIV/AIDS). 1999a. *Fact Sheet on Differences in HIV Spread in African Cities.* Geneva: UNAIDS. Available at: http://www.unaids.org/html/pub/Publications/IRC-pub03/lusaka99_en_html.htm.

UNAIDS (Joint United Nations Programme on HIV/AIDS). 1999b. *Listen, Learn, Live: Challenges for Latin America and the Caribbean.* Geneva: UNAIDS. Available at: http://www.unaids orUNAIDS (Joint United Nations Programme on HIV/AIDS). 2000a. *HIV and AIDS-Related Stigmatization, Discrimination and Denial: Forms, Contexts and Determinants.* UNAIDS/00.16E. Geneva: United Nations.

UNAIDS (Joint United Nations Programme on HIV/AIDS). 2002. *Report on the Global HIV/AIDS Epidemic, June 2002.* Geneva: United Nations. Available at: http://www.unaids.org.

UNAIDS (Joint United Nations Programme on HIV/AIDS). 2004. *Report on the Global HIV/AIDS Epidemic.* Geneva: United Nations. Available at: http://www.unaids.org.

UNDP (United Nations Development Programme). 1998. *Human Development Report.* New York: Oxford University Press.

UNDP (United Nations Development Programme). 1999. *Human Development Report.* New York: Oxford University Press.

UNDP (United Nations Development Programme). 2000. *Human Development Report.* New York: Oxford University Press.

UNDP (United Nations Development Programme). 2003a. *Human Development Report.* New York: Oxford University Press. Available at: http://www.undp.org/hdro/indicators.html.

UNDP (United Nations Development Programme). 2003b. *The Roma of Central and Eastern Europe: Avoiding the Dependency Trap. A Regional Human Development Report.* New York: Oxford University Press. Available at: http://roma.undp.sk/.

UNDP (United Nations Development Programme). 2004. *Human Development Report.* New York: Oxford University Press.

UNFPA (United Nations Population Fund). 1999. *AIDS Update 1999.* New York: UNFPA.

UNICEF. 2003. *Social Monitor 2003.* Florence: Innocenti Research Center. Available at: http://www.unicef-icdc.org/publications/pdf/monitor03/monitor2003.pdf.

Urassa, W., S. Kapiga, G. Msamanga, et al. 2001. "Risk Factors for Syphilis among HIV-1 Infected Pregnant Women in Dar es Salaam, Tanzania," *African Journal of Reproductive Health* 5(3):54–62.

U.S. Census Bureau. 1999. *HIV/AIDS Surveillance Data Base.* Washington, D.C.: Government Printing Office. Available at: http://www.census.gov/ipc.

USAID (U.S. Agency for International Development). 2001. *Leading the Way: USAID Responds to HIV/AIDS.* Washington, D.C.: USAID.

USAID (U.S. Agency for International Development). 2003. Country Profile, HIV/AIDS: Rwanda. Washington, D.C.: USAID. Available at: http://www.usaid.gov/pop_health/aids/countries/africa/rwanda.html.

van Vliet, C., K. Holmes, B. Singer, and J.D.F. Habbema. 1997. *The Effectiveness of HIV Prevention Strategies under Alternative Scenarios: Evaluation with the STDSIM Model.* Washington, D.C.: World Bank. Available at: http://www.iaen.org/files.cgi/6925_confront_aids_chapter_11.pdf.

Varney, James. 2000. "Plague on Honduras," *Times-Picayune* (New Orleans), February 27, p. A1.

Vaughan, P., E. Rogers, A. Singhal, and R. Swalehe. 2000. "Entertainment-Education and HIV/AIDS Prevention: A Field Experiment in Tanzania," *Journal of Health Communication* 5(Suppl.):81–100.

Verhoeff, F., B. Brabin, L. Chimsuku, et al. 1999. "Increased Prevalence of Malaria in HIV-Infected Pregnant Women and Its Implications for Malaria Control," *Tropical Medicine and International Health* 4:5–12.

von Braun, Joachim, Tesfaye Teklu, and Patrick Webb. 1999. *Famine in Africa: Causes, Responses, and Prevention.* Baltimore: Johns Hopkins University Press.

Vos J., M. W. Borgdorff, and E. G. Kachidza. 1990. "Cost and Output of Mobile Clinics in a Commercial Farming Area in Zimbabwe," *Social Science and Medicine* 31(11):1207–1211.

Walker, D. 2001. "Cost and Cost-Effectiveness Guidelines: Which Ones to Use?" *Health Policy and Planning* 16(1):113–121.

Walker, Damian. 2003. "Cost and Cost-Effectiveness of HIV/AIDS Prevention Strategies in Developing Countries: Is There an Evidence Base?" *Health Policy and Planning* 18(1):4–17.

Walker, Damien, and Julia Fox-Rushby. 2000. "Economic Evaluation of Parasitic Diseases: A Critique of the Internal and External Validity of Published Studies," *Tropical Medicine and International Health* 5(4):237–249.

Walsh, J. A., and K. S. Warren. 1979. "Selective Primary Health Care: An Interim Strategy for Disease Control in Developing Countries," *New England Journal of Medicine* 301(18):967–974.

Wapnir, Raul. 2000. "Zinc Deficiency, Malnutrition and the Gastrointestinal Tract," *Journal of Nutrition* 130:1388S–1392S.

Warner, Dennis. 2001. "Environmental Sanitation and Child Health," in Ernest Bartell and Alejandro O'Donnell (eds.), *The Child in Latin America: Health, Development, and Rights,* pp. 97–120. Notre Dame, Ind.: University of Notre Dame Press.

Wawer, Maria, M. Sewankambo, D. Serwadda, et al. 1999. "Control of Sexually Transmitted Diseases for AIDS Prevention in Uganda: A Randomised Community Trial," *Lancet* 353:525–535.

WDI (World Development Indicators). 2004. Washington, D.C.: World Bank. Available at: http://devdata.worldbank.org/dataonline.

Webster, Linda, J. Greenspan, A. Nakashima, and R. Johnson. 1993. "An Evaluation of Surveillance for *Chlamydia trachomatis* infections in the United States, 1987–1991," *Morbidity and Mortality Weekly* 42(SS-3):21–27.

Weidenreich, F. 1946. *Apes, Giants, and Man.* Chicago: University of Chicago Press.

Whitaker, Rupert. 1997. "Re-assessing the Virological Approach to HIV Pathogenesis: Can It Explain AIDS as an Immunological Disease?" *Journal of Theoretical Biology* 187(1):45–56.

Whitworth, J., D. Morgan, M. Quigley, et al. 2000. "Effect of HIV-1 and Increasing Immunosuppression on Malaria Parasitaemia and Clinical Episodes in Adults in Rural Uganda: A Cohort Study," *Lancet* 356(9235):1051–1056.

WHO (World Health Organization). 1987. *Global Schistosomiasis Atlas.* Geneva: WHO. Available at: http://www.who.int/wormcontrol/documents/who_docs/en.

WHO (World Health Organization). 1996 last updated/2003 accessed. *Schistosomiasis.* Fact Sheet No. 115. Geneva: WHO. Available at: http://www.who.int/inf-fs/en/fact115.html.

WHO (World Health Organization). 1997. *Health and Environment in Sustainable Development: Five Years after the Earth Summit.* WHO/EHG/97.8. Geneva: WHO.

WHO (World Health Organization). 1998a. *African Trypanosomiasis (Sleeping Sickness) Control.* Geneva: WHO. Available at: http://www.who.int/ctd/html/trypano.html.

WHO (World Health Organization). 1998b. *Intestinal Parasites Control.* Geneva: WHO. Available at: http://www.who.int/ctd/html/intest.html.

WHO (World Health Organization). 1998c. *Malaria Prevention and Control.* Geneva: WHO. Available at: http:/www.who.int/ctd/html/malaria.html.

WHO (World Health Organization). 1998d. *Schistosomiasis Control.* Geneva: WHO. Available at: http:/www.who.int/ctd/html/schisto.html.

WHO (World Health Organization). 2000a. *Lymphatic Filariasis.* Fact Sheet No. 102. Geneva: WHO. Available at: http://www.who.int/inf-fs/en/fact102.html.

WHO (World Health Organization). 2000b. *Maternal Mortality in 2000: Estimates*

Developed by WHO, UNICEF and UNFPA. Geneva: WHO. Available at: http://www.who.int/reproductive-health/publications/maternal_mortality_2000/index.html.

WHO (World Health Organization). 2001a. *African Trypanosomiasis or Sleeping Sickness.* Fact Sheet No. 259. Geneva: WHO. Available at: http:/www.who.int/inf-fs/en/fact259.html.

WHO (World Health Organization). 2001b. *Geographical Distribution.* Geneva: WHO. Available at: http:/www.who.int/emc/diseases/tryp/trypanogeo.html.

WHO (World Health Organization). 2003a. *Expert Group Stresses That Unsafe Sex Is the Primary Mode of Transmission of HIV in Africa.* Geneva: WHO. Available at: http:/www.who.int/mediacentre/statements/2003/statements5/en/print.html.

WHO (World Health Organization). 2003b. *Tuberculosis Epidemiological Surveillance Report.* Geneva: WHO. Available at: http:/www.who.int.

WHO (World Health Organization). 2003c. *Unsafe Injection Practices: A Plague of Many Health Care Systems.* Geneva: WHO. Available at: http:/www.who.int/injection_safety/about/resources/BackInfoUnsafe/en/.

WHO (World Health Organization). 2004. *Tuberculosis.* Fact Sheet No. 104. Geneva: WHO. Available at: http:/www.who.int.

Wolday, D., S. Mayaan, Z. Mariam, et al. 2002. "Treatment of Intestinal Worms Is Associated with Decreased HIV Plasma Viral Load," *Journal of Acquired Immune Deficiency Syndromes* 31:56–62.

Woodward, Bill. 1998. "Protein, Calories, and Immune Defenses," *Nutrition Reviews* 56(1, Part 2):S84–92.

World Bank. 1993a. *Investing in Health: World Development Report 1993.* Washington, D.C.: World Bank.

World Bank. 1993b. *Sexually Transmitted Infections: Prevention and Care Project, Zimbabwe.* Staff Appraisal Report No. 11730-ZIM. Washington, D.C.: World Bank.

World Bank. 1997. *Confronting AIDS: Public Priorities in a Global Epidemic.* Oxford: Oxford University Press.

World Bank. 1998. "Nutritional Status and Poverty in Sub-Saharan Africa," *Findings* 108, April.

World Bank. 1999. *World Development Report, 1998/1999.* New York: Oxford University Press.

World Bank. 2003a. *AIDS and Transport in Africa.* Washington, D.C.: World Bank.

World Bank. 2003b. *School Deworming at a Glance.* Washington, D.C.: World Bank. Available at: http:/www.worldbank.org/hnp.

World Bank. 2004. *World Development Report, 2005.* New York: Oxford University Press.

Xiao, L, S. Owen, D. Rudolph, et al. 1998. "*Plasmodium falciparum* Antigen-Induced Human Immunodeficiency Virus Type 1 Replication Is Mediated through Induction of Tumor Necrosis Factor-alpha," *Journal of Infectious Diseases* 177:437–445.

Young, T. Kue. 1998. *Population Health: Concepts and Methods.* New York: Oxford University Press.

Zbarskaya, Irina. 2002. "Poverty and Welfare Trends in the Russian Federation over the 1990s." Background paper for the *Social Monitor (2002),* UNICEF.

Index